THE ORIGINS OF
ENGLISH NONSENSE

Also by Noel Malcolm

De Dominis 1560–1624:
Venetian, Anglican, Ecumenist and Relapsed Heretic

George Enescu: His Life and Music

Sense on Sovereignty

Bosnia: A Short History

The Correspondence of Thomas Hobbes (2 vols)
in the Clarendon Edition of
the Works of Thomas Hobbes

The
Origins
of
English
Nonsense

Noel
Malcolm

HarperCollins*Publishers*

HarperCollins*Publishers*
77–85 Fulham Palace Road,
Hammersmith, London w6 8jb

Published by HarperCollins*Publishers* 1997
1 3 5 7 9 8 6 4 2

A catalogue record for this book is
available from the British Library

ISBN 0 00255827 0

Set in Postscript Adobe Caslon by
Rowland Phototypesetting Ltd,
Bury St Edmunds, Suffolk

Printed and bound in Great Britain by
Caledonian International Book Manufacturing Ltd, Glasgow

For Euthymia,
and in memory of her father,
John

Estrangement
Se fet mun quer dolent,
Quant me purpens,
Que jo ai gaste mun tens
Sanz rimer de aucun sens

The poet 'Richard', in E. M. Stengel (ed.)
Codicem manu scriptum Digby 86
in bibliotheca bodleiana asservatum
(Halle, 1871), p. 118

Nonsense (when all is said and done) is still nonsense.
But the study of nonsense, that is science.

Saul Lieberman, introducing Gershom Scholem's
lectures on the Cabbala: quoted in S. Schama,
Landscape and Memory (London, 1995), p. 134

CONTENTS

PREFACE

ONE MIGHT ASSUME that the period of English literature which lies between the major works of Shakespeare and Milton was a peculiarly well-ploughed field, where little remained to be explored. Yet the purpose of this volume is to make known a genre which enjoyed real popularity in precisely that period, and which has never yet been discussed in any detail. I am not aware of a single study, not even a short article, that sets out to describe or explain the history of this minor but fascinating literary phenomenon.

It would not be true to say that the poetry itself is entirely unknown. Individual poems have been printed in anthologies such as John Broadbent's *Signet Classic Poets of the Seventeenth Century* and Alastair Fowler's *New Oxford Book of Seventeenth Century Verse*.[1] Several of the poems printed and discussed in this volume have appeared in general nonsense anthologies, the fullest selection being provided by Hugh Haughton's valuable *Chatto Book of Nonsense Poetry*. But I know of no collection specifically devoted to these seventeenth-century nonsense poems.

Nor would it be fair to suggest that literary scholars have never noticed or alluded to the existence of such a genre. Some acknowledgements of the presence of this vein of nonsense writing can be found in the scholarly literature; but notices and allusions are all that they amount to. Thus Wallace Notestein, in his path-breaking study of John Taylor, merely comments:

---

1 Broadbent prints two of Taylor's 'Certaine Sonnets' (poem 8 in the present collection): ii, pp. 55–6. Fowler prints an extract from Taylor's *Sir Gregory Nonsence* (poem 11 in the present collection): pp. 167–8.

'He was, I think, the first writer of nonsense verse. In *The Essence . . . of Nonsence upon Sence* (1653) he gives us nonsense verse and not without skill.'[2] Similarly, a standard work on the comic poetry of the Restoration period discusses at length the 'drolleries' or collections of light poetry, but devotes only one sentence to the nonsense poems which they contained: 'There are not many of these in the drolleries, but there are some.'[3] Even Bernard Capp's excellent study of John Taylor, the only full-length work ever to have been published on this seminal nonsense poet, makes only passing references to his nonsense writing, and does not attempt to assess his place in the development of the genre itself.[4] The best discussion known to me of the seventeenth-century nonsense tradition is given in Timothy Raylor's recent study of Sir John Mennes and James Smith; but it amounts to no more than two suggestive paragraphs.[5]

In more general works of literary history, the ignorance of this genre is even more striking. Standard works on nonsense poetry either pass over the seventeenth century in silence, or allude briefly to one or two poems which have appeared in modern nonsense anthologies without investigating the genre to which they belonged.[6] Entries on 'Nonsense' in reference works such as the *Princeton Encyclopaedia of Poetry and Poetics* make no allusion whatsoever to the seventeenth-century material. More surprisingly, there is no overall history of nonsense poetry in medieval and Renaissance European literature,

---

2 W. Notestein, *Four Worthies: John Chamberlain, Anne Clifford, John Taylor, Oliver Heywood* (London, 1956), p. 206. The date given by Notestein for *The Essence of Nonsence upon Sence* is that printed on the title-page; from Thomason, however, we know that the work did not appear until Feb. 1654.
3 D. Farley-Hills, *The Benevolence of Laughter: Comic Poetry of the Commonwealth and Restoration* (London, 1974), p. 32.
4 B. Capp, *The World of John Taylor the Water-Poet, 1578–1653* (Oxford, 1994), esp. pp. 43, 54, 76, 92, 159, 186.
5 T. Raylor, *Cavaliers, Clubs, and Literary Culture: Sir John Mennes, James Smith, and the Order of the Fancy* (Newark, NJ, 1994), pp. 99–100.
6 See, for example, A. Liede, *Dichtung als Spiel: Studien zur Unsinnspoesie an den Grenzen der Sprache*, 2 vols. (Berlin, 1963), which mentions Corbet (i, p. 158), but only because he is included in the Everyman anthology.

even though specific aspects of this subject, and works by specific authors, have been discussed separately in some detail.[7] In Chapter 3 of the Introduction to this collection I have tried to put together for the first time an overall history of medieval and Renaissance nonsense poetry in Europe, and, in doing so, to suggest some of the lines of transmission which tie together the nonsense literatures of different periods and countries.

Why bother to take such serious trouble over such a self-evidently ridiculous subject-matter? One reason must be that nonsense poetry, like any comic genre, is part of the larger literary culture which it inhabits, and to which it is connected in many ways, both direct and indirect: understanding more about those connections can only shed light on other areas of literature too. It can tell us about the ways in which writers and readers regarded the literary fashions, stylistic conventions, and canons of taste and diction of the day. In Chapter 2 of the Introduction I have tried to show how intimately the earliest seventeenth-century nonsense poetry was bound up with the development of late Elizabethan dramatic and satirical poetry. Nonsense poetry is also connected, in more tangential ways, with a wide range of minor genres, sources and traditions in European literary history; I have offered some examples of these connections in Chapter 4. Also in that chapter, I have tried to set out some more general conclusions about the nature and origins of nonsense poetry, which may be valid for other periods too; these conclusions run contrary to the theories about 'carnivalesque' humour which nowadays dominate most discussion of early modern comic writing.

But the most important reason for collecting these poems should not be left altogether unsaid. At their best, they are supremely enjoyable – exuberant, sonorous, and (within the confines of some soon-to-be-familiar routines) richly inventive. The best sections of Taylor's two large-scale nonsense works (*Sir Gregory Nonsense* and *The Essence of Nonsense upon Sence*: poems

7 See the works referred to in the notes to Chapter 3 of the Introduction.

II and 17 in this collection) contain some of the most splendid nonsense poetry in the English language, which can be enjoyed by anyone who possesses even a slight acquaintance with the 'serious' literature of the period. Of course, reading page after page of this material will jade any reader's appetite, like feasting on chocolate; and in any case not all the poems in this collection are of high quality. Nevertheless, the most important aim of this book is not to trade arguments with scholarly specialists, but to share the pleasure of these poems with all interested readers.

For that reason, notes have been added to explain words and allusions; some of these may seem unnecessary to those readers who have a thorough grounding in classical mythology or a specialist knowledge of seventeenth-century vocabulary. A few 'Longer Notes' are presented on pp. 289–94. Otherwise, I have placed all explanatory notes at the foot of each page, rather than collecting them in a single glossary at the end of the book. This has been done for two reasons: first, for the ease of the reader, and secondly, because some of the words which need explanation would not obviously strike the reader as requiring it. (In the phrase 'Ale and Wigs', for example, the 'Wigs' are bread-rolls, not hairpieces; but it would not occur to most readers to look up 'Wigs' in a glossary.) I hope that readers will be patient with the inevitable degree of repetition which this method entails (repeated explanations have been dispensed with only within the unit of a single page), and remember that the repetitions are there for their own convenience.

The annotations also contain occasional textual notes (distinguished by the key-words being printed in italics), recording material variants between texts and my own formal emendations of the copy-text; the sources referred to in these notes are listed at the end of each poem. But my emendations are few and far between. With a few exceptions (recorded in the notes) I have preserved original spellings and punctuations; the only changes which I have made systematically and silently are to convert initial 'v' to 'u', medial 'u' to 'v', 'i' to 'j' (where appropriate) and long 's' to normal 's'. Otherwise the degree of emendation is as light as possible. Some of these poems use word-play, or ingenious Hudibrastic rhymes, which would disappear from view in a modernized spelling of the text. Others, which are in gibberish, cannot of course be modernized at all. And where textual emendations are concerned, it is necessary to bear in mind that nonsense poetry overturns all the usual rules of procedure. Normally, where different stages of manuscript transmission survive, corruptions to the text can be identified by an editor on the grounds that a corrupted text makes less sense than the original. In the case of nonsense poetry, the opposite is true: corruption involves the introduction of sense. 'O that my lungs could bleat' is, for example, a corruption of 'O that my wings could bleat'. The most insidious error a modern editor can commit, therefore, is to introduce any further corruptions of this kind into the text. Some strange examples of this were perpetrated by Charles Hindley, the diligent Victorian editor of one collection of John Taylor's works: 'Sinderesis of Wapping', for instance, was emended by Hindley to 'Cinderesses of Wapping.'[8] This brings to mind the logic of the (perhaps legendary) German editor of Shakespeare, who 'corrected' one famous passage to make it read: 'stones in the running brooks, Sermons in books'. It is a logic which I have tried to avoid.

Finally, a few words about definitions, or the lack of them. Readers will note that I use the term 'genre' in a fairly loose, non-technical way. Readers will also observe that at no point in this book do I attempt to frame a precise definition of nonsense. Such definition-making is not necessary for practical reasons, any more than it is necessary for studies of lyric poetry or comedy to begin with watertight definitions of those terms. These are things which, usually, we recognize when we see them. But close definition is not desirable for theoretical reasons either, since these literary types are cluster-concepts: they have a core on which all can agree, and a more variable periphery

8 J. Taylor, *Works*, ed. C. Hindley (London, 1872), sect. 6, p. 2.

on which disagreement is always possible. The 'high' literary nonsense of Hoskyns, Taylor and Corbet clearly belongs at the core of any notion of nonsense poetry; some of the other items in this collection are closer to the periphery.

I am grateful to the Bodleian Library, Oxford, for permission to print the texts of poems 14, 19, 20, and 32; to the British Library, London, for permission to print the text of poem 30; and to Nottingham University Library for permission to print the text of poem 21. I should like to record my thanks to the staff of not only those libraries, but also the Cambridge University Library, where much of the research for this edition was done.

The notes record specific sources of information, but I have not thought it necessary to give such sources for general information contained in standard reference works. Of such works, the most useful in preparing this edition have been the following: *The Oxford English Dictionary*, *The Dictionary of National Biography*, Brewer's *Dictionary of Phrase and Fable*, Brewer's *Reader's Companion*, *The Oxford Companion to Classical Literature*, Lemprière's *Classical Dictionary*, Sugden's *Topographical Dictionary to the Works of Shakespeare*, Stow's *Survey of London*, Kent's *Encyclopaedia of London* and Partridge's *Dictionary of Historical Slang*. Full details of these works are given in the bibliography.

Finally, I am particularly grateful to Dr Colin Burrow, Dr Richard Luckett, Mr Richard Ollard and Dr Timothy Raylor for reading this work in typescript and giving me their comments. I should also like to express my gratitude to Dr Edward Chaney for suggesting the Inigo Jones drawings which ornament the cover of this book, and to thank his Grace the Duke of Devonshire and the Trustees of the Chatsworth Settlement for permission to reproduce them. Last but not least, I owe a special word of thanks to Stuart Proffitt for showing such an interest in this book, and to Arabella Quin for seeing it expertly through the press.

INTRODUCTION

CHAPTER 1

The origins and development of English seventeenth-century nonsense poetry

THERE ARE TWO COMMON BELIEFS about the literary genre of nonsense poetry in England, and both of them are false. The first holds that nonsense poetry was the exclusive product of the nineteenth century, more or less the creation of Edward Lear and Lewis Carroll. 'Considered as a genre', argues a recent study by a specialist in this field, 'we cannot, indeed, trace the origins of nonsense literature beyond the nineteenth century, when it first appeared in Victorian England.'[1] Another modern writer has argued in all seriousness that nonsense poetry began in 1846 and ended in 1898, after which date 'it can no longer exist'.[2] The second common belief about this genre is that nonsense is not so much a cultural-historical product as a timeless, universal category, which therefore has only instances rather than origins. This was the view of some of the earliest modern writers on nonsense literature, G. K. Chesterton and Émile Cammaerts, and it seems to be implied by those modern studies of nonsense which explore its dependence on formal

---

1 W. Tigges, 'An Anatomy of Nonsense', in Tigges (ed.), *Explorations in the Field of Nonsense*, DQR Studies in Literature 3 (Amsterdam, 1987), pp. 23–46. Tigges finds two underlying historical reasons for the advent of nonsense poetry: first, 'the rise of philology during the Romantic period', and secondly, capitalism, which ensured that 'Victorian households . . . were inundated with "things"'. This second line of explanation might perhaps be described as nonsense-Marxism.
2 K. Reichert, *Lewis Carroll: Studien zum literarischen Unsinn* (Munich, 1974), p. 103.

procedures of inversion, repetition, serialization, circularity and simultaneity.[3]

That those procedures in themselves are universal, to be found in the literature and folklore of different cultures from various times and places, is clear. They can be found too in English popular writing and folk materials: drinking songs, humorous ballads, folktales, nursery rhymes, and so on. But full-scale nonsense poetry as an English literary phenomenon is not a timeless thing, springing up here, there and everywhere of its own accord; still less is it something that wells up from folk culture. It is, rather, a literary genre with a particular history or histories, developed by individual poets and possessing a peculiarly close relationship – largely a parodic one – to the 'high' literary conventions of its day. After a brief flowering in the late Middle Ages (discussed in Chapter 3 of this Introduction), literary nonsense poetry in England was re-invented in the early seventeenth century. It then enjoyed an extraordinary vogue for more than fifty years, and was still being printed in the popular 'drolleries' of the Restoration period. This efflorescence was due partly to the stylistic conditions of English declamatory poetry in the early seventeenth century (discussed in Chapter 2 of this Introduction), which were so ideally suited to nonsensification. But the success of high literary nonsense poetry in this period was due above all to the skills and energies of the individual poets who created and developed the genre. As it happens, it is possible to attribute the origins of this genre to one poet in particular, and to explain how, when and why he created it. The literary nonsense poetry of the seventeenth century was invented by a lawyer, rhetorician, minor poet and wit, Sir John Hoskyns, in

3 Chesterton, 'A Defence of Nonsense', first published in the *Defender*, 1901; reprinted in E. Rhys (ed.), *A Century of English Essays* (London, n.d.), pp. 446–50. Cammaerts, *The Poetry of Nonsense* (New York, 1925). On inversion see R. Benayoun's introduction to his anthology, *Le Nonsense* (Paris, 1977). On repetition and serialization see E. Sewell, *The Field of Nonsense* (London, 1952). On all of these formal characteristics see S. Stewart, *Nonsense: Aspects of Intertextuality in Folklore and Literature* (Baltimore, 1979).

1611. Since this fact has never been properly recognized hitherto, it is worth setting out in some detail the story of how nonsense poetry sprang, almost fully armed, out of Hoskyns's head into the English literary world.

John Hoskyns was born in 1566, to a humble family of Welsh origins living in the Herefordshire village of Mounckton or Monnington.[4] He was sent to Winchester College, where he displayed a prodigious memory as well as a special talent for Latin verse composition; at Winchester he was, in John Aubrey's words, 'the flower of his time'. His friends and contemporaries there included several who later became well-known poets and littérateurs: John Davies (also from Herefordshire), Henry Wotton, the epigrammatist John Owen, and the poet Thomas Bastard. With Wotton and Owen he went on to New College, Oxford, where he matriculated in early 1585. He proceeded BA in 1588 and MA in 1592; but at the 'Act' (the degree-giving ceremony) on that latter occasion he caused serious offence to the University authorities. He had been chosen to perform at the 'Act' as *Terrae filius*, the mock-orator whose role it was to make a humorous speech which might contain topical and personal allusions in a satirical vein. These traditionally elaborate and boisterous rhetorical performances, like much of the material in the comic University dramas of the period (the Cambridge *Parnassus* plays being the best known), cultivated parodic routines and in-jokes. But Hoskyns carried the joke too far, to the point where its humour was no longer apparent. One modern biographer has ingeniously reconstructed his offence, suggesting that his declamation satirized the recently deceased Chancellor of Oxford University, Sir Christopher

---

4 For this and all further biographical details about Hoskyns, see J. Aubrey, *'Brief Lives', chiefly of Contemporaries, set down by John Aubrey, between the Years 1669 & 1696*, ed. A. Clark, 2 vols. (Oxford, 1898), i, pp. 416–25; L. B. Osborn, *The Life, Letters, and Writings of John Hoskyns 1566–1638* (New Haven, Conn., 1937), pp. 16–61; B. W. Whitlock, *John Hoskyns, Serjeant-at-Law* (Washington, DC, 1982).

5

Hatton.[5] The punishment was severe: as Aubrey later put it, 'he was so bitterly satyricall that he was expelled and putt to his shifts'.[6]

After a brief period as a schoolmaster in Somerset, Hoskyns travelled to London in early 1593 and was admitted as a student of the law at one of the Inns of Court, the Middle Temple. He may have been persuaded to take this step by his friend John Davies, who had been at the Middle Temple since 1588. The Inns of Court (Gray's Inn, Lincoln's Inn, the Inner Temple and the Middle Temple) formed a kind of legal counterpart to the universities of Oxford and Cambridge; many sons of merchants and country gentry studied there, not in order to become professional lawyers, but merely to acquire a grounding in legal procedures which would see them through the innumerable lawsuits of their adult lives. But with so many connections between the lawyers, the parliamentarians and the court wits, the Inns of Court also formed the basis of much of the literary culture of London during this period. Not only did they produce lawyers with wide-ranging intellectual and literary interests (such as Francis Bacon and John Selden); but also whole coteries of poets and writers were fostered within their walls. Hoskyns and Davies were later joined at the Middle Temple by their old friend Henry Wotton, the poet and dramatist John Marston, the minor poet Charles Best, and the 'character'-writer Thomas Overbury. Thomas Campion was at Gray's Inn during this period, and John Donne was at Lincoln's Inn. One modern critic has described Donne's works of the 1590s as products of 'a typical Inns of Court poet', characterizing them as follows: 'In his verse epistles occur many instances of his recondite learning and startling wit, but the tone is always that of an easy intimacy, of someone speaking to an audience of

5 Whitlock, *John Hoskyns*, p. 82.
6 Aubrey, *Brief Lives*, i, p. 417.

equals; often he appears to be improvising entertainment for their amusement.'[7]

The Inns were famous for their elaborate Christmas revels, whole sequences of speeches, mock-trials, comic plays, processions, banquets and dances, which extended through December and January. A leader of the revels was chosen before Christmas; he was given the title of 'Prince d'Amour' at the Middle Temple and 'Prince of Purpoole' at Gray's Inn (after the parish in which the Inn was situated). He would appoint members of his princely 'court', and organize and preside over the revels; on Candlemas night (2 February) the Prince would die, and a final banquet would be held. Fortunately, texts survive from the Gray's Inn revels of 1594–5 (*Gesta Grayorum*, first published in 1688), and from the Middle Temple revels of 1597–8 (*Le Prince d'Amour*, published in 1660), giving us the full flavour of these performances.[8] The Gray's Inn materials consist mainly of mock-edicts issued by the Prince of Purpoole, and mock-correspondence between him and the Russian Tsar. The edicts indicate the kind of legal-parodic word-play which was the staple of Inns of Court humour; one announcement excuses all those within the Prince's domains of

> all manner of Treasons, Contempts, Offences, Trespasses, Forcible Entries, Intrusions, Disseisins, Torts, Wrongs, Injustices, Over-throws, Over-thwartings, Cross-bitings, Coney-catchings, Frauds, Conclusions, Fictions, Fractions, Fashions, Fancies, or Ostentations: . . . All Destructions, Obstructions and Constructions: All Evasions,

---

7 P. J. Finkelpearl, *John Marston of the Middle Temple* (Cambridge, Mass., 1969), p. 30. Finkelpearl gives an excellent account of the literary culture of the Inns of Court, which he presents as the formative influence on Marston. See also A. Wigfall Green, *The Inns of Court and Early English Drama* (New Haven, Conn., 1931), and Whitlock, *John Hoskyns*, pp. 92–4.

8 On the *Gesta Grayorum* see the introduction by W. W. Greg to his edition of it (Malone Society Reprints, Oxford, 1914 [1915]). On the dating of the *Prince d'Amour* revels see Hoskyns, *Directions for Speech and Style*, ed. H. H. Hudson (Princeton, NJ, 1935), pp. 108–9.

> Invasions, Charges, Surcharges, Discharges, Commands, Countermands, Checks, Counter-checks and Counter-buffs: ... All, and all manner of Mis-feasance, Non-feasance, or too much Feasance ...⁹

And the flourish of seigneurial titles with which the Prince begins each document strikes a typically mock-heroic note, with its conjuncture of aristocratic style and bathetic London place-names:

> *Henry* Prince of *Purpoole*, Arch-Duke of *Stapulia* and *Bernardia*, Duke of *High* and *Nether Holborn*, Marquis of St. *Giles's* and *Tottenham*, Count Palatine of *Bloomsbury* and *Clerkenwell*, Great Lord of the Canton of *Islington*, *Kentish-Town*, *Paddington* and *Knights-bridge*, Knight of the most Heroical order of the *Helmet*, and Sovereign of the same ...¹⁰

The surviving text of the Middle Temple revels of 1597-8 is a similar affair, centring on a mock-trial before a grand jury. One of the speeches is attributed in two manuscript versions to Hoskyns; in the printed version its speaker is described as 'Clerk of the Council' to the Prince d'Amour – in other words, one of the senior figures chosen to help organize the revels by the Prince, who on this occasion was Hoskyns's friend Richard Martin.¹¹ The same qualities of verbal dexterity which had qualified Hoskyns to be *Terrae filius* at Oxford must also have distinguished him at the Middle Temple; but this time he employed that talent not in biting satire but in something altogether more harmless and fantastical. After a speech by the Prince's 'Orator', Charles Best, Hoskyns was (according to one of the manuscript

9 *Gesta Grayorum*, ed. Greg, p. 15.

10 Ibid., p. 14; 'Stapulia' and 'Bernardia' were Staple Inn and Bernard's Inn, minor Inns which were subsidiary to Gray's Inn.

11 See Hoskyns, *Directions*, ed. Hudson, pp. 108–10. On Martin, the friend of Ben Jonson (and dedicatee of his *Poetaster*) who later became Recorder of the City of London, see Aubrey, *Brief Lives*, ii, pp. 47–53.

sources) 'importuned by ye Prince & Sr Walter Raleigh'.[12] He obliged with a speech which was a classic example of the 'fustian' style of parodic prose.[13] The reputation of this speech lived on long after its author's death. When compiling his notes on Hoskyns in the 1680s or 1690s, John Aubrey jotted down: 'Memorandum: – Hoskyns – to collect his nonsense discourse, which is very good'.[14] The speech is not in any strict sense 'nonsense', but it is so important as a preliminary to Hoskyns's invention of English nonsense poetry that it is reproduced here in full:

> Then (*Mr. Orator*) I am sorry that for your *Tufftaffata* Speech, you shall receive but a *Fustian* Answer. For alas! what am I (whose ears have been pasted with the Tenacity of your Speeches, and whose nose hath been perfumed with the Aromaticity of your sentences) that I should answer your Oration, both Voluminous and Topical, with a Replication concise and curtal? For you are able in Troops of *Tropes*, and Centuries of Sentences to muster your meaning: Nay, you have such Wood-piles of words, that unto you *Cooper* is but a Carpenter, and *Rider* himself deserves not a Reader. I am therefore driven to say to you, as *Heliogabalus* said to his dear and honourable servant *Reniger Fogassa*, If thou dost ill (*quoth he*) then much good do thee; if well, then snuffe the candle. For even as the Snow advanced upon the points vertical of cacuminous Mountains, dissolveth and discoagulateth itself into humorous liquidity; even so by the frothy volubility of your words, the Prince is perswaded to depose himself from his Royal Seat and Dignity, and to follow your counsel with all contradiction and reluctation; wherefore I take you to

---

12 BL MS Add. 25,303, fo. 184ᵛ. Raleigh's presence very possibly accounts for the choice of tobacco as one of the main topics of this speech. Benjamin Rudyerd, who drew up the MS record of these revels which was printed in the *Prince d'Amour*, explains it by saying that Best had taken tobacco in the middle of his own oration (*Le Prince d'Amour; or the Prince of Love. With a Collection of Several Ingenious Poems and Songs by the Wits of the Age* (London, 1660), p. 83), but this may be a later rationalization on Rudyerd's part.

13 On the 'fustian' style, and on the significance of the term itself, see below, pp. 30–41.

14 Aubrey, *Brief Lives*, i, p. 424.

be fitter to speak unto stones, like *Amphion*, or trees, like *Orpheus*, than to declaim to men like a Cryer, or to exclaim to boyes like a Sexton: For what said *Silas Titus*, the Sope-maker of Holborn-bridge? For (*quoth he*) since the States of *Europe* have so many momentary inclinations, and the Anarchical confusion of their Dominions is like to ruinate their Subversions, I see no reason why men should so addict themselves to take *Tabacco* in *Ramus Method*; For let us examine the Complots of Polititians from the beginning of the world to this day; What was the cause of the repentine mutiny in *Scipio's* Camp? it is most evident it was not *Tabacco*. What was the cause of the Aventine revolt, and seditious deprecation for a Tribune? it is apparent it was not *Tabacco*. What moved me to address this Expostulation to your iniquity? it is plain it is not *Tabacco*. So that to conclude, *Tabacco* is not guilty of so many faults as it is charged withal; it disuniteth not the reconciled, nor reconcileth the disunited; it builds no new Cities, nor mends no old Breeches; yet the one, the other, and both are not immortal without reparations: Therefore wisely said the merry-conceited Poet *Heraclitus*, Honourable misfortunes shall have ever an Historical compensation. You listen unto my speeches, I must needs confess it; you hearken to my words, I cannot deny it; you look for some meaning, I partly believe it; but you find none, I do not greatly respect it: For even as a Mill-horse is not a Horse-mill; nor Drink ere you go, is not Go ere you drink; even so Orator Best, is not the best Orator. The sum of all is this, I am an humble Suitor to your Excellency, not only to free him from the danger of the Tower, which he by his demerits cannot avoid; but also to increase dignity upon his head, and multiply honour upon his shoulders, as well for his Eloquence, as for his Nobility. For I understand by your Herald that he is descended from an Ancient house of the *Romans*, even from *Calpurnius Bestia*, and so the generation continued from beast to beast, to this present beast. And your Astronomer hath told me that he hath Kindred in the *Zodiack*; therefore in all humility I do beseeche your Excellency to grant your Royal Warrant to the *Lo. Marshal*, and charge him to send to the Captain

of the Pentioners, that he might send to the Captain of
the Guard to dispatch a Messenger to the Lieutenant of
the Tower, to command one of his Guards to go to one
of the Grooms of the Stable, to fetch the Beadle of the
Beggars, *ut gignant stultum*, to get him a stool; *ut sis foris
Eloquentiae*, that he may sit for his Eloquence. I think I
have most oratoriously insinuated unto your apprehension,
and without evident obscurity intimated unto your good
consideration, that the Prince hath heard your Oration,
yea marry hath he, and thinketh very well of it, yea marry
doth he.[15]

The generic relation of this sort of prose to nonsense literature
is obvious: it plays on a contradiction between form and content,
the form being that of an oration arguing strenuously about
high matters, and the content being perversely inconsequential.
But most of the sentences or phrases in this composition are
not in themselves nonsensical; they merely use a tightly packed
succession of comic devices such as stilted diction, bathos, puns
and exaggerated intensification. Here and there, however, one
sees touches of a more radically nonsensical sensibility: the
phrase 'to take *Tabacco* in *Ramus Method*', for instance, uses
precisely that kind of category-mistake (applying a logical
method to a physical object) which was to become one of the
standard building-blocks of nonsense literature.

In 1604 Hoskyns was elected a Member of Parliament for
the city of Hereford. During the years in which this parliament
sat (until 1611) he must have spent much of his time in London.
'His great witt quickly made him be taken notice of', writes
Aubrey: 'In shorte, his acquaintance were all the witts then about
the towne.'[16] A jocular Latin poem survives about a 'convivium
philosophicum' (philosophical banquet) held at the Mitre tavern
in London, probably in 1611. It lists fourteen individuals as participants, including Hoskyns, Richard Martin, John Donne,
Christopher Brooke (a close friend of Donne and a known friend

---

15 *Prince d'Amour*, pp. 37–9.
16 Aubrey, *Brief Lives*, i, pp. 417–18.

of Hoskyns) and the suddenly famous travel-writer, Thomas Coryate.[17] This group of wits formed the nucleus of the original 'Mermaid Club', which romanticizing literary historians were later to populate with Raleigh, Shakespeare and other poets and dramatists. The only definite contemporary reference to any such club comes in one of Coryate's letters from India, which is addressed to 'the High Seneschall of the Right Worshipfull Fraternitie of Sirenaical Gentlemen, that meet the first Fridaie of every month at the signe of the Mere-Maide in Bread-streete in London'. In a postscript to this letter Coryate asked to be remembered to a number of writers and wits, including Jonson, Donne, Christopher Brooke, Richard Martin, William Hakewill (a member, like Brooke, of Lincoln's Inn) and John Hoskyns.[18]

Coryate himself appears to have played a strangely central part in this group – strangely, that is, because he was its least typical member, being neither a lawyer nor a poet. He was born in the Somerset village of Odcombe, where his father was rector of the parish. He studied at Oxford and acquired a considerable amount of classical learning, but seems never to have contemplated a university or church career. Instead, he was briefly employed in the household of the young Prince Henry, where his position 'seems to have been that of an unofficial court jester'.[19] Then, in May 1608, he began the first of the two adventures which were to ensure his fame: he sailed to Calais and travelled, mainly on foot, through France and northern Italy to Venice, returning via Switzerland, Germany and the Netherlands. On his return to London in October he began converting the copious travel-notes he had taken into a long, continuous narrative, which, thanks to 'the importunity of some of my deare

17 For the text of the poem, with a contemporary English translation, see ibid., ii, pp. 50–53. For a discussion of its dating, authorship and significance, see M. Strachan, *The Life and Adventures of Thomas Coryate* (London, 1962), pp. 142–4, 302–3.
18 See Strachan, *Life of Coryate*, pp. 144–8, which convincingly demythologizes the traditional account of the club.
19 Ibid., p. 13.

friends who prevailed with me for the divulging of the same', he decided to publish. Following the custom of the period, he asked for commendatory verses from his most distinguished literary friends (whose acquaintance he had made either through Prince Henry's court, or through the man who was his local patron in Somerset, the eminent lawyer and member of the Middle Temple, Sir Edward Phelips). 'But word of what was afoot soon spread', writes his modern biographer, 'and with the encouragement of Prince Henry himself, the courtiers and wits set about composing mock panegyrics with gusto. It became the fashion to make fun of Coryate and his book.'[20] Anyone who reads Coryate's narrative, with its long quotations from Latin poetry and its serious and observant descriptions of European cities, may wonder why this work should have provoked such a storm of hilarity and ridicule. Many of the court wits had evidently not read the work, and chose to assume that it was full of tall stories and traveller's tales. But most of them, it seems, had seen an advance copy of the engraved title-page, which contained a number of vignettes illustrating the most bizarre episodes in the book: Coryate being pelted with eggs by a courtesan in Venice, for instance, or being hit over the head by a German peasant for picking a bunch of grapes in a vineyard. Each vignette was linked to an explanatory couplet by Ben Jonson, which helped to set the tone for the other wits' performances: for example,

> Here France, and Italy both to him shed
> Their hornes, and Germany pukes on his head.

And the very title Coryate had chosen was also an incitement to jocular metaphor-making: *Coryats Crudities Hastily gobled up in five Moneths of travell. . . Newly digested in the hungry aire of Odcombe in the County of Somerset, & now dispersed to the nourishment of the travelling Members of this Kingdome.*

In the end no fewer than fifty-six authors sent in their humor-

20 Ibid., p. 124.

ous commendations to be printed; and Coryate was under express orders from Prince Henry not to omit a single one. There were poems in seven languages, including Spanish and Welsh. John Donne contributed a macaronic quatrain which combined Latin, English, Italian, French and Spanish:

> *Quot, dos haec*, linguists perfetti, *Disticha* fairont,
>   *Tot* cuerdos States-men, *hic* livre fara tuus.
> Es *sat* a my l'honneur estre *hic* inteso; Car I leave
>   L'honra, de personne nestre creduto, *tibi*.[21]

And Coryate himself rounded off the collection of verses with thirty-four lines of more traditionally Latinate macaronics of his own:

> Ille ego qui didici longos andare caminos
>   Vilibus in scrutis, celeri pede, senza cavallo;
> Cyclico-gyrovagus coopertos neigibus Alpes
>   Passavi, transvectus equo cui nomina, Ten-toes . . .[22]

Two of the contributions bring us very close to nonsense poetry. One, by Henry Peacham, is described as 'In the Utopian tongue' (poem 2 in the present collection). It uses a few words of gibberish language more reminiscent of the 'Antipodean' spoken by Rabelais's Panurge than of the specimen of 'Utopian' provided by More.[23] Most of its lexical material, however, consists of place-names, some of them belaboured into puns ('Not A-rag-on ô *Coryate*'). Nonsense language is, of course, a type of nonsense; it presents the form of meaning while denying us the substance. But the denial is so complete that it can go no further; it is unable to perform that exploration of nonsense possibilities in which proper nonsense literature excels. Apart from creating a generic nonsense effect, gibberish is capable of performing only one trick, which is to make funny noises. To

21 Coryate, *Crudities*, sig. d4ʳ.
22 Coryate, *Crudities*, sig. 11ᵛ.
23 Rabelais, bk. 2, ch. 9 (*Oeuvres complètes*, ed. J. Boulenger (Paris, 1951), p. 230); Sir Thomas More, *Utopia*, ed. E. Surtz and J. H. Hexter (New Haven, Conn., 1965), pp. 18–19.

achieve any other effects, it must dilute itself with words (or at least recognizable vestiges of words) which are not nonsense. The few other examples of gibberish poems in the present collection will illustrate the nature of this problem.

The second piece of near-nonsense poetry among the prefatory verses to Coryate's book is an English poem (poem 3), with mock-learned footnotes, by 'Glareanus Vadianus' – probably the witty cleric John Sanford.[24] Although the poem itself is comical rather than nonsensical, it contains several phrases which verge on nonsense, either through the compression of a conceptual metaphor into an incongruously physical description ('the shoing-horne of wine', meaning something which makes wine slip down more easily) or through the deflection of a familiar metaphor into an unfamiliar, unexpectedly literal form. (Thus 'Sometimes he warbleth sweet as a stewd prune' takes the taste-metaphor implied in a common adjective for beautiful singing, and makes it absurd by giving it a literal embodiment.)[25] But it is the notes to this poem which come closest to pure literary nonsense: the term 'Bologna sawcidge', for example, is explained as 'A French *Quelque chose* farced with oilet holes, and tergiversations, and the first blossoms of Candid Phlebotomie'. These notes belong to the humanist comic tradition of mock-scholarship, a tradition which runs from Rabelais to Sterne and is an important part of the background to nonsense literature.

For the first specimen of full-blown English literary nonsense poetry in the seventeenth century, we must turn to John Hoskyns's contribution to the mock-praise of Coryate. An explanatory note at the head of these lines describes them as 'Cabalisticall Verses, which by transposition of words, syllables, and letters make excellent sense, otherwise none'. Without further ado, we are launched on literary nonsense at high tide:

> Even as the waves of brainlesse butter'd fish,
> With bugle horne writ in the Hebrew tongue,

24 For this identification see Strachan, *Life of Coryate*, p. 290.
25 'Stewed prune' was also a slang term for a whore, by association with 'stews'.

> Fuming up flounders like a chafing-dish,
> That looks asquint upon a Three-mans song . . .[26]

That explanatory note was, needless to say, only mock-explanatory. Contributing as he was to a collection of poems written for show (which includes pattern-poems and acrostic verses), Hoskyns pretended that he was performing an even more elaborate formal exercise. Although there was little general knowledge of cabbalistic matters in England in this period (the 'briefe Index, explayning most of the hardest words' appended to the 1611 edition of Sylvester's translation of du Bartas explicates 'Cabalistick' as 'mysticall Traditions among the Jewes Rabbins'), Hoskyns's learned friends would probably have been aware of the interest shown in the Jewish cabbalistic tradition by Renaissance scholars such as Reuchlin and Pico della Mirandola.[27] They may have had some knowledge of the techniques of verbal and numerical analysis applied by cabbalists to the Hebrew scriptures, of which the most complex method, 'themurah' or 'transposition', involved a combination of letter-substitution and anagrammatic interchanges of the resultant letters.[28]

A well-known anti-astrological work published by the Earl of Northampton in 1583 had included a section on the 'Arte of Cabolistes' which observed: 'Another kinde of mysterie they had lykewise, which consisted eyther in resolving wordes of one sentence, and letters of one word that were united, or uniting letters of one word, or wordes of one sentence that were dissevered.' 'But', the Earl continued, 'I declaime against the follies of the foolishe Jewes of this tyme, and some other giddy cockbraynes of our own, which by the resolution or transporting of letters, syllables and sentences, are not ashamed to professe the

---

26 Poem 1.
27 G. du Bartas, *Divine Weekes and Workes*, trans. J. Sylvester (London, 1611), sig. Hhh8ʳ. On early modern knowledge of the cabbala, see J. L. Blau, *The Christian Interpretation of the Cabala in the Renaissance* (New York, 1944), and F. Secret, *Les Kabbalistes chrétiens de la renaissance* (Paris, 1964).
28 Blau, *Christian Interpretation of the Cabala*, pp. 8–9.

finding out of secrete destinies.'[29] That last sentence is quite closely echoed in Hoskyns's own phrasing ('which by transposition of words, syllables, and letters'); and this fact makes it possible to reconstruct the precise mental process by which Hoskyns was led to compose his seminal nonsense verses. The most likely explanation is that Hoskyns, prompted by one of the incidents described by Coryate and depicted in his title-page (an encounter between Coryate and a Rabbi in the Venetian Ghetto, when the parson's son from Odcombe immediately tried to convert the Rabbi to Christianity), had leafed through his books in search of an idea for a witty pseudo-Rabbinical conceit, and had stumbled on this passage in the Earl of Northampton's account. Perhaps it was the reference to 'giddy cockbraynes' which alerted him to the possibility of a comic application to Coryate.

Those twelve lines of high nonsense were, apparently, the only such verses Hoskyns ever wrote. The genre of nonsense poetry might now have died in infancy, were it not for the intervention of another minor poet, who adopted it and made it his own. He was John Taylor, the 'Water-poet', and once again it was Tom Coryate who provided the catalyst.

Taylor was the son of a Gloucestershire barber-surgeon; born in 1580, he was briefly educated at Gloucester Grammar School before being packed off to London and apprenticed to a waterman (the Thames equivalent of a gondolier).[30] During his apprentice years he also served several times in the Navy: the Thames watermen were frequently used as a kind of naval reserve. In 1598 Taylor took up the waterman's trade. Resident in Southwark, the play-house and low-life district on the south

---

29 H. Howard, Earl of Northampton, *A Defensative against the Poyson of Supposed Prophecies* (London, 1583), sig. Ccii'.
30 Taylor's life is briefly summarized in the entry in the *DNB*, and in Notestein, *Four Worthies*, pp. 169–208. These studies are now largely superseded by Capp, *World of John Taylor*. For a brief, sympathetic account of Taylor, see Schama, *Landscape and Memory*, pp. 320–28.

bank of the river, he formed many friendships with actors and writers. In 1612 he joined the ranks of the latter when he published the first of what was to become a torrent of minor literary productions, many of them in humorous quasi-doggerel verse. Although the title of this pamphlet was probably designed to cash in on the fame of Coryate's book (*The Sculler, rowing from Tiber to Thames: with his Boat laden with a Hotch-potch, or Gallimawfrey of Sonnets, Satyres, and Epigrams*), it was not primarily directed against Coryate; Taylor was not pretending to have travelled to Italy himself, the reference to the 'Tiber' merely alluding to the fact that the first group of epigrams consisted of fierce attacks on the Papacy and the Roman Catholic clergy. But one of the poems in this work was entitled 'To Tom Coriat', and it addressed him in tones of genial disrespect:

> What matters for the place I first came from
> I am no Duncecomb, Coxecomb, Odcomb *Tom*
> Nor am I like a wool-pack, crammed with Greek,
> *Venus* in *Venice* minded to goe seeke . . .[31]

This seems to have cut Coryate to the quick: 'it was one thing for the wits and gallants to flatter him with their notice by laughing at his antics and quite another to be publicly called a dunce by an upstart waterman.'[32] Although he did not stoop to reply in print, his reaction was reported by Taylor in a later work:

> He frets, he fumes, he rages and exclaimes,
> And vowes to rouze me from the River Thames.[33]

Taylor had a talent for self-publicizing, and would not allow the opportunity to slip. He quickly turned out another pamphlet, entitled *Laugh, and be Fat: or, a Commentary upon the Odcombyan Banket*, in which he supplied a humorous running commentary on the prefatory verses to Coryate's *Crudities*. His reaction

---

31 J. Taylor, *All the Workes* (London, 1630), sig. Bbb3^r.
32 Strachan, *Life of Coryate*, p. 149.
33 Taylor, *Workes*, sig. Ff4^r.

to Sanford's poem was one of bemusement rather than emulation:

> Thou fatall impe to Glastonburie Abbey,
> The Prophecie includes thou art no baby . . .[34]

To Peacham's poem in 'the Utopian Tongue' he responded in kind, filling his own version of gibberish with semi-submerged fragments of abuse (poem 5). And on reaching Hoskyns's poem he paused only to indulge in a little trans-linguistic pun ('Cabalistical, or Horse verse') before launching himself into headlong imitation:

> Mount *Malvorn* swimming on a big-limb'd gnat,
> And *Titan* tilting with a flaming Swanne . . .[35]

This was Taylor's induction into the art of nonsense poetry, an art of which he was to become, in his own time if not in ours, the acknowledged master.

In 1613 Taylor renewed his ridicule of Coryate with another poetical pamphlet, *Odcombs Complaint*. Coryate had set out in October 1612 on his second great adventure, a journey to India, and Taylor's new work was a set of spoof elegies, based on the supposition that Coryate had drowned on his way to Istanbul. These included an 'Epitaph in the *Barmooda* tongue, which must be pronounced *with the accent of the grunting* of a hogge' (poem 6 – this resembles a later gibberish poem by Taylor 'in the Barbarian tongue', ridiculing tobacco-taking: poem 9), another in the 'Utopian tongue' (poem 7), and finally an exuberant sextet of sonnets in the high Hoskyns nonsense style (poem 8). Thomas Coryate did eventually die on his travels, succumbing to a 'flux' at Surat in December 1617; and within a few years Taylor had emancipated his own nonsense writing from the narrow confines of his feud with Coryate. At the end of a humorous prose pamphlet on fasting and feasting published in 1620, *Jack a Lent*, Taylor added twenty-three lines of nonsense

---

34 Taylor, *Workes*, sig. Gg3ᵛ.
35 Poem 4.

verse, entitled 'Certaine Blanke Verses written of purpose to no purpose' (poem 10). The genre was now a firmly established part of his repertoire.

Two years later Taylor issued the first of his two large-scale nonsense works, *Sir Gregory Nonsence His Newes from No Place* (poem 11); and in 1630 all his hitherto published nonsense poems received a much wider circulation when he published a fat volume of his collected works, which, as he proudly announced on the title-page, were 'Sixty and three in Number'. Taylor was now a celebrity, and his nonsense poetry was one of the things that helped to make him famous. A comedy by the minor playwright Henry Glapthorne, published in 1640, includes a scene in which a master instructs his servant to buy books. '*John Taylor*, get me his nonsense,' he commands; to which the servant replies, 'You mean all his workes sir.'[36] And three years after the republication of *Sir Gregory Nonsence* in Taylor's *Workes*, another poet, the balladeer Martin Parker, published an explicit homage to Taylor, entitled *The Legend of Sir Leonard Lack-Wit, sonne in law to Sir Gregory Nonsence*. Most of this work was in nonsense prose, of a by now quite recognizable type:

> The petty-foggers of *Virginia* set *Hercules* and *Caucasus* together by the eares, about the drinking of fryed Harti-chokes. The blue bores of Islington Forrest leapt over Pancrasse Church to invade the Turkes Army in Bosworth Field: these things (with diligent negligence) were told to the Emperour of *Pyramedes*, who sent foure dripping pannes to tell great *Tamberlaine*, that *London* had never a Cuckold in it.[37]

And so on, for all of eighteen pages. Parker's one venture into nonsense poetry in this production (poem 12), on the other hand, illustrates the surprising difficulty of the genre: organized

---

36 H. Glapthorne, *Plays and Poems*, ed. R. H. Shepherd, 2 vols. (London, 1874), p. 170 (from *Wit in a Constable*, I.i). For a discussion of this and further evidence of Taylor's popularity, see Capp, *World of John Taylor*, pp. 69–73, 189–90.
37 M. Parker, *The Legend of Sir Leonard Lack-Wit, sonne in law to Sir Gregory Nonsence* (London, 1633), sig. A8ʳ.

in rigid rhetorical patterns and constantly veering into sense, it may at least function as a tribute to Taylor by demonstrating the superiority of his own nonsense.

Another trace of Taylor's influence can be found in a nonsense poem which can confidently be attributed to the minor poet James Smith (poem 25); first published in 1658, it was probably written in the mid 1640s.[38] The mock-scholarly footnotes attached to this work place it in the tradition of academic self-parody to which the poem by John Sanford (poem 3) also belonged. But a comparison between the texts of these two poems clearly shows that, somewhere in between, the influence of Taylor's own nonsense poetry has interposed itself. Smith's line 'But then an *Antelope* in Sable blew' recalls Taylorian lines such as 'With that grim *Pluto* all in Scarlet blue'; other lines, such as 'And to the butter'd Flownders cry'd out, *Holla*', or 'And mounting straight upon a Lobsters thigh', betray both Taylor's habitual parodying of Marlowe (discussed below, pp. 42–4), and that gastronomic obsession with marine delicacies which characterizes so much of the nonsense poetry in the Hoskyns–Taylor tradition.

Smith's involvement in writing nonsense poetry is significant too in the light of a recent discovery about a London literary club or coterie of the late 1620s and early 1630s, the 'Order of the Fancy', to which he belonged. A denunciation of Smith in a legal document of 1633 affirmed: 'That for 4 yeares last past James Smith hath bin a Common and ordinary frequenter of tavernes alehouses playhouses, and players Companye . . . and he with them and others stiled themselves of *the order of the fancye* whose practise was to drinke excessively, and to speake non sence . . .' Another witness declared: 'That he heard James Smith say and . . . bragge that he was one of the Cheifest and first founders of that societye, and that he of that Company that could speake best non sence was Counted the best man,

---

38 For the attribution and dating see Raylor, *Cavaliers, Clubs, and Literary Culture*, pp. 182–5, 226–7.

which was him selfe . . .'[39] The modern scholar who discovered this evidence has painstakingly reconstructed the possible membership of the 'Order', which probably included the playwright Philip Massinger, the poets John Mennes, Robert Herrick and William Davenant, and several other known London wits and members of the Inns of Court.[40] There is thus a clear similarity (though not, it seems, a direct connection) between this group and the grouping of wits at the Mitre tavern which helped give rise to the first nonsense poem by Hoskyns. Nor is this surprising, since the self-parodic routines of nonsense poetry are characteristic products of enclosed, self-conscious institutions such as clubs. The 'non sence' spoken by Smith and his friends may of course have been closer to the 'fustian' style of Hoskyns's nonsense speech (a style which, as we shall see, was by now becoming almost an obligatory party trick for undergraduates in at least one Oxford college) than to the concentrated nonsense poetry practised by Taylor.[41] But it is quite inconceivable that any gathering of London wits and players in the 1630s could have been ignorant of John Taylor's well-known contributions to the genre.

Thanks to his tremendous efforts at self-publicizing, Taylor was by now almost a public institution. He was famous not only for his poetry and pamphlets but also for his 'travels' – journeys to different parts of the British Isles, announced by prospectus in advance and described in pamphlet-form soon after their completion. Most of these had the nature of stunts, such as his much-trumpeted journey to Edinburgh and back without spending, borrowing or stealing any money on the way. One stunt, reminiscent of the famous wager-journeys of Elizabethan comedians such as Will Kemp, might almost be described as a nonsense journey: he attempted to scull from London to Queenborough (on the Isle of Sheppey, off the Kentish coast)

39 Ibid., pp. 60–61.
40 Ibid., pp. 84–97.
41 On the performance of 'nonsense' by Oxford undergraduates, see below, p. 34.

in a brown paper boat with oars made out of salted dried fish.[42] But many of Taylor's travelogues supply valuable descriptions of ordinary English life, and two of his more entrepreneurial publications are important source-materials for modern historians: his catalogue of taverns in the Home Counties, and his directory of carrier services from all the provincial towns of England to their terminus-points at different London inns.[43]

A few months after the outbreak of the Civil War Taylor was publicly accused of royalism and 'popery'; and in early 1643 he refused to pay a parliamentary tax. Soon afterwards he fled, first to Windsor and then to Oxford (the royalist garrison town and seat of government), where he remained until 1646.[44] Taylor's own royalism was not in doubt; he wrote elegies on Charles I after his execution in 1649, and later that year was arrested for espionage and/or corresponding with the King's friends.[45] Taylor's devotion to the Crown spurred him into another literary feud, this time against an old friend, the Puritan poet George Wither. Wither had supported the King against the Scots in 1639, but by 1642 he had gone over to the parliamentary side. When the Civil War broke out he raised his own troop of cavalry; his next book of poems, entitled *Campo-Musae* (1643), was written while serving in the field as a captain.[46] Taylor, in one of his several pamphlets written in the form of proclamations by the Devil and ironically praising the war, referred in 1644 to 'our dear sons *Mercurius Britannicus*, *George Wither* (the Gull's Darling) and *Booker*, the Aetheriall Planeteriall learned Preterpluperfect Asse-trologian, with the rest of our *English and*

---

42 This and Taylor's other journeys are discussed in Capp, *World of John Taylor*, pp. 18–28, 58, 158–62.
43 *Taylor's Travels and Circular Perambulation* (London, 1636); *The Carrier's Cosmographie* (London, 1637).
44 Capp, *World of John Taylor*, pp. 150–51.
45 Ibid., p. 158; Notestein, *Four Worthies*, p. 188.
46 See C. S. Hensley, *The Later Career of George Wither* (The Hague, 1969), pp. 67, 89–91.

Scottish Doves, Scoutes, Scoundrells and Lyurnall-makers'.[47] In the same year he issued his *Aqua-Musae: or, Cacafogo, Cacadaemon, Captain George Wither Wrung in the Withers*, which concluded with a brief nonsense poem (poem 15). A final quatrain following this poem made – for the first time in Taylor's output – a claim about the ideological significance of nonsense poetry:

> And is not this rare Nonsence, prethee tell,
> Much like thy writing, if men marke it well:
> For Nonsence is Rebellion, and thy writing,
> Is nothing but Rebellious Warres inciting.[48]

If this were the only surviving specimen of nonsense poetry, it would be tempting to take this comment and construct on its foundation a whole theory about the political significance of nonsense as an expression of the satirical-political 'world turned upside-down' theme during the Civil War. That this theme appealed to Taylor is evident from a poem he wrote to accompany a woodcut (of which it provides a full and accurate description) in 1642:

> This Monstrous Picture plainely doth declare
> This land (quite out of order) out of square.
> His Breeches on his shoulders do appeare,
> His doublet on his lower parts doth weare;
> His Boots and Spurs upon his Arms and Hands,
> His Gloves upon his feet (whereon he stands)
> The Church or'eturnd (a lamentable show)
> The Candlestick above, the light below,
> The Cony hunts the Dogge, the Rat the Cat,
> The Horse doth whip the Cart (I pray marke that)
> The Wheelbarrow doth drive the man (oh Base)
> And Eeles and Gudgeon flie a mighty pace.[49]

47 *Mercurius Infernalis; or Orderlesse Orders, Votes, Ordinances, and Commands from Hell, established by a Close Committee of the Divell and his Angels* (London, 1644), p. 6. 'Booker' was John Booker, parliamentarian propagandist and author of popular astrological works.
48 *Aqua-Musae*, p. 11.
49 Taylor, *Mad Fashions, Od Fashions* (London, 1642).

But possessing, as we do, the earlier history of nonsense poetry, we can see that it was a literary phenomenon long before it became an ostensibly political one; Taylor's remarks about nonsense and rebellion at the end of poem 15 are just another example of his talent for turning whatever materials he had at hand to an immediate topical use.

This poem was followed by two brief extensions of the same theme (poem 16), added at the start and finish of a pamphlet which Taylor published in the form of a mock-news-sheet in 1648, *Mercurius Nonsensicus*. These verses are of interest for two other reasons. The first is their curious mixture of literary aims and conventions, which makes them unlike the rest of Taylor's nonsense output. Some of the lines are examples of the 'impossibilia' tradition, which is discussed below (pp. 78–88). At the same time they are a direct parody (again, untypical of Taylor) of a popular poem on man's mortality:

> Like as the damask rose you see,
> Or like the blossom on the tree,
> Or like the dainty flower of May,
> Or like the morning to the day . . .[50]

The second point of interest here is that the original idea for subjecting those trite lines to nonsensical parody seems to have come from another minor poet, Richard Corbet – who was probably, therefore, the third writer of such concentrated nonsense poetry in English. In 1641 a collection of humorous verse had published a similar parody in three stanzas (poem 14); the author's name was not stated there, but some of the early manuscripts containing this poem ascribe it to Corbet. A later collection, published in 1658, included another nonsense poem (poem 13) under the title 'A non sequitur, by Dr. Corbet'. Both poems show the evident influence of Taylor, containing some of his

---

50 First printed in M. Sparke, *The Crums of Comfort* (London, 1628), and since attributed to Francis Quarles, Francis Beaumont and Henry King, among others; see N. Ault (ed.), *Seventeenth Century Lyrics*, 2nd edn. (London, 1950), pp. 42–4, 492.

own most characteristic images, such as lobsters and bag-puddings; but the second poem is in an elaborate classical form (the Pindaric ode) which Taylor seems never to have attempted. Since the two poems are clearly quite closely connected, their separate attributions to Corbet can be taken as mutually reinforcing evidence of his authorship of both.[51] Although he rose to be Bishop first of Oxford (1628) and then of Norwich (1632; he died in 1635), Corbet was best known for his wit and high spirits; Aubrey described him as 'very facetious, and a good fellowe'.[52] He may have read Taylor's *Workes* and the first printed version of the mortality poem at roughly the same time (1630); or he may have been familiar with the latter as it circulated, like so much of the poetry of this period, in manuscript. His own nonsense verses had evidently been circulating in this way for many years before they appeared in print.

Also circulating in manuscript were several more or less close imitations of Taylor. One of these (poem 21), which seems never to have been published, appears in a manuscript together with a copy of Taylor's verses from *Jack a Lent*: it is so close to Taylor's style that it could indeed be attributed to him, were it not for the fact that the manuscript attributes it to 'T. W.'. Another (poem 20) in a much more bitter and scatological vein than anything that survives from Taylor's own pen, is entitled 'A sonnett to cover my Epistles taile peece'. This suggests that it was intended to be printed at the end of a dedicatory epistle; but it has not yet been located in any printed work. Two other reasonably successful imitations of Taylor's style were printed in collections of humorous poetry which appeared in 1641 (poem 22) and 1655 (poem 23); a more elementary fragment in a similar vein appeared in another such collection in 1656 (poem 26). As always with anonymous poems printed in miscellanies of this kind, it is impossible to know for how long they had been

---

51 They are placed in the category 'Dubia' by Corbet's modern editors: Corbet ['Corbett'], *Poems*, ed. J. A. W. Bennett and H. R. Trevor-Roper (Oxford, 1955), pp. 95–7, 162–4.
52 Aubrey, *Brief Lives*, i, p. 184.

circulating, by manuscript or by word of mouth, before they were finally printed.

The one fragment of nonsense by Taylor which seems to have undergone widespread circulation in manuscript (and, evidently, in recitation and memory) was contained in a work published in February 1654, just two months after his death: *The Essence, Quintessence, Insence, Innocence, Lye-sence, & Magnificence of Nonsence upon Sence: or, Sence upon Nonsence* (poem 17).[53] This was Taylor's longest and most ambitious nonsense performance; only three of its twenty-three pages are not in nonsense verse. (Those three pages contain a doggerel about 'the death of a Scottish nag', which includes what is probably the longest list of horse-diseases in English poetry, but is not reproduced in the present collection.) This little volume, as published in 1654, was in fact the end-product of a cumulative process: the first part had been published as *Nonsence upon Sence* in 1651, and that work had then been reissued in the following year with additional material, under the title *Nonsence upon Sence, or, Sence upon Nonsence: Chuse you either, or neither.* Curiously, it was the very last set of additional verses, written in the final weeks of Taylor's life and appearing for the first time in the posthumous *Essence of Nonsence upon Sence*, that yielded the most popular and enduring of all Taylor's nonsense poems. One section of this work, beginning 'O that my wings could bleat like butter'd pease', recurs in several manuscript copies, usually with 'lungs' instead of 'wings'; together with twenty extra lines, probably by a subsequent imitator, this acquired a separate existence as a nonsense poem (poem 18) and was printed in a popular anthology three years after Taylor's death.[54] (A similar extension or

---

53 The date of publication is given as 10 February 1654 by Thomason (BL E 1465 (1)); Taylor was buried on 5 December 1653 (Capp, *World of John Taylor*, p. 162).
54 *Wit and Drollery* (London, 1656), p. 233. It has been reprinted in J. Ashton (ed.), *Humour, Wit, and Satire of the Seventeenth Century* (London, 1883), pp. 3–4; C. Wells (ed.), *A Nonsense Anthology* (New York, 1958), pp. 16–17; G. Grigson (ed.), *The Faber Book of Nonsense Verse, with a Sprinkling of Nonsense Prose* (London, 1979), p. 34; and H. Haughton (ed.), *The Chatto Book of Nonsense Poetry* (London, 1988), p. 104.

adaptation of Taylor's last nonsense poem exists, in somewhat fragmentary form, in a manuscript compilation; it is printed here as poem 19.) Two years later, another imitation of Taylor was published in a collection of 'Such Voluntary and Jovial Copies of Verses, as were lately receiv'd from some of the Wits in the Universities'; this poem, by 'T. C.' (poem 24), pays direct homage to Taylor by borrowing one of his most characteristic phrases for its title ('Upon the Gurmundizing Quagmires . . .'), and is perhaps the most successful of all the attempts to replicate his style.[55]

To follow the history of English nonsense poetry beyond the seventeenth century would be outside the scope of this Introduction. However, one suggestive link can be made between Taylor's last poem and the genre of nonsense poetry in the nineteenth century. A poem published in 1815 by the minor American author Henry Coggswell Knight, entitled 'Lunar Stanzas', has long been recognized as one of the path-breaking works of nineteenth-century nonsense: Carolyn Wells called it 'among the best examples of the early writers', and one recent study has described it as 'one of the most astonishing nonsense-poems of the period'.[56] Two lines in this poem,

> Yet, 'twere profuse to see for pendant light,
> A tea-pot dangle in a lady's ear;

are so directly reminiscent of one of the most striking conceits in Taylor's poem,

> I grant indeed, that Rainbows layd to sleep,
> Snort like a Woodknife in a Ladies eyes,

---

55 The phrase is borrowed from Taylor's 'Certaine Sonnets' (poem 8), sonnet 5: 'The Gormundizing Quagmires of the East'.

56 Wells, 'The Sense of Nonsense', *Scribner's Magazine*, xxix (January–June 1901), pp. 239–48; here p. 241; D. Petzold, *Formen und Funktionen der englischen Nonsense-Dichtung im 19. Jahrhundert*, Erlanger Beiträge zur Sprach- und Kunstwissenschaft, xliv (Nuremberg, 1972), p. 122. The full text is given by both those writers, and by Grigson (*Faber Book of Nonsense Verse*, p. 75) and Haughton (*Chatto Book of Nonsense Poetry*, pp. 201–2).

that it is surely necessary to conclude that Knight had read either Taylor's original text or the version of these lines printed in the later anthology. We know that seventeenth-century texts were eagerly devoured by early nineteenth-century 'library cormorants' such as Robert Southey, who attempted to revive interest in Taylor with a long and sympathetic essay on the water-poet in his *Lives and Works of the Uneducated Poets* (1831). In this essay Southey quoted ten lines from Taylor's *Sir Gregory Nonsence*, describing them as 'verses of grandiloquous nonsense . . . honest right rampant nonsense'.[57] It is not impossible, therefore, that, more than 150 years after his death, Taylor's grandiloquous nonsense played some part, however indirectly, in stimulating the growing fashion for nonsense poetry which was to find its finest examples in the works of Edward Lear and Lewis Carroll.

57 *The Lives and Works of the Uneducated Poets*, ed. J. S. Childers (London, 1925), p. 43.

CHAPTER 2

Fustian, bombast and satire:
the stylistic preconditions of
English seventeenth-century nonsense poetry

THE 'FUSTIAN' SPEECH performed by John Hoskyns in the winter of 1597–8 (above, pp. 9–11) belonged to a genre which formed an important part of the background to the nonsense poetry of this period. Many seventeenth-century writers would use the terms 'nonsense' and 'fustian' almost interchangeably. This may surprise the modern reader, to whom it is obvious that most instances of fustian prose have a definite sense, albeit one expressed in needlessly obscure or elaborate terms. But the association of fustian with nonsense must be taken seriously. It helps to show that in this period nonsense writing was thought of primarily in terms of a parodic stylistic exercise: to write nonsense was not to express the strangeness of unconscious thought but to engage in a highly self-conscious stylistic game. The history of fustian prose still waits to be written; a brief account can be given here.

The phenomenon itself was older than its name. Many writers in the sixteenth century were acutely conscious of the fact that large quantities of vocabulary were being lifted out of Latin (either directly or via French) and added to the English language. A few (such as the Bible translators William Tyndale and John Cheke) deliberately resisted this trend; others welcomed the enrichment of the language, but were aware at the same time that English was acquiring new registers of ornate and lofty diction which could easily be abused. Two varieties of misuse could be distinguished: the excessively 'aureate' language of the would-be courtier, and the deliberate obscurity of the would-be scholar. Since both of these involved the use of cumbersome Latinate terminology, they were easily conflated into a single stylistic fault: the use of 'inkhorn terms'. One very influential English handbook, Wilson's *Arte of Rhetorique* (first edition 1553; revised edition 1560), put it as follows:

> The unlearned or foolish phantasticall, that smelles but of learning ... will so Latin their tongues, that the simple can not but wonder at their talke, and thinke surely they speake by some revelation. I know them that thinke *Rhetorique* to stande wholie upon darke wordes, and hee that can catch an ynke horne terme by the taile, him they coumpt to be a fine Englisheman, and a good *Rhetorician*.[1]

To illustrate his point, Wilson printed a preposterous letter, sent (as he claimed, with tongue in cheek) by a Lincolnshire man to an acquaintance in the household of the Lord Chancellor:

> Pondering, expending, and revoluting with my selfe, your ingent affabilitie, and ingenious capacity for mundane affaires: I cannot but celebrate, & extol your magnifical dexteritie above all other. For how could you have adepted such illustrate prerogative, and dominicall superioritie, if the fecunditie of your ingenie had not been so fertile and wonderfull pregnant ...[2]

This still retains some power to impress the modern reader; it requires an effort of the imagination, however, to realize now just how outlandish this sounded in the mid sixteenth century, when so many of these words were newly minted.

Wilson may not have invented this parodic genre in English, but he certainly helped to ensure its widespread popularity. By the 1590s, as we have already seen, it was standard fare at the Inns of Court revels; and it is quite certain that Hoskyns had studied Wilson's book carefully, since some of the word-play in

1 G. H. Mair (ed.), *Wilson's Arte of Rhetorique 1560* (Oxford, 1909), p. 162.
2 Ibid., p. 163.

his own 'fustian speech' is taken from another section of *The Arte of Rhetorique*.[3] But Wilson was not the only popularizer of the genre. Sir Philip Sidney, writing in the 1580s, had also given a fine specimen of it in the person of Rombus, the learned fool in his *Arcadia*:

> Why you brute Nebulons have you had my corpusculum so long among you, and cannot tell how to edifie an argument? Attend and throw your ears to me, for I am gravidated with child, till I have endoctrinated your plumbeous cerebrosities. First you must divisionate your point, quasi you would cut a cheese into two particles, for thus must I uniforme my speeche to your obtuse conceptions . . .[4]

So popular was this passage that an allusion to 'plumbeous cerebrosities' became a common hallmark of later fustian speeches.

At the time when Sidney was completing his *Arcadia*, English prose was experiencing a huge intensification of stylistic self-consciousness as a result of the influence of John Lyly's *Euphues*. Ornate, mellifluous and elaborate, 'Euphuistic' prose was a non-stop succession (and superimposition) of stylistic devices, especially alliteration and the balancing and echoing of clauses, in a diction both lofty and pretty. This style encouraged courtly, 'aureate' prose to attempt new heights, while at the same time slightly blurring the line between extravagant achievement and self-parody. Thomas Coryate supplied a very blurred instance of this when he printed the 'orations' he had made when delivering copies of his *Crudities* to members of the royal family in 1611. His address to Prince Henry, for example, began:

> Most scintillant *Phosphorus* of our British *Trinacria*, Even as the Christalline deaw, that is exhaled up into the ayre out of the cavernes & spungie pores of the succulent Earth,

3 Ibid., p. 203 (the play on 'horse-mill' and 'mill-horse'). Hoskyns refers to this instance of the rhetorical figure 'antimetabole' in his own MS treatise on rhetoric, 'Directions for Speech and Style', printed in Osborn, *Life of Hoskyns*, pp. 114–66: here p. 129.

4 *The Countess of Pembroke's Arcadia*, ed. A. Feuillerat (Cambridge, 1926), p. 335.

doeth by his distillation descend, and disperse it selfe
againe upon the spacious superficies of his mother *Earth*,
and so consequently fecundate the same with his bountifull
irrigation . . .[5]

This is quite close to the sort of thing 'fustian' prose parodied.
But the essence of fustian was that it parodied the language of
scholars, rather than courtiers. In Act III of Jonson's *Every
Man out of his Humour* (first performed in 1599) Carlo Buffone
says to his companion: 'prithee, let's talk fustian a little, and
gull 'em: make 'em believe we are great scholars'. The speech
he proceeds to make (which, more than any other instance of
fustian prose, verges on the fully nonsensical) depends for its
'fustian' effect not on devices such as alliteration but on the
sheer density of inkhorn terms:

> Now, sir, whereas the ingenuity of the time and the soul's
> synderesis are but embryons in nature, added to the paunch
> of Esquiline and the intervallum of the zodiac, besides
> the ecliptic line being optic and not mental, but by the
> contemplative and theoric part thereof doth demonstrate
> to us the vegetable circumference, and the ventosity of the
> Tropics . . .[6]

That fustian prose normally retained some element of scholarly
or academic pretensions is hardly surprising, since it was the
rituals of places of learning – the Inns of Court and the universities – that kept it going as a popular genre. Anthony Wood
supplies a valuable description of the Christmas traditions he
experienced at Merton College, Oxford, in 1647. Fires were lit
in the College hall on every feast-day and holiday from All
Saints to Candlemas:

> At all these fires every night, which began to be made a
> little after five of the clock, the senior undergraduats would
> bring into the hall the juniors or freshmen between that

5 *Coryats Crambe* (London, 1611), sig. A2.
6 III. iv. 19–24: Jonson, *Complete Plays*, ed. G. A. Wilkes, 4 vols. (Oxford, 1981–2),
i, p. 341.

time and six of the clock, and there make them sit downe on a forme in the middle of the hall, joyning to the declaiming desk: which done, every one in order was to speake some pretty apothegme, or make a jest or bull, or speake some eloquent nonsense, to make the company laugh.[7]

Wood also recorded the 'eloquent nonsense' which he himself spoke on that occasion: 'Most reverent Seniors, may it please your Gravities to admit into your presence a kitten of the Muses, and a meer frog of Helicon to croak the cataracts of his plumbeous cerebrosity before your sagacious ingenuities . . .'[8] Writing in the 1680s, Wood apologetically observed that this illustrated 'the folly and simplicity of those times'; at some time between 1647 and the restoration of Charles II in 1660, he wrote, 'it was disused, and now such a thing is absolutely forgotten'.[9] In this last claim he was not quite accurate. A few examples of fustian can be found in publications of the late seventeenth century; the generation which had been at Oxford or Cambridge in the 1640s and 1650s still formed a significant part of the reading public, and one would not expect the genre to become 'absolutely forgotten' until that generation itself was no more. One late example can be found in a compilation of humorous letters edited by Charles Gildon and published in 1692. Introduced as a letter 'From a conceited Fellow that affects to write fine Language, tho' he makes his Letter perfect Nonsense', and signed 'Jehoiachim Balderdash', it begins:

> *Obscenical Sir,*
> I could not recognise upon any Substance since I was so Malheureus in your transcendent Conversation, which the Philosophy of the *Cymerians* most abtrusly demonstrated, tho' I must confess, I for those Ecclarisments,

7 A. Wood, *The Life and Times of Anthony Wood, Antiquary, of Oxford, 1632–1695, as Described by Himself,* ed. A. Clark, 5 vols., Oxford Historical Society, xix, xxi, xxvi, xxx, xl (Oxford, 1891–1900), i, p. 133.
8 Ibid., i, p. 139.
9 Ibid., i, pp. 139–40.

and doubtful Disputations have no small Antiquity, and
yet the extraordinary Regret that Humidity, and
Preter-natural turn of your Wit superseded them, makes
me desire a fresh Excrement from you to nourish my
Intellectuals . . .[10]

Reading this, one becomes aware of a more fundamental reason
for the decline of the genre: whereas much latinate vocabulary
was still either off-puttingly scholarly or completely new-minted
in the late sixteenth century, such large quantities of it had been
absorbed into the language during the next hundred years that
it was becoming impossible to achieve the same effects of sheer
density and outlandishness any longer.

As the 'fustian' speech in Jonson's *Every Man out of his
Humour* and Hoskyns's performance of the previous year dem-
onstrate, the term 'fustian' was well established by the late 1590s.
It is, however, hard to say exactly when this name had come into
use. The *OED* draws a comparison between the development of
this term and the use – which is datably earlier – of the word
'bombast'; other metaphors of cloth or material, such as 'taffeta',
were also used in this period, and their meanings were eventually
conflated. But the more closely one looks into the history of
each term, the further apart their original meanings seem to
stand. Bombast (a kind of coarse cotton-wool) was used by
tailors for padding, and its natural metaphorical application was
to poetry or oratory which was padded out with redundancies
or puffed up to impress. This was a matter of rhetorical extravagance and excessive grandeur rather than pretentious obscurity:
when George Puttenham drew up his list of stylistic defects in
The Arte of English Poesie (written in the 1570s and 1580s) he
kept his strictures on 'inkhorn terms' and over-Latinate diction
quite separate from his attack on what he called '*Bomphiologia*,
or Pompious speech', in which he observed: 'Others there be
that fall into the contrary vice [contrary, that is, to the vice of

10 C. Gildon (ed.), *The Post-boy rob'd of his Mail: or, the Pacquet broke open*
(London, 1692), pp. 83–4.

excessively mean diction] by using such bombasted wordes, as seeme altogether farced full of winde, being a great deal to high and loftie for the matter, whereof ye may finde too many in all popular rymers'.[11] By the end of the 1580s there was one style above all that attracted this criticism: the extravagant poetic oratory of Marlowe. In 1589 Thomas Nashe pointed unmistakably at Marlowe's *Tamburlaine* when he referred to those playwrights 'who, mounted on the stage of arrogance, think to out-brave better pens with the swelling bumbast of a bragging blanke verse'. Swelling and bragging, rather than affecting obscurity, were the original connotations of 'bombast'.

Fustian, on the other hand, was a 'velure' cloth made either from cotton or from a mixture of flax and wool, so silky in appearance that it could be used in place of velvet. A modern historian of costume observes that 'Elizabethan statutes of apparel limiting the use of silk materials to rich nobility made fustian a fashionable substitute for middle-class persons'.[12] So the natural metaphorical use of the term was for the pretentious and the bogus – things which appeared more valuable or exotic than they really were. The earliest known use of the word as a linguistic metaphor comes in a popular work which itself used the device of representing the social and moral world by means of differences in cloth and clothing: Robert Greene's *A Quip for an Upstart Courtier: or, a quaint Dispute between Velvet-breeches and Cloth-breeches* (1592). A description of a fashionable barber includes the following: 'Then comes he out with his

11 G. Puttenham, *The Arte of English Poesie*, ed. G. D. Willcock and A. Walker (Cambridge, 1936), pp. 259–60. The criticisms of inkhorn affectation are on pp. 144–5, 252–3. Puttenham's use of the word 'farced' serves as a chance reminder that the literary terms 'bombast' and 'farce' have coincidentally similar origins: a farce was originally (in medieval France) something 'stuffed in' as a comic interpolation or interlude.

12 M. C. Linthicum, *Costume in the Drama of Shakespeare and His Contemporaries* (Oxford, 1936), p. 106. In England, the manufacture of fustian (using a cotton weft and a linen warp) began in the late 16th century; by 1621 40,000 pieces of fustian were being produced each year, chiefly in Lancashire (A. C. Wood, *A History of the Levant Company* (London, 1935), pp. 74–5).

fustian Eloquence, and ... saith, Sir, Will you have your Worships Hair cut after the *Italian* Manner, short and round, and then frounct with the curling Yrons, to make it looke like to a Halfmoone in a Mist?'[13] Two years later Thomas Nashe used the term in his *The Terrors of the Night*, referring to mountebank astrologers 'with their vaunting and prating, and speaking fustian in steede of Greeke'.[14] This usage by Nashe (unlike that by Greene) does show that the term had already acquired some connotations of pseudo-scholarliness; but in the early 1590s it was obviously not quite tied to the stylistic phenomenon of addiction to inkhorn terms. When Nashe himself had mounted one of the most famous attacks on that phenomenon in his verbal assault on Gabriel Harvey, *Strange Newes, of the Intercepting certain Letters* (1592), he had made no use of the term 'fustian', preferring 'inkehornisme' instead.[15]

Another influential passage using the term 'fustian' also dates from the early 1590s: it comes in one of the comic interludes in Marlowe's *Dr Faustus*, which may have been written for a performance in 1594. One modern scholar has suggested that they were written by Nashe himself; Nashe's modern biographer argues, more plausibly, that they were written by someone who was influenced by Nashe's writings.[16] The passage is an exchange between Faustus' assistant, Wagner, and a 'clown':

> *Wagner*　Vilaine, call me Maister *Wagner*, and let thy left eye be diametarily fixt upon my right heele, with *quasi vestigias nostras insistere.*
>
> *Clown*　God forgive me, he speakes Dutch fustian.

There are several possible levels of allusion here. Wagner was

13 Greene, *Life and Complete Works*, ed. A. B. Grosart, 15 vols. (London, 1881–6), xi, pp. 246–7.
14 Nashe, *Works*, ed. R. B. McKerrow, rev. F. P. Wilson, 5 vols. (Oxford, 1966), i, p. 364.
15 Ibid., i, p. 316.
16 P. H. Kocher, 'Nashe's Authorship of the Prose Scenes in *Faustus*', *Modern Languages Quarterly*, iii (1942), pp. 17–40; C. Nicholl, *A Cup of News: The Life of Thomas Nashe* (London, 1984), pp. 96–7.

himself 'Dutch' (high Dutch, i.e. German). German fustian was the coarsest and cheapest of all the commonly imported varieties: so substituting 'Dutch fustian' for velvet would be the height of false pretension.[17] It is also conceivable that some word-play on 'Faustian' was intended.

The use of cloth-metaphors for speech features prominently in another play, written probably in 1593–4: Shakespeare's *Love's Labours Lost*. Here it the poetical wooer Berowne finally abjures

> Taffeta phrases, silken terms precise,
> Three-pil'd hyperboles, spruce affection,
> Figures pedantical

and declares:

> Henceforth my wooing mind shall be express'd
> In russet yeas and honest kersey noes ...[18]

('Three-pil'd' refers to the deepest-piled variety of plush velvet; 'spruce' is used in its ordinary sense of 'neat' or 'dapper', as applied to dress; and 'affection' here means 'affectation'.) Taffeta was a fine material made of glossy silk, worn by the ostentatious and the fashion-conscious: in Thomas Overbury's 'character' of 'an Innes of Court man' we read that 'His very essence he placeth in his outside, and his chiefest praier is, that his revenues may hold out for taffeta cloakes in the summer, and velvet in the winter'.[19] Shakespeare varies the metaphor according to the type of language: shimmering cloths for fine, poetic or courtly speech, and soft plush fabric for hyperbole (where the metaphor, as with 'bombast', works on tactile or three-dimensional, rather than

---

17 The cheapest imported varieties were 'Holmes', from Ulm, and 'osbrow' or 'Osborough', which was sold at Antwerp (Linthicum, *Costume in Shakespeare*, p. 107). The latter was manufactured in Augsburg.

18 V. ii. 406–8, 412–13.

19 Overbury, *The Miscellaneous Works*, ed. E. F. Rimbault (London, 1856), p. 104. This character first appeared in the edition of 1616. In his note to this passage Rimbault quotes Henry Peacham: 'a proud coxcombe in the fashion, wearing *taffata* ... thinkes all that weare cloth, and are out of fashion, to be clownes, base, and unworthie his acquaintance': *The Truth of òur Times* (London, 1638), p. 57.

visual, qualities).[20] The metaphor of 'taffeta' here operates in a quite different way from that of 'fustian': it is meant as a genuinely pretty and luxurious material.

'Tuft-taffeta' or 'tufftaffeta', however, brought further implications into play. This was a 'tufted' variety of the material, which meant that it was woven with raised stripes or spots. 'These stripes, upon being cut, left a pile like velvet, and, since the tufted parts were always a different colour from the ground, beautiful colour combinations were possible.'[21] Tufftaffeta could also appear to change its colour, according to the angle at which it was viewed or the way in which it was brushed. The mixture of colours could be associated, in the metaphor, with a mixture of different meanings. ('Motley' was similarly used as a metaphor for absurd speech: this was not the parti-coloured fool's costume we now associate with the term, but a variegated cloth made from different colours of wool.)[22]

When Hoskyns made his 'fustian' oration at Christmas 1597 he began with the apology: 'I am sorry that for your *Tufftaffeta* Speech, you shall receive but a *Fustian* Answer.' Since the tufftaffeta speech itself does not survive, we cannot tell whether he was alluding to any difference in style, or merely playing on the fact that fustian was the cheaper material. Already, any original distinctions between terms such as 'fustian', 'taffeta' and 'bombast' had begun to break down. Earlier that year, Shakespeare had written the scene in *Henry IV Part Two* where Doll Tearsheet complains of Pistol, who has been declaiming

20 Modern critics tend to blur these distinctions: Keir Elam describes the cloth-imagery of this play in general terms of 'deceptive disguise' or even 'transvestism', in a section which is headed 'Taffeta phrases' but is really concerned with hyperbole (*Shakespeare's Universe of Discourse* (Cambridge, 1984), pp. 297–8). The editor of the Arden edition adds a misleading note to these lines in Berowne's speech, suggesting that the reference to taffeta alludes to the type of clothing worn by actors. Any variety of stage-costume would have done for that purpose; the point of taffeta here is that it is a genuinely fine material.

21 Linthicum, *Costume in Shakespeare*, p. 124.

22 The idea of mixture or mix-up forms the basis of the many metaphors for verbal muddle or nonsense which come from food or drink: balderdash (a mixture of drinks), farrago (a stirred-together animal feed), mishmash and hotchpotch.

mangled passages from Marlowe: 'I cannot endure such a fustian rascal' (II. iv. 184).

The association of Marlovian poetic oratory with fustian was a powerful one, and it helped to make the terms 'fustian' and 'bombast' almost interchangeable. This was encouraged too by another idiom, the origins of which are very obscure: 'fustian fumes', the special condition of the humours that prompted people to indulge in furious invective. As a speaker in Lodge and Greene's *A Looking-Glasse for London and England* related, 'At last in a great fume, as I am very cholericke, and sometimes so hotte in my fustian fumes, that no man can abide within twentie yards of me, I start up, and so bombasted the divell, that sir, he cried out and ranne away.'[23] Another work of 1600 explained: 'Testines and furie, bee fonde effects that proceede from certaine fantasticall humours in their heades, whom wee commonly call testie & fustian fooles'.[24] It may be conjectured that this term derived not from the cloth but from an association with 'fusty'. It may have meant the fumes given off by stale liquors which are undergoing fermentation – a process which can cause bottles (like testy fools) to explode. In Shakespeare's *Troilus and Cressida* Ulysses describes how Patroclus parodied the oratorical style of Agamemnon:

> 'Tis like a chime a-mending, with terms unsquar'd,
> Which, from the tongue of roaring Typhon dropp'd,
> Would seem hyperboles. At this fusty stuff
> The large Achilles, on his press'd bed lolling,
> From his deep chest laughs out a loud applause . . .[25]

The comparison here with the volcanic Titan of classical mythology suggests that 'fusty' must surely be intended here in the sense of 'fustian fumes', i.e. explosive bombast, rather than in the sense of 'mouldy' (which, the editor of the Arden text

23 Greene, *Works*, vi, p. 93.
24 T. Garzoni, *The Hospitall of Incurable Fooles*, trans. anon. (London, 1600), p. 103. This passage concludes with a prayer to Tesiphon: 'great daughter of night, and Acheron, remoove a little thy fustian fumes from these men' (p. 107).
25 I. iii. 159–63.

believes, 'suits the rest of the food imagery in the play'). By the time this play was written (probably in 1602), bombast and fustian had almost fused into one.

Some of the linguistic factors in that process have now been described: the original overlap between bombast and fustian in their use of latinate terms; the natural conflation of cloth metaphors; and the probably coincidental use of the word 'fustian' in 'fustian fumes'. But the convergence between bombast and fustian can also be explained in terms of a literary development: the appropriation of elements of the Marlovian style by the satirical poet John Marston. And this in turn brings us close to the stylistic heart of seventeenth-century English nonsense. The development of nonsense poetry in the hands of its master, John Taylor, would have been unthinkable had it not been preceded by Marlowe and Marston. This is not just a matter of the models which Taylor parodied. The combination of Marston and Marlowe made possible a radical destabilizing of poetic diction; and of that resulting instability, Taylor's nonsense poetry was both a parody and an even more radical expression.

Marlowe's declamatory style – above all, that of *Tamburlaine* – made a huge impression on his contemporaries. It was highly rhetorical; but the rhetoric was of a different kind from that employed by earlier English tragedians. In his use of blank verse, Marlowe not only dispensed with the end-stopping of rhymed couplets, but also turned away from the enclosed pattern-making rhetorical devices which that end-stopping had encouraged: devices of alliteration and word-symmetry within the line or the couplet. Instead, his rhetoric depended much more on the nature of the diction he employed. This, together with the motoric force which blank verse made possible (with the play of declamatory speech-rhythms against the metre), created effects which could best be placed in the category of 'energy' rather than that of 'order'. One modern analysis, by Alvin Kernan, of the Marlovian grand style singles out the following seven characteristics, the majority of which are peculiarities of diction:

(1) the steady, heavy beat of 'Marlowe's mighty line' . . .
(2) the consistent use of present participles for adjectives
– 'shining' for 'bright', 'rising' for 'high' – expressing a
mind always in movement and always aspiring; (3) frequent
appearance of such 'rising' words as 'soar', 'mount' and
'climb'; (4) persistence of the rhetorical figure Hyperbole,
conveying a constant striving for a condition beyond any
known in this world . . . (5) parataxis, the joining together
of several phrases and clauses by 'and' – and . . . and . . .
and – to create a sense of endless ongoing, of constant
reaching; (6) the use of the privative suffix in words which
state limits – 'topless', 'quenchless', 'endless'; (7) frequent
use of ringing popular names and exotic geographical
places to realise the sensed wideness, brightness and rich-
ness of the world.[26]

Readers of John Taylor's nonsense verse will recognize many
of these characteristics in it. The steady onward movement of
Marlowe's mighty line is the least obvious of these in Taylor's
verses, whose movement tends to be more steady than onward.
For most of his nonsense poems he could not resist the comic-
doggerel potentialities of rhyme; and in any case the fragmentation of sense in such writing was not conducive to large-scale
cumulative effects. (Hence also the general lack of cumulative
'and . . . and' parataxis in these verses.) Taylor first made use of
blank verse for his nonsense writing in *Jack a Lent*: here the
diction is certainly Marlovian, but the rhythmical effects are
undistinguished and the thinking still comes in couplets:

Great *Jacke-a-Lent*, clad in a Robe of Ayre,
Threw mountaines higher then *Alcides* beard:
Whilst Pancradge Church, arm'd with a Samphier blade,
Began to reason of the businesse thus:
You squandring Troglodites of Amsterdam,
How long shall *Cerberus* a Tapster be?

26 A. Kernan, 'The Plays and the Playwrights', in J. L. Barroll, A. Leggatt, R.
Hosley and A. Kernan, *The Revels History of Drama in English*, iii (London, 1975),
pp. 237–474; here pp. 255–6.

'You squandring Troglodites of Amsterdam' is, however, a piece of pure mock-Marlowe, with a participial adjective, an exotic term and a resonant place-name, all wrapped up in the declamatory vocative. The most sustained piece of Marlovian nonsense achieved by Taylor was in the opening section of *Sir Gregory Nonsence his Newes from No Place* (poem 11); and there the management of large-scale syntactical structure through whole paragraphs of verse is much more assured, with the rhythmical character of the poetry also gaining in the process.

But it was Marlowe's diction that Taylor imitated most closely. Grandiose participial adjectives recur in his six sonnets in praise of Coryate: 'Conglomerating *Ajax*, in a fogge'; 'And with conglutinating haughty pride'; 'Whilst thunder-thwacking *Ossa* limps and halts'. These sonnets also exhibit the 'rising' syndrome ('gan to swell'; 'leaps and vaults'), as does the opening section of *The Essence of Nonsence upon Sence* (poem 17):

> Then mounted on a Windmill presently
> To Dunstable in Derbyshire I'le flie . . .
> From thence I'le soare to silver Cynthia's lap,
> And with Endimion take a nine years nap . . .

As for hyperbole, one of the most essential techniques of this type of nonsense poetry is to out-hyperbolize hyperbole, doing to hyperbole what hyperbole itself does to ordinary speech. The privative suffix does not play a prominent part in these poems, but exotic geographical (and classical) names are omnipresent:

> Then shall the Perecranians of the East . . .
> All knuckle deep in Paphlagonian Sands,
> Inhabite Transylvanian Netherlands . . .

And one other stylistic tic of Marlowe's poetry (not mentioned by Kernan) is also picked up by Taylor: the citing of large numbers. Where Marlowe had written

> My lord, the great commander of the world,
> Besides fifteen contributory kings
> Hath now in arms ten thousand janizaries . . .

43

> Two hundred thousand footmen that have served
> In two set battles fought in Graecia . . .[27]

Taylor could write:

> Then did the Turntripes on the Coast of *France*,
> Catch fifteene hundred thousand Grasshoppers,
> With fourteene Spanish Needles bumbasted,
> Poach'd with the Egs of fourscore Flanders Mares[28]

That Marlowe's style invited parodic imitation seems clear; and yet, a direct parody of it (which Taylor's verses are not) was curiously difficult to achieve. Its most obvious feature, heightened diction, could scarcely be heightened any further. The best early parody of it, Pistol's ranting in *Henry IV Part Two*, keeps the diction at more or less the same level and dislocates the sense:

> Shall packhorses,
> And hollow pamper'd jades of Asia,
> Which cannot go but thirty mile a day,
> Compare with Caesars, and with Cannibals,
> And Troiant Greeks? Nay, rather damn them with
> King Cerberus; and let the welkin roar.[29]

The full comic potentialities of this sort of declamatory poetry could only be exploited after it had undergone another transformation (not itself parodic), at the hands of the satirist John Marston.

Marston's two sets of satires were published in 1598: 'Certaine Satyres' as the second half of the volume *The Metamorphosis of Pigmalions Image*, and ten further satires published as *The Scourge of Villanie* later in the year. These poems were modelled in the first place on the satires of Persius and Juvenal; but they were also steeped in the Marlovian style of declamatory verse. They abound in exclamations ('O Hecatombe! o Catastrophe!'; 'O

---

27 *Tamburlaine, Part 1*, III. iii. 13–19.
28 Poem 11 (p. 172).
29 II. iv. 154–9.

hidden depth of that dread Secrecie'),[30] rhetorical questions ('Nay, shall a trencher slave extenuate, / Some *Lucrece* rape? and straight magnificate / Lewd *Jovian* lust?'),[31] and vocative constructions brimming with classical names:

> Ambitious *Gorgons*, wide-mouth'd *Lamians*,
> Shape-changing *Proteans*, damn'd *Briareans*,
> Is *Minos* dead? is *Radamanth* a sleepe?
> That ye thus dare into *Joves* Pallace creepe?[32]

Although deeply influenced by Marlowe, Marston was not trying simply to reproduce his style. Following his Roman models, he aimed at a more concentrated and crabbed type of invective; and this meant increasing the linguistic density of the verse. One way to do this was to pile up adjectives or nouns ('O what a tricksie lerned nicking straine / Is this applauded, sencles, modern vain!'; 'Fidlers, Scriveners, pedlers, tynkering knaves, / Base blew-coats, tapsters, brod-cloth minded slaves').[33] Another way of thickening the diction was to mix in inkhorn terms such as 'circumference', 'esculine' and 'capreall': this conveyed a sense of intellectual intensity to match the intensity of feeling. But at the same time Marston was also trying to give his denunciations an unprecedented sense of gross physical disgust: for this purpose he repeatedly exploited a range of vocabulary which included 'slime', 'dung', 'muddy', 'reeking', 'stinking', 'slimie' and 'putrid'. And so, intermixed with his high latinate diction and resounding classical names was an utterly different register of language, which not only referred to slime and dung but also described the material props and settings of vice in late sixteenth-century England: it alluded, for example, to aphrodisiac foods in a manner unthinkable in high classical diction ('marrow pies, and yawning Oystars'; 'A Crab's baked guts, a Lobster's

30 'Certaine Satyres' 5, line 15; *Scourge of Villanie* 4, line 161 (Marston, *Poems*, ed. A. Davenport (Liverpool, 1961), pp. 87, 123).
31 *Scourge of Villanie* 3, lines 191–3 (ibid., p. 117).
32 'Certaine Satyres' 5, lines 1–4 (ibid., p. 87).
33 *Scourge of Villanie* 9, lines 44–5; 'In Lectores' 33–4 (ibid., pp. 159, 97).

buttered thigh'),[34] and alongside the place-names of classical mythology it referred to scenes of contemporary vice such as Pickt-hatch and Stourbridge Fair. Marston had brought Marlovian declamation out of Persia and Syria and placed it in the streets – and gutters – of Elizabethan England.

This stylistic mixture was improbable, unstable and potentially explosive. It deliberately violated all the canons of taste which distinguished high diction from low. It was sustained only by the sheer intensity of the satirical charge with which Marston managed to invest it; and the moment that the reader ceased to believe in this, the entire project could become almost hysterically funny. The anonymous authors of the Cambridge *Parnassus* plays (1598–1601) were quick to seize on its comic potential: they introduced a Marston-figure, 'Furor poeticus', whose outpourings characteristically combine Marlowe, inkhorn terms and low diction:

> The great projector of the Thunder-bolts,
> He that is wont to pisse whole clouds of raine
> Into the earthes vast gaping urinall,
> Which that one ey'd subsizer of the skie,
> *Don Phoebus*, empties by caliditie:
> He and his Townesmen *Planets* bring to thee
> Most fatty lumps of earths faelicitye.[35]

Ben Jonson contributed to the ridicule of Marston in his *Poetaster* (1601), where the character Crispinus (representing Marston) declaims the following poem:

> Ramp up, my genius; be not retrograde:
> But boldly nominate a spade, a spade.
> What, shall thy lubrical and glibbery Muse
> Live, as she were defunct, like punk in stews?
> Alas! That were no modern consequence,
> To have cothurnal buskins frighted hence.

---

34 *Scourge of Villanie* 2, line 36; 3, line 73 (ibid., pp. 107, 113).
35 J. B. Leishman (ed.), *The Three Parnassus Plays* (London, 1949), pp. 317–18.

No; teach thy incubus to poeticize;
And throw abroad thy spurious snotteries . . .[36]

Later in the play a purge is administered to Crispinus, who spews up fustian words such as 'turgidous', 'ventositous', 'furibund' and 'fatuate'. Jonson had in fact already ridiculed Marston's fustian tendencies: most of the obscure terms in the fustian speech in *Every Man out of his Humour* (quoted above, p. 33) were drawn either from *The Scourge of Villanie* or from Marston's *Histriomastix*.[37] And to some extent Marston had himself invited this treatment, since he had not only denounced 'fustian' poetry in *The Scourge of Villanie*:

Here's one, to get an undeserv'd repute
Of deepe deepe learning, all in fustian sute
Of ill-plac'd farre-fetch'd words attiereth
His period, that all sence forsweareth

but also described his own satires as 'my fustian'.[38]

So by the turn of the century several stylistic ingredients had come together. Marlovian bombast had become intermixed not only with a deliberately coarse vernacular, but also with the fustian of Marston's inkhorn terms; and the fashion had already begun of submitting the resultant mixture to ludicrous parodizing routines. The comic potentialities of such a style were peculiarly rich and various. A consistently high style can be guyed, of course, using effects of bathos and incongruity; but the incongruity is then likely to be systematic, depending on a sustained contrast between high level and low (as in the two forms of burlesque, mock-heroic and travesty). The starting-point for English seventeenth-century nonsense, on the other hand, was a style with built-in incongruities of several kinds, constantly working their effects at the local level. In exploiting these parodically, nonsense poetry could shake out a kaleidoscopic mixture of comic effects. Hence both its strength and its weakness. Its

36 Jonson, *Complete Plays*, ii, pp. 211–12.
37 See Leishman's analysis in his *Parnassus Plays*, pp. 84–5.
38 *Scourge of Villanie* 4, lines 55–8, 83 (Marston, *Poems*, p. 137).

strength was its exuberant multifariousness, which included its ability to make use of shreds of other genres at the same time (sententious or proverbial lines, ballad-material, etc.). And its weakness was its inherent tendency to fragmentation, its inability to develop large-scale poetic designs.

Finally, one other literary influence on Taylor's nonsense poetry must also be mentioned, though its effect is hard to measure in any precise way: the prose of Thomas Nashe. It is clear that Taylor idolized Nashe, and tried to model his own comic-rhapsodic-satirical prose on Nashe's style. One of Taylor's works even took the form of an account of a visit by Nashe from beyond the grave:

> there appeared unto me a poore old swarty fellow, with stareing haire, Neglected beard, Ashy Gastly look, with a black Cloath Cloak upon his back, which hee had worne as thin as if it had been Searge (whereby I conceiv'd him to be a Poet) . . . Quoth he, my name is *Thomas* or *Tom* Nashe, who when this Ayerie shadow of mine had a corporeall substance, I had a yerking, firking, jerking, Satiricall and Poeticall veine . . .[39]

Nashe had contributed to the ridicule of fustian, both in his polemic against Gabriel Harvey and in the bizarrely grandiloquent speech of one of the characters in his *The Unfortunate Traveller*, 'a bursten belly inkhorne orator called *Vanderhulke*'.[40] In several of his writings, Nashe had pursued a method of fantastical metaphor-development which expanded the frontiers of the comic grotesque. And in his final (1599) and most extraordinary work, *Lenten Stuffe* (a kind of prose rhapsody in praise of Great Yarmouth and its smoked herrings), he had developed the mock-encomium to the point where it too, like Taylor's nonsense poetry, contained a kaleidoscopic mixture of high and low styles, shaken together with almost manic linguistic energy:

39 Taylor, *Crop-Eare Curried, or, Tom Nashe his Ghost* (n.p. [Oxford], n.d. [1644]), pp. 1–2.
40 Nashe, *Works*, i, pp. 315–17 (against Harvey); ii, pp. 247–8 (Vanderhulke).

A colony of criticall *Zenos*, should they sinnow their sillogisticall cluster-fistes in one bundle to confute and disprove moving, were they, but during the time they might lap up a messe of buttred fish, in Yarmouth one fishing, such a motion of toyling *Mirmidons* they should be spectators of and a confused stirring to and fro of a *Lepantalike* hoast of unfatigable flud-bickerers and foame-curbers, that they woulde not move or stir one foote till they had disclaimd and abjurd their bedred spittle-positions.[41]

Even in his most energetic prose, Taylor never came close to this; but one may still sense the ghost of Tom Nashe hovering over many of Taylor's works, including his nonsense poetry.

The purpose of this chapter has been to place the nonsense style of Taylor and his imitators in a particular literary context: a collocation of stylistic forces which came together in the last decade of the sixteenth century and the first decade of the seventeenth. Those were the two decades that contributed most to Taylor's formation as a poet. He was evidently a voracious reader and theatre-goer with a very retentive memory; no doubt he absorbed a great deal of Shakespeare as well as Marlowe, Marston, Dekker, Middleton and Jonson. Some of his best lines, indeed, are pure nonsense-Shakespeare, such as 'From out the heels of squemish magnitude' or 'Then smoth thy brow with milk-white discontent'. Although written by a Thames waterman rather than a sophisticated court wit, Taylor's nonsense poetry was nevertheless a highly literary phenomenon, closely tied to the literary culture which it parodied and celebrated.

And this in turn helps to explain why the genre died away in the second half of the seventeenth century. After Taylor's death in 1653, nonsense poetry was kept going by the comic anthologies or 'drolleries' which started up in Cromwellian England and became a major publishing industry after the Restor-

41 Ibid., iii, p. 185.

ation.[42] If one looked only at the printing-history of the genre, one might even think that the writing of nonsense poetry underwent a revival during this period. But this impression is misleading; the truth is that the compilers of the Restoration drolleries were scouring all available manuscripts – and memories – for comic material to meet a seemingly insatiable public demand. (Similarly, it was during this period that printers made use of the manuscripts of the Middle Temple and Gray's Inn revels, which they published in 1660 and 1688 respectively.) In the process, the drollery-editors picked up quite a few nonsense verses; they seem also to have concocted one or two further poems in the same manner. But in terms of internal literary history, we can see that a genre which was so closely linked to poetic styles of the turn of the century could not properly flourish once those styles themselves had become antiquated and remote. For a while it was insulated by its own oddity; it may be true that by the 1670s it had, like its stylistic sources, become strange-sounding stuff, but of course it was in the very nature of nonsense poetry to sound strange. The point is not that it became unreadable, but that the impetus to write it had gone.

However, another part of the internal literary-historical explanation for the decline of nonsense poetry adds a further paradoxical twist. Far from distancing itself from nonsense poetry, ordinary poetry had, so to speak, encroached on the domain of nonsense itself. One of the stylistic mechanisms of nonsense poetry, namely the exploitation of remote and incongruous metaphors, had itself been absorbed into the mainstream of English poetry. Under the influence of continental theories of the special nature of creative 'wit', which emphasized the role of novelty and surprise,[43] the later metaphysical poets had

---

42 On the drolleries see C. C. Smith, 'The Seventeenth-Century Drolleries', *Harvard Library Bulletin*, vi (1952), pp. 40–51; J. Wardroper (ed.), *Love and Drollery* (London, 1969), pp. xiv–xix; Farley-Hills, *Benevolence of Laughter*, pp. 21–45; Raylor, *Cavaliers, Clubs, and Literary Culture*, pp. 203–7; and the listings in A. E. Case, *A Bibliography of English Poetical Miscellanies, 1521–1750* (Oxford, 1935).
43 See J. A. Mazzeo, *Renaissance and Seventeenth-Century Studies* (New York, 1964), pp. 29–43.

developed techniques of metaphor-making which verged on self-parody – giving the nonsense poet little left to do. When John Cleveland can describe a girl's hand as 'So soft, 'tis ayr but once remov'd, / Tender, as 'twere a Jellie glov'd', or conjure up kisses with the lines, 'Love prints his Signets in her smacks, / Those Ruddy drops of squeezing wax',[44] it is not clear that the comic effects of such ingeniousness could be far overtaken by any attempt at incongruity for incongruity's sake. Nor is it altogether absurd that one modern anthology of nonsense poetry should include some extracts from Marvell's *Upon Appleton House*.[45] In her *Poems and Fancies* (1653), Margaret Cavendish, Marchioness of Newcastle, provided a kind of *reductio ad absurdum* of this new poetic, stringing together her conceits or 'fancies' with ostentatious disregard for the demands of congruity:

> *Life* scummes the *Cream* of *Beauty* with *Times Spoon*,
> And drawes the *Claret Wine* of *Blushes* soon.
> There boiles it in a *Skillet* cleane of *Youth*,
> Then thicks it well with crumbl'd *Bread* of *Truth* . . .

'I must intreat my *Noble Reader*', the Marchioness explained, 'to read this part of my *Book* very slow, and to observe very strictly every word they read, because in most of these *Poems*, every word is a *Fancy*'.[46] The comic fragmentation of sense could hardly go any further than that.

---

44 Cleveland, *Poems*, ed. B. Morris and E. Withington (Oxford, 1967), pp. 58, 49.
45 Haughton (ed.), *The Chatto Book of Nonsense Poetry*, pp. 110–11.
46 M. Cavendish, *Poems and Fancies* (London, 1653), pp. 128, 123.

CHAPTER 3

A short history of nonsense poetry in medieval and Renaissance Europe

LITERARY NONSENSE POETRY was virtually unknown to readers of English when Hoskyns wrote his lines in praise of Coryate in 1611. But although this kind of nonsense poem was absent (so far as we know) from classical literature, various literary genres of nonsense or near-nonsense had existed in Germany, France, Italy and Spain in the medieval and Renaissance periods. Some of these forms (above all, the vigorous and elaborate Italian nonsense poetry of the fifteenth and sixteenth centuries) are so close to the kind of poem Hoskyns introduced that it is hard to believe that he had no knowledge of them.

A full history of early European nonsense has never been written; many of the details remain very obscure. The general pattern which emerges from this material, however, is one of a complex and overlapping succession of styles and genres, undergoing the kind of development – through the ordinary mechanisms of individual invention, transmission to later poets, influence on (and from) neighbouring genres, and so on – which other literary forms also experienced. Nonsense poetry was, in other words, a typically or even a quintessentially literary phenomenon. It was not something dwelling, like dreams or madness, in the collective unconscious of Europe, liable to break out here, there or everywhere through its own spontaneous energies. On the contrary, it was something invented, learned and transmitted; something which existed only in a literary culture; and indeed something which, because of its essentially parodic nature, had a peculiarly intimate connection with the literary world – as intimate as that between a parasite and its host.

The earliest known nonsense poetry was written by a German Minnesinger, 'Reinmar der alte', who died in 1210. Just a few lines of unmistakable nonsense survive in his oeuvre, forming the first stanza of a three-stanza poem. They list a series of bizarre reversals of the natural order, using the traditional poetic-rhetorical device of 'impossibilia' (discussed more fully below, pp. 78–88).

> Blatte und krone wellent muot willik sin,
> so waenent topfknaben wislichen tuon,
> So jaget unbilde mit hasen eber swin,
> so ervliuget einen valken ein unmehtik huon,
> Wirt dan[ne] der wagen vür diu rinder gende,
> treit dan[ne] der sak den esel zuo der müln,
> wirt danne ein eltiu gurre z'einem vüln:
> so siht man'z in der werlte twerhes stende.[1]

> Breastplate and crown want to be volunteer soldiers,
> Boys playing with a top think they are acting wisely,
> The boar hunts with hares, setting a poor example,
> A feeble hen flies up and catches a falcon.
> Then the cart goes in front of the oxen,
> The sack drags the donkey to the mill,
> An old nag turns into a filly:
> This is what one sees in the world turned upside-down.

Since the rest of the poem is a love poem, the overall purpose of this initial stanza is clear: it is to set out a vision of a world in which the miraculous becomes the norm, in order then to describe the miracle of requited love. In the overall context of the poem, therefore, the first stanza is not free-standing nonsense but merely an extended rhetorical device. It even concludes by stating explicitly that it refers to that inversion of reality, the

---

1 F. von der Hagen, *Minnesänger: deutsche Liederdichter des zwölften, dreizehnten und vierzehnten Jahrhunderts*, 4 vols. (Leipzig, 1838), i, p. 197 (no. 53).

world turned upside-down, and any work which makes such a statement is confirming that it knows which way up the world really is. Nevertheless, the sheer bizarrerie and extended invention of this stanza make it possible for it to be read as if it were a piece of nonsense with no larger sense-making rhetorical purpose; and that indeed seems to be the way in which its influence was felt.

Several poets wrote similar pieces during the thirteenth century, establishing a kind of genre with its own stock forms and conventions. A typical piece is the following, by Reinmar von Zweter:

> Ich kwam geriten in ein lant,
> uf einer gense, da ich affen, toren vant,
> ein kra mit einem habche die viengen vil der swine in einer
>   bach;
> Ein hase zwene winde zoch,
> der jagte einen valken, den vienk er in den lüften hoch;
> schachzabel spilten mukken zwo, meisen einen turn ich muren
>   sach;
> Da saz ein hirz unt span vil kleine sien;
> da huote ein wolf der lember in den widen;
> ein krebze vlouck mit einer tuben
> ze wette, ein pfunt er ir ab gewan;
> drie groze risen erbeiz ein han:
> (unt) ist daz war, so naet ein esel huben.[2]

> I came riding on a goose
> Into a land where I found apes and fools;
> A crow and a hawk seized many pigs in a stream;
> A hare who turned two windlasses
> Hunted a falcon, which he caught high in the air;
> I saw two flies playing chess, and titmice building a tower;
> A stag sat there spinning many small silk threads;
> The lamb kept watch over a wolf in the meadow;
> A crab flew with a dove,
> It made a bet with her, and won a pound;

2 Ibid., i, p. 206 (no. 161).

Three big giants bit a hen to death;
And if that is true, then a donkey can stitch bonnets.

As this example shows, the overall pretext of the poem was usually that it was an eye-witness narrative, a tall story related by the poet: in this way the nonsense genre was able to stand more freely in its own right as a display of the poet's own inventiveness, no longer limited by the function of a mere rhetorical device in a love poem. This medieval German genre is therefore known as 'Lügendichtung', or lie-poetry.[3]

The general idea of a fibber's or boaster's narrative was not new, of course, either in literature or in folklore. One example of a lying tale comes in a Latin poem written in Germany in the tenth or eleventh century, the 'Modus florum': it describes how a king offered the hand of his daughter to whoever could tell the best lie, and presents the lying story of the man who won – a story which involves killing a hare, cutting it open and finding inside it huge quantities of honey and a royal charter.[4] This is bizarre, but it is not a nonsense poem; although scholars have traditionally identified this Latin poem as the origin of the 'Lügendichtung' genre, its relationship to the medieval German poems is remote and quite tangential.[5]

The general idea of the tall story may have been absorbed by the Lügendichtung as, so to speak, its form, but its content came from adapting a range of other stock literary devices. These included, most obviously, several types of impossibilia: the reversal of roles by animals (hens seizing hawks), the animation – or, to be more precise, the animal-ization – of inanimate objects (flying millstones being particularly common), and the performance by animals of complex human activities (such as spinning

---

3 See C. Müller-Fraureuth, *Die deutschen Lügendichtungen bis auf Münchhausen* (Halle, 1881), esp. pp. 3–13.
4 K. Strecker (ed.), *Die Cambridger Lieder*, Monumenta Germaniae historica (Berlin, 1926), pp. 44–6.
5 For traditional identifications see Müller-Fraureuth, *Die deutschen Lügendichtungen*, p. 3; W. Stammler and K. Langosch (eds.), *Die deutsche Literatur des Mittelalters: Verfasserlexikon*, 5 vols. (Berlin, Leipzig, 1933–55), iv, col. 729.

or building).[6] Two other ways in which animals were treated in these poems seem to have reflected particular literary influences. First, the common imagery of animals playing musical instruments suggests a connection with the form of ecclesiastical-satirical writing in which church music and other functions were performed by animals.[7] And secondly, the increasingly frequent references to contests and battles between different animals (and/or inanimate objects) reflects the influence of a mock-heroic or burlesque tradition which stemmed from the pseudo-Homeric *Batrachomyomachia*, the battle of the frogs and the mice. Given the huge popularity of the *Roman de Renart*, which itself depended on the device of using animals as humorous substitutes for the heroes of epic or romance, it is not surprising that this particular literary-parodic function – the function of burlesque – should have grown in importance in these German nonsense poems. And at the same time more indirect or glancing parodic relationships may have been at work with several of the other forms of beast poetry which were so popular in the Middle Ages, including the most fundamental of them all, the fable.[8]

6 See the comments on the 'somewhat limited thematic range' of these poems in S. Westphal-Wihl, 'Quodlibets: Introduction to a Middle High German Genre', in H. Heinen and I. Henderson (eds.), *Genres in Medieval German Literature*, Göppinger Arbeiten zur Germanistik, no. 439 (Göppingen, 1986), pp. 157–74. She notes: 'The standardization of the adynata [i.e. impossibilia] in the lying quodlibets speaks against the commonly held theory that they were freely composed from random elements . . . On the contrary, the surviving examples of this most fanciful of genres were composed according to strict formulae that must have been preserved by unchanging audience expectations' (pp. 166–7).
7 See W. Schouwink, 'When Pigs Consecrate a Church: Parodies of Liturgical Music in the *Ysengrimus* and some Medieval Analogies', *Reinardus: Yearbook of the International Reynard Society*, v (1992), pp. 171–81, and R. Hammerstein, *Diabolus in musica* (Munich, 1974). One of the poems in the *Carmina Burana*, 'Florebat olim studium' (dating probably from the 13th century), includes asses playing the lute and oxen dancing: see E. R. Curtius, *European Literature and the Latin Middle Ages*, trans. W. R. Trask (London, 1953), pp. 94–5.
8 For a useful general treatment see H. R. Jauss, *Untersuchungen zur mittelalterliche Tierdichtung* (Tübingen, 1959); and for a valuable study of the earlier medieval Latin material see J. Ziolkowski, *Talking Animals: Medieval Latin Beast Poetry, 750–1150* (Philadelphia, 1993).

The 'Lügendichtung' genre of German nonsense poetry enjoyed a long life; but its high point was undoubtedly reached in the fourteenth and fifteenth centuries.[9] One very popular example from the fourteenth century was the 'Wachtelmäre' or 'quail-story' (so called because of a refrain which counts quails in a sack, alluding to a proverbial saying about hunters who tell fibs). A long and elaborate narrative, it tells the story of a vinegar-jug who rides out to joust against the King of Nindertda in the land of Nummerdummernamen, which lies beyond Monday. Heroes of courtly epic such as Hildebrand and Dietrich of Bern also come into the story, which develops into a great battle between a hedgehog and a flying earthworm, a battle which is eventually decided by a swimming millstone.[10] This poem was unusual, however, in having such a unified narrative structure; most of the Lügendichtungen are little more than strings of impossibilia, with images which are built up over a few lines at most:

> Ein schweizer spiss ein helnparten
> Die tanczten in einem hopffengarten
> Eins storchs pein und eins hasenfuss
> Die pfiffen auf zum tancz gar suss . . .[11]

9 See the discussions in Müller-Fraureuth, *Die deutschen Lügendichtungen*, pp. 12–13; Westphal-Wihl, 'Quodlibets'; and E. Schröder, 'Die "Lügenpredigt" und das "Quodlibet"', *Anzeiger für deutsches Altertum und deutsche Literatur*, 1 (1930), p. 214. The Lügendichtung lived on thereafter in Germany, appearing both in the form of prose narratives during the 16th and 17th centuries (the ancestors of Baron Münchhausen) and popular poems (published usually in broadsides) of the 16th, 17th and even 18th centuries. The best-known book of prose narratives was *Der Finckenritter* (1559); for examples of broadside poems see F. M. Böhme, *Altdeutsches Liederbuch: Volkslieder der Deutschen nach Wort und Weise aus dem 12. bis zum 17. Jahrhundert*, pp. 361–2 (nos. 277a, 277b). For a 17th-century Dutch example, see G. Kalff, *Het Lied in de Middeleuwen*, 2nd edn. (Leiden, 1884), p. 486.
10 The text is printed in W. Wackernagel, *Deutsches Lesebuch*, 5 vols. (Basel, 1872–8), i (entitled *Altdeutsches Lesebuch*), cols. 1149–56.
11 From a late 15th-century poem, probably by Hans Rosenplüt, printed in K. Euling, 'Eine Lügendichtung', *Zeitschrift für deutsche Philologie*, xxii (1890), pp. 317–20; here p. 317.

A Swiss lance and a halbard
Were dancing in a hop-field;
A stork's leg and a hare's foot
Were playing sweet dance-tunes on the pipe . . .

This medieval German nonsense poetry seems to have influenced writers in both England and France. The transmission is easiest to see in the English case (though it has not apparently been noticed there before); the influence on France, which has been suggested by a number of modern writers, remains more shadowy and uncertain.

In the case of England, just a handful of narrative animal nonsense poems survive from the Middle Ages, written probably in the mid fifteenth century. They all bear a strikingly close resemblance to the German Lügendichtung. One is a brief account of an animal battle:

> The krycket & the greshope wentyn here to fyght,
> With helme and harburyone all redy dyght;
> The flee bare the baner as a dughty knyght,
> The cherubed trumpyt with all hys myghth . . .[12]

> The cricket and the grasshopper went out to fight,
> Already dressed in helmet and coat of mail;
> The fly carried the banner, as a doughty knight,
> The scarab-beetle trumpeted with all his might . . .

Another is a short but more chaotic description of animals and other objects fighting and making music:

> The hare and the harthestone hurtuld to-geydur,
> Whyle the hombul-be hod was hacked al to cloutus
> Ther schalmod the scheldrake and schepe trumpyd,

---

12 R. H. Robbins (ed.), *Secular Lyrics of the XIVth and XVth Centuries* (Oxford, 1952), p. 104 (no. 115). (I have substituted 'gh' for the character *yogh*, and turned double 'gh' into single.) The source is a 15th-century manuscript in the National Library of Wales; it also contains a Latin version of the same poem, but the strict rhyme-pattern of the English and the lack of any such patterning in the Latin suggest that the English must have come first.

[The] hogge with his hornepype hyod hym belyve,
And dansyd on the downghhyll, whyle all thei day lasted . . .[13]

The hare and the hearth-stone collided with each other,
While the bumblebee's hood was hacked to shreds;
The salmon, the sheldrake and the sheep trumpeted,
The hog came on quickly with his hornpipe
And danced on the dunghill, so long as the day lasted . . .

Another poem is a more ambitious narrative. Beginning with
the sort of brief introductory formula which one finds in the
German poems of this period, it moves quickly into a dense
mass of comic animal impossibilia:

Herkyn to my tale that I schall to yow schew,
For of seche mervels have ye hard bot few;
Yf any of them be ontrue that I schall tell yow aftur,
Then wax I as pore as tho byschop of Chestur.
As I rode from Durram to Dowre I fond by tho hee strete
A fox and a fulmarde had XV fete;
Tho scate scalldyd tho rydlyng and turnede of hys skyn;
At the kyrke dore called the codlyng, and badd lett hym yn.
Tho salmond sang tho hee mas, tho heyrying was hys clarke,
On tho orgons playde tho porpas, there was a mere warke . . .
I toke a peyny of my purse, and offerd to hom all.
For this offerand was made, tho sothe yf I schall sey,
When Midsomer evyn fell on Palmes sounnday.
Fordurmore I went, and moo marvels I founde;
A norchon by the fyre rostyng a greyhownde.
There was dyverse meytes, reckyn hom yf I schall;
Ther was raw bakon, and new sowrde all.
Tho breme went rownd abowte, and lette hem all blode;
Tho sow sate on hye benke, and harpyd Robyn-Howde . . .[14]

---

13 T. Wright and J. O. Halliwell (eds.), *Reliquiae antiquae: Scraps from Ancient Manuscripts, Illustrating chiefly Early English Literature and the English Language*, 2 vols. (London, 1841–3), i, p. 84.
14 Ibid., i, pp. 81–2; another version of the same poem, from a manuscript of the 1460s or 1470s, is also printed on pp. 85–6.

Hearken to my tale, which I shall tell you,
For you have heard few such marvels;
If any of the ones I shall tell you are untrue,
Let me become as poor as the Bishop of Chester.
As I rode from Durham to Dover, I found in the high street
A fox and a polecat which had fifteen feet;
The skate scalded the redshank and skinned him;
The codling called at the church door, and asked to be let in.
The salmon sang the high mass, the herring was his clerk,
The porpoise played the organ, there were merry goings-on . . .
I took a penny from my purse, and offered it to them all.
Now, this offering was made, to tell the truth,
When Midsummer day fell on Palm Sunday.
I went further, and found more marvels:
A hedgehog by the fire, roasting a greyhound.
There were various things to eat, let me tell you what they
    were:
There was raw bacon, and new soured ale.
The bream went round and took blood from them all;
The sow sat on a high bench, playing 'Robin Hood' on her
    harp . . .

The close connection between these poems and the German
genre is self-evident. Of course, the basic idea of listing animal
or natural impossibilia was so widespread that it would have
been known to English writers from many other sources too;
but those other sources, and their English imitators, generally
used it in a non-nonsensical way, as a rhetorical device to fortify
satire or complaint – usually about the impossibility of female
constancy. (One well-known example is a fifteenth-century
poem which begins: 'Whane nettuls in wynter bryng forth rosys
red'; the end-line of each stanza is: 'Than put women in trust
and confydens.')[15] Humorous-miraculous narratives were not
unknown either, the most famous being the early fourteenth-
century poem 'The Land of Cockaygne'.[16] But that poem is a

15 T. Silverstein (ed.), *English Lyrics before 1500* (York, 1971), pp. 151–3 (no. 137).
16 Printed in E. Mätzner, *Antenglische Sprachproben*, 2 vols. (Berlin, 1867–1900),
i, pp. 147–52.

straightforward narrative description of extraordinary things; it lacks the density, energy and chaotic intermingling of different kinds of impossibilia which mark out the German poems and the small group of English poems which follow them so closely.

Finally, one other type of impossibilia cultivated by the German genre should also be mentioned, since it seems to have given rise to another short English poem: this type has been described as 'the subcategory of adynata [i.e. impossibilia] in which incapacitated persons act as if they had full, or even extraordinary possession of their faculties'.[17] The lame dance (or, frequently, catch hares), the dumb sing, the naked put things in their pockets, and so on. This idea is taken up by another fifteenth-century English poem:

> I saw thre hedles playen at a ball;
> On hanles man served them all;
> Whyll thre mouthles men lay and low
> Thre legles away hem drow.[18]

> I saw three headless men playing ball;
> One handless man served them all;
> While three mouthless men lay and laughed
> Three legless men drove him away.

This looks like a small fragment extracted from a Lügendichtung and turned into a free-standing pseudo-gnomic poem, which might then have entered the stock of orally transmitted folk poetry. The only other genre in medieval English literature which cultivated impossibilia for their own sake was that of the mock-recipe or mock-prescription: this genre, one instance of which was available in print to seventeenth-century readers, will be discussed in the next chapter.

Apart from these two examples, it is doubtful whether any

---

17 Westphal-Wihl, 'Quodlibets', p. 167.
18 Silverstein (ed.), *English Lyrics*, p. 145 (no. 130). On this theme, and its percolation (apparently from German sources) through various folk-literatures, see J. Bolte and P. Polívka, *Anmerkungen zu den Kinder- und Hausmärchen der Brüder Grimm*, 5 vols. (Leipzig, 1913–32), iii, pp. 116–18.

of the small number of medieval English nonsense poems which have come down to us were known to writers of the sixteenth or seventeenth centuries.[19] The torch of nonsense poetry seems to have been more or less extinguished in England after its brief flaming in the fifteenth century. When it was re-lit by Hoskyns in 1611, he may well have been writing under the influence of continental nonsense genres; if so, seventeenth-century English nonsense poetry was in part the final product of a more circuitous transmission, in which literary nonsense had travelled in relays from Germany, first to France, and then to Italy.

The earliest French nonsense poetry which has come down to us was written in northern France (in Artois and the Île-de-France region) during the second half of the thirteenth century. Known as 'fatrasies', these early poems survive in two main collections, one by the poet Philippe de Rémi, sieur de Beaumanoir (1250–96), and the other, a group of poems called 'Les Fatrasies d'Arras', by an unknown writer (or writers).[20] One example from the latter group will give the flavour of the genre:

> Vache de pourcel,
> Aingnel de veël,
> Brebis de malart;
> Dui lait home bel
> Et dui sain mesel,
> Dui saiges sotart,
> Dui emfant nez d'un torel

19 The late medieval poem in this genre which begins 'I saw a dog sethying sows / And an ape thatching an house' (Haughton (ed.), *Chatto Book of Nonsense Poetry*, p. 59), for example, was preserved in a manuscript at Balliol College, Oxford, and published only in the 20th century.
20 See L. C. Porter, *La Fatrasie et le fatras: essai sur la poésie irrationnelle en France au moyen âge* (Geneva, 1960); P. Zumthor, 'Fatrasie et coq-à-l'âne', in G. De Poerck, M. Piron, et al. (eds.), *Fin du moyen âge et renaissance: mélanges de philologie offerts à Robert Guiette* (Antwerp, 1961), pp. 5–18; W. Kellermann, 'Über die altfranzösischen Gedichte des uneingeschränkten Unsinns', *Archiv für das Studium der neueren Sprachen und Literaturen*, ccv (1968–9), pp. 1–22; and G. Angeli, *Il mondo rovesciato* (Rome, 1977). The origin of the word is uncertain; it may have the same origin as 'farce', meaning something stuffed in, impromptu.

Qui chantoient de Renart,
Seur la pointe d'un coutel
Portoient Chastel Gaillart.[21]

Cow born of a pig,
Lamb born of a calf,
Sheep born of a duck;
Two ugly handsome men
And two healthy lepers,
Two wise idiots,
Two children born of a bull,
Who sang about Reynard,
Carried Château Gaillard
On the point of a knife.

The precise origins of this type of poetry are obscure. One modern scholar has tried to show that these poems were riddles with specific personal and political meanings.[22] It is possible that they developed in connection with some kind of literary game, perhaps involving the parodying of gnomic or over-elaborate courtly poetry; this may have been the work of Philippe de Rémi, whose verses are probably earlier than those of the Arras collection.[23] These French nonsense poems have a distinctive character: they lack the unifying narrative structure of the German poems, and their impossibilia are generally less visual or physical, less energetic and not so densely packed. But on the other hand the basic similarity with the German poems of the thirteenth century is inescapable. The very idea of putting together strings of impossibilia, not for their traditional rhetorical purpose but simply for the effect of comic absurdity which

---

21 Les Fatrasies d'Arras, no 33, in Porter, *La Fatrasie*, p. 130.
22 M. Ungureanu, *La Bourgeoisie naissante. Société et littérature bourgeoises d'Arras aux XIIe et XIIIe siècles*, Mémoires de la commission des monuments historiques du Pas-de-Calais, viii, no. 1 (Arras, 1955), pp. 267–71. This is a common reaction to nonsense poetry, compensating for a lack of meaning in the explicandum by an excess of meaning in the explanation. As Leibniz demonstrated, there is no pattern of points on a graph so random that a formula cannot be constructed for a line which would generate them all.
23 Kellermann, 'Über die altfranzösischen Gedichte', pp. 15–16.

they produced on their own, is fundamental to both the German and the French poems, and it is very unlikely that this idea was just invented independently on two occasions, within the same century, in two neighbouring countries.[24] Literary influences flowed to and fro between the French and German vernaculars throughout the Middle Ages (as the complex development of the *Roman de Renart* shows). The universities of northern France were frequented by large numbers of German students; one fourteenth-century German lament for the decay of Orléans University says that the sound of the German language was once so loud in the streets of Orléans that one would have thought oneself in the Fatherland.[25] It is highly likely that an ingenious new style of poetry invented by German Minne-singers, even though it may have been a minor experimental genre known only through a few examples, should eventually have percolated into French poetic culture too.

As the genre developed in France during the fourteenth and fifteenth centuries (in a slightly different verse-form, known as the 'fatras'), it was treated simply as a form of humorous poetry, and described also as a 'frivole' or 'folie'. Not all of the 'fatras' were nonsense poems putting together impossible collocations of ideas; such versions of the 'fatras' died out in the early fifteenth century.[26] Nonsense poetry thus enjoyed a much shorter continuous history in France than it did in Germany. But something of the spirit of the 'fatras' was revived in the sixteenth century by the poet Clément Marot, in a form of his own invention known as the 'coq-à-l'âne'.[27]

---

24 Modern scholars who accept the idea of German influence on the fatrasies include Kellermann (ibid.); Angeli (*Il mondo rovesciato*, pp. 96–7); and Westphal-Wihl, who notes: 'The impossibilities expressed in the Old French poems, and their fluid internal structure, are very reminiscent of the German lying quodlibets' ('Quodlibets', p. 166).
25 H. Waddell, *The Wandering Scholars*, 7th edn. (London, 1934), p. 147.
26 Porter, *La Fatrasie*, p. 75.
27 See E. Picot, 'La Sottie en France', *Romania*, vii (1878), pp. 236–326 (here p. 237); Zumthor, 'Fatrasie et coq-à-l'âne', p. 16; C. E. Kinch, *La Poésie satirique de Clément Marot* (Paris, 1940), pp. 130–90; C. Marot, *L'Enfer, les coq-à-l'âne, les élégies*, ed. C. A. Mayer (Paris, 1977), pp. x–xix (Mayer's comments), 22–66 (texts).

The French literary historian Paul Zumthor has made a useful distinction between 'relative' and 'absolute' nonsense poetry.[28] In relative nonsense, each line or couplet makes sense in itself, and it is only the juxtaposition of them in the verse that is without meaning; whereas in absolute nonsense the transgressions of sense occur within the smallest units of the poetry. As the example given above makes clear, the 'fatrasie' was capable of thorough-going absolute nonsense. Other types of French medieval poetry exploited the techniques of relative nonsense: foremost among them was the 'resverie', which put together a pointless sequence of personal statements, sententious remarks or fragments of conversation.[29] Each statement was a distich of unequal length, linked to the next by rhyme (ab, bc, cd, etc.): this strongly suggests that the form had its origin in a dialogue-game between two poets. Thus, for example:

> Nul ne doit estre jolis
> S'il n'a amie.
> J'aime autant crouste que mie,
> Quant j'ai fain.
> Tien cel cheval par le frain,
> Malheüreus! . . .[30]

> No-one should be happy
> Without a girl he loves.
> I like the crust as much as the dough,
> When I'm hungry.
> Take this horse by the bridle,
> Miserable man! . . .

This kind of poem seems to have been, originally, a peculiarly French phenomenon. Its most ambitious development took place on the French stage, where the writers of comic drama during the fifteenth and sixteenth centuries delighted in stringing together such sequences of inconsequentialities, known as

28 Zumthor, 'Fatrasie et coq-à-l'âne', pp. 5–18.
29 On the resverie see Angeli, *Il mondo rovesciato*, pp. 15–53.
30 From a late 13th-century poem, printed in ibid., p. 108.

'menus propos'; one classic work, the *Sottie des menus propos*, consists quite simply of three speakers playing this game for a total of 571 lines.[31] But this French nonsense genre in turn gave rise to similar types of nonsense in two other countries. One was Germany, where a form of inconsequential platitude poem known as the 'quodlibet' grew up in the fourteenth and fifteenth centuries. It consisted, as the classic modern study by Hanns Fischer puts it, of a succession of small units, containing general statements of the obvious and ironic pieces of moral instruction, 'the comedy of which lies above all in the inconsequentiality with which they are put together'.[32] Thus:

> Nu hör wie gar ain tor ich bin
> Ich trunck durch die wochen win
> Für laster wiche wasser
> Von baden wirt man nasser . . .[33]

> Now hear what an utter fool I am:
> I drank wine for weeks;
> In order to be vicious, avoid water.
> Bathing makes you wetter . . .

The standard view, formulated by Fischer, is that the quodlibet was the overall genre, of which the Lügendichtung was a peculiar sub-species. (He therefore renamed the Lügendichtung the 'Lügenquodlibet'.) However, the Lügendichtungen were more common than these platitude-quodlibets, of which only three instances are known.[34] It makes more sense, surely, to

---

31 The best discussion of the 'menus propos' is in R. Garapon, *La Fantaisie verbale et le comique dans le théâtre français du moyen âge à la fin du XVIIᵉ siècle* (Paris, 1957), pp. 48–63. The *Sottie des menus propos* is printed in E. Picot (ed.), *Recueil général des sotties*, 3 vols. (Paris, 1902–12), i, pp. 65–71.
32 H. Fischer, *Studien zur deutschen Märendichtung*, 2nd edn., ed. J. Janota (Tübingen, 1983), p. 43.
33 J. von Lassberg, *Lieder-Saal: Sammlung altdeutscher Gedichte*, 4 vols. (n.p., 1820; photo-reproduction, Hildesheim, 1968), iii, p. 561 (no. 248). For another example see K. Euling, 'Ein Quodlibet', *Zeitschrift für deutsche Philologie*, xxii (1890), pp. 312–17.
34 This point is made by Westphal-Wihl, who provides a full listing of the poems and their manuscripts: 'Quodlibets', pp. 158–9, 172–3.

suppose that these German platitude-poems reflected an impor-
tation into Germany of the French resverie. The fact that the
French version has a slightly more complicated ab, bc, cd rhyme-
scheme, while the German has the simpler aa, bb, cc form (in
which each unit of sense usually occupies one couplet), strongly
suggests that if there were any relation between the two, it was
the German version which was an adaptation of the French,
and not vice-versa.

The other country which seems to have been influenced by
the resverie was Italy. Two types of relative nonsense developed
in Italian poetry in the fourteenth century: the 'motto confetto'
and the 'frottola'. Both operated by stringing together inconsequential series of remarks, the former in elegantly sententious
literary language, and the latter in a much more personal and
colloquial style.[35] The frottola never crossed the frontiers of absolute nonsense, but it did expand in its subject-matter into four
large areas: the descriptive, the gnomic, the political, and the
poem of personal confession.[36] And it attracted the interest of
major poets of the fourteenth century, such as Franco Sacchetti
(*c.*1332–1400), who were exploring various kinds of ostentatiously
anti-'poetic' poetry – 'burlesque' or 'realist' poetry which used
colloquial language and described the real conditions of the
poet's often poverty-stricken life.[37]

It is quite possible that Sacchetti had also come across speci-

---

35 On the motto confetto see Angeli, *Il mondo rovesciato*, p. 54. Antonio da
Tempo, writing in the 1330s, observed that the motto confetto was wrongly but
'vulgariter' (commonly) called the frottola: *Trattato delle rime volgari*, ed. G. Giron
(Bologna, 1970), p. 153. On the frottola see R. Russell, *Generi poetici medioevali*,
Studi e testi di bibliologia e critica letteraria, viii (Naples, 1982), pp. 147–61; P.
Orvieto, 'Sulle forme metriche della poesia del non-senso (relativo e assoluto)',
Metrica, i (1978), pp. 203–18 (emphasizing its connection with the resverie); and
S. Verhulst, *La frottola (XIV–XV sec.): aspetti della codificazione e proposte esegetiche*,
Rijksuniversiteit te Gent, Werken uitgegeven door de Faculteit van de Letteren
en Wijsbegeerte, clxxvii (Ghent, 1990).
36 See Russell, *Generi poetici medioevali*, pp. 148–9.
37 See C. Previtera, *La poesia giocosa e l'umorismo dalle origini al rinascimento*
(Milan, 1939), pp. 143–230; and F. Massèra (ed.), *Sonetti burleschi e realistici dei
primi due secoli*, 2 vols. (Bari, 1920).

mens of absolute-nonsense fatrasies; this cannot be proved, though it is known that French 'jongleurs' did visit Florence during the fourteenth and fifteenth centuries.[38] Whether prompted in this way or not, Sacchetti seems to have developed what was, for Italian readers, a new form of nonsense poetry: something much more concentratedly nonsensical than any verses in the resverie-frottola tradition. His most famous poem in this style was the following:

> Nasi cornuti e visi digrignati,
> nibbi arzagoghi e balle di sermenti
> cercavan d'Ipocrate gli argomenti
> per mettere in molticcio trenta frati.
>   Mostrava la luna a' tralunati,
> che strusse già due cavalier godenti;
> di truffa in buffa e' venian da Sorenti
> lanterne e gufi con fruson castrati.
>   Quando mi misi a navicar montagne
> passando Commo e Bergamo e 'l Mar rosso,
> dove Ercole ed Anteo ancor ne piagne,
>   alor trovai a Fiesole Minosso
> con pale con marroni e con castagne,
> che fuor d'Abruzzi rimondava il fosso,
>   quando Cariodosso
>   gridava forte: 'O Gian de' Repetissi,
>   ritruova Bacco con l'Apocalissi'.[39]

Horned noses, teeth-gnashing faces,
Sophistical kites and bales of vine-branches
Were seeking arguments from Hippocrates
For putting thirty friars in tanning vats.
The moon was showing itself to staring eyes;
It had already melted two pleasure-taking gentlemen;
From Truffa in Buffa and from Sorrento there came
Lanterns and owls with castrated finches.
When I began to navigate mountains
Passing Como and Bergamo and the Red Sea,

38 See E. Faral, *Les Jongleurs en France au moyen âge* (Paris, 1910), p. 95.
39 Sonnet 222 in F. Sacchetti, *Il libro delle rime*, ed. A. Chiari (Bari, 1936), p. 266.

Where Hercules and Antaeus are still weeping,
I then found Minos at Fiesole
With shovels, mattocks and chestnuts,
Cleaning up the ditch outside the Abruzzi,
When Cariodosso
Cried out loud: 'Oh, Giovanni de' Repetissi
Rediscovers Bacchus with the Apocalypse!'

This style of absolute nonsense was developed in a desultory way by a few other late fourteenth- or early fifteenth-century poets, notably Andrea Orcagna (who died in 1424).[40] Later in the fifteenth century, however, it became almost a popular fashion, thanks to the talents of one highly idiosyncratic poet who took up the genre and made it his own: the Florentine Domenico di Giovanni, who was known by his nickname, 'il Burchiello'.

Born in 1404, Burchiello developed some contacts with literary circles in Florence while plying his trade as a barber in the 1420s. He had to leave the city (either for political reasons or, more probably, because of unpaid debts) in the early 1430s; in 1439 he was imprisoned in Siena for theft and brawling. He later moved to Rome, where he resumed his trade before dying in early 1449.[41] In addition to his nonsense poems, he also wrote comic and satirical poetry of extraordinary vividness and verbal density. All his poems seem to have been written for the delight of his friends; they were collected only after his death (in many cases from people who had learned the verses by heart). Once his poetry began to be published in 1475, its wider popularity was assured: there were ten further editions in the fifteenth century, and eleven during the sixteenth.[42] Lorenzo de' Medici kept only seven books in his bedroom: the Gospels, Boethius, a medical treatise, Dante, Petrarch, Boccaccio, and Burchiello.[43]

40 See Previtera, *La poesia giocosa*, pp. 229–30.
41 For biographical details see C. Mazzi, *Il Burchiello, saggio* (Bologna, 1877); M. Messina, 'Domenico di Giovanni detto il Burchiello: sonetti inediti', *Biblioteca dell' 'Archivum Romanicum'*, ser. 1, xxxiii (1952); and R. Watkins, 'Il Burchiello (1404–1448) – Poverty, Politics, and Poetry', *Italian Quarterly*, xiv, no. 54 (1970), pp. 21–57.
42 Messina, 'Domenico di Giovanni', pp. 25–6.
43 Watkins, 'Il Burchiello', p. 23.

The fashion of writing nonsense 'alla burchia' continued after Burchiello's death, through the fifteenth and sixteenth centuries and well into the seventeenth – despite the occasional efforts of Counter-Reformation cardinals and inquisitors to have Burchiello's works burnt.[44] The greatest master of this style after Burchiello was the exuberant Bolognese poet Giulio Cesare Croce (1550–1609), whose colossal output of pamphlets, broadsides, occasional poems and other fantastic literary performances in the late sixteenth century included several extended nonsense poems, one of which was explicitly described as being 'alla burchiellesca'.[45] In view of his prolific output, humble origins (he was a blacksmith by trade) and talent for zany self-advertisement, Croce might well be called the Bolognese equivalent of John Taylor; his works were widely known in Italy, and it is worth noting that he was writing almost up until the very year in which the art of English literary nonsense poetry was re-launched by John Hoskyns.

One of Burchiello's best-known nonsense sonnets exemplifies the Italian genre:

> Nominativi fritti, e Mappamondi,
>   Et l'Arca di Noè fra due colonne,
>   Cantavan tutti Chirieleisonne

---

44 Messina, 'Domenico di Giovanni', p. 33. The imitators included Baldassare da Fossombrone (on whom see G. Crocioni, 'Il "Menzionero" di Baldassare da Fossombrone', *La rinascita*, vi, no. 31 (1943), pp. 224–57), Bernardo Bellincioni, Antonio Cammelli, known as 'il Pistoia', and Alessandro Adimari: for poems by these last three see E. Giovannetti (ed.), *Antologia burchiellesca* (Rome, 1949), pp. 161–84.

45 G. C. Croce, *Spalliera in grottesco alla burchiellesca* (Bologna, n.d. [164?]). Other works by Croce in this style, also issued in undated reprints in Bologna during the 1640s, include his *Dono, over presente, di varii, e diversi capricci bizzari; Nel tempo che la luna buratava, operetta bellissima, dove s'intendano alcune stantie ridicolose*; and *La scatola*. On Croce's life and writings see O. Guerrini, *La vita e le opere di Giulio Cesare Croce* (Bologna, 1879); and P. Camporesi, *La maschera di Bertoldo: G. C. Croce e la letteratura carnevalesca* (Turin, 1976). For listings of his almost innumerable works see M. Rouch, 'Bibliografia delle opere di Giulio Cesare Croce', *Strada maestra*, xvii (1984), pp. 229–72; and R. Bruni, R. Campioni and D. Zancani, *Giulio Cesare Croce dall'Emilia all'Inghilterra: cataloghi, biblioteche e testi* (Florence, 1991).

Per l'influenza de' Taglier mal tondi.
La Luna mi dicea, che non rispondi?
  Et ei rispose io temo di Giasonne,
  Però chi' odo che'l Diaquilonne
  E buona cosa a fare i capei biondi.
Per questo le Testuggini e i Tartufi
  N'hanno posto l'assedio alle Calcagne
  Dicendo noi vogliam che tu ti stufi.
E questo fanno tutte le Castagne;
  Pe i caldi d'hoggi non si grassi i Gusi
Ch'ognun non vuol mostrar le sue magagne
  E vide le lasagne
Andare a Prato, a vedere il sudario,
E ciascuna portava l'inventario.[46]

Fried nominatives, geographical globes
And Noah's Ark standing between two columns
Were all singing Kyrie Eleison
Under the influence of badly rounded trenchers.
The moon said to me: 'Why don't you answer?'
And I replied: 'I am afraid of Jason,
Because I hear that diachylum ointment
Is just the thing for dyeing your hair blond.
That is why the tortoises and the truffles
Have not put the heels under siege,
Saying, 'We want you to be fed up.'
This is what all the chestnuts do;
In today's heat, the pea-pods do not get fat;
So that everyone is reluctant to show his blemishes
And sees the lasagne
Going to Prato, to see St Veronica's handkerchief,
And each person was carrying the inventory.

This style defies rational analysis or exposition: that is its whole point. One early editor of Burchiello, Anton Francesco Doni, did offer detailed allegorical and historical exegeses of the

---

46 Burchiello, *Le rime*, ed. A. F. Doni (Venice, 1566), p. 42. For a detailed discussion of this poem, see A. Tartaro, *Il primo quattrocento italiano* (Bari, 1971), pp. 97–100. Tartaro suggests that 'fritti' ('fried') may also mean 'exhausted by constant use', as in the expression 'fritti e rifritti'.

poems, but his explanations themselves turn out to be mock-explanations, solemnly parodying the art of learned commentary.[47] A modern scholar has suggested that many of Burchiello's apparent absurdities are in fact obscene allusions, locked up in a code of bawdy imagery and Florentine slang; he has to admit, however, that such meanings as he can find are only local, and that no Burchiellesque nonsense poem makes sense as a whole.[48] If there is any general purpose in Burchiello's style, it is to ridicule the highly wrought, emotionally intense and imagery-laden poetry of Petrarch and the Petrarchists.[49] Occasionally this aim becomes quite explicit, as in the following parody of Petrarchan heart-ache:

> Sospiri azzurri, di speranze bianche
>> Mi vengon nella mente: e tornan fuori,
>> Seggonsi à piè dell'uscio con dolori
>> Perche dentro non son deschetti, ò panche ...[50]

> Blue sighs, born of white hopes,
> Come into my mind – and go out again,
> Walking in a line out of the exit, sorrowfully,
> Because there are no desks or benches inside ...

But in general Burchiello's nonsense poetry, and that of his many followers, is neither single-mindedly parodic nor directly satirical. It seems to pursue nonsense for nonsense's sake.

Outside Italy, nonsense poetry flourished in one other country during the Renaissance period: Spain. Here the earliest examples were written by Juan del Encina (1468–1529), and published in

---

47 See Burchiello, *Rime*, and the comments by Crocioni in 'Il "Menzionero" di Baldassare da Fossombrone', p. 237n.
48 J. Toscan, *Le Carnaval du langage: le lexique érotique des poètes de l'équivoque de Burchiello à Marino (XVe–XVIIe siècles)*, 4 vols. (Paris, 1981): i, pp. 72–95.
49 See ibid., i, p. 70, and A. Lanza, *Polemiche e berte letterarie nella Firenze del primo quattrocento: storia e testi* (Rome, 1971), pp. 171–227.
50 Burchiello, *Rime*, p. 129.

the edition of his poems issued at Salamanca in 1496.[51] The most famous (and influential) of these poems begins as follows:

> Anoche de madrugada,
> ya después de mediodía,
> vi venir en romería
> una nuve muy cargada,
> y un broquel con un espada
> en figura de hermitaño,
> cavallero en un escaño,
> con una ropa nesgada,
> toda sana y muy rasgada . . .[52]

> One night, at dawn,
> Already after mid-day,
> I saw coming on a pilgrimage
> A heavily-laden cloud,
> And a shield with a sword
> In the form of a hermit,
> A knight on a bench,
> With cross-cut clothes,
> Which were quite sound and very torn . . .

Del Encina entitled this poem 'Disparates trobados'; the word 'disparate', which apparently derives from the Latin 'disparatus' in its sense of 'divided' or 'contradictory', quickly became the general term for this type of poetry. It is possible that del Encina was also influenced by some confused knowledge of the Italian genre of popular poetry known as the 'disperata' or lament, which could in its most extreme forms express the ravings of unrequited love.[53] Whether he was familiar with any of Burchiello's nonsense poetry cannot now be known, though the chronology is of course suggestive: these earliest 'disparates' were written towards the end of precisely that period, the last quarter

---

51 B. Periñan, *Poeta ludens: disparate, perqué y chiste en los siglos XVI y XVII* (Pisa, 1979), p. 23.
52 J. del Encina, *Obras completas*, ed. A. M. Rambaldo, 4 vols. (Madrid, 1978–83), ii, p. 8.
53 Watkins, 'Il Burchiello', p. 27.

of the fifteenth century, when the reprinting of Burchiello's poems was at its most intensive.[54] The disparates did exhibit many of the small-scale devices of absolute nonsense: reifications of abstract terms, personifications of place-names, anthropomorphizing of objects, and vividly impossible combinations of concepts: 'hedgehog's feathers', 'baskets of water', and so on.[55]

On the other hand, it is clear that as this Spanish genre developed during the sixteenth century, it took a rather different course, verging more towards 'relative' nonsense in the manner of the resverie or the frottola. One favourite type of disparate was the mock-prognostication or 'perogrullada' (so-called after a famous poem in this style, the 'Profecías de Pero Grullo'), which not only used tautologies and mock-profundities to satirize the art of astrological prediction, but also contained genuine social and political satire, referring to the inevitable oppression exercised by princes and prelates.[56] Many such works were printed, often anonymously, during the sixteenth and seventeenth centuries. Some of these entered the popular imagination, and were still being printed or recited from memory in the nineteenth and twentieth centuries: one mid twentieth-century writer records having heard them recited at Carnival time, or at festive pig-killings, on both the Catalan and the French sides of the Pyrenees.[57]

Finally, the influence of the Burchiellesque style can also be seen in a brief revival of high literary nonsense poetry in France at the turn of the sixteenth and seventeenth centuries. The

54 See above, n. 42. For evidence of the strong influence of Italian poetry on Spanish writers during this period, see B. Sanvisenti, *I primi influssi di Dante del Petrarca e del Boccaccio sulla letteratura spagnuola* (Milan, 1902). A. L. Martín discusses the influence of Italian comic poets on Spain in the 15th and 16th centuries, and concludes: 'the Spanish comic poets of this period remain closely tied to their Italian models' (*Cervantes and the Burlesque Sonnet* (Berkeley, Calif., 1991), p. 65).
55 For a thorough analysis of these various devices, see Periñan, *Poeta ludens*, pp. 44–53.
56 See ibid., pp. 54–8; for the earliest example see del Encina, *Obras completas*, ii, pp. 15–24.
57 J. Amades, 'El habla sin significado y la poesía popular disparatada', *Revista de dialectologia y tradiciones populares*, xv (1959), pp. 274–91.

key author here was a minor nobleman, Charles-Timoléon de
Beauxoncles, seigneur de Sigogne (1560–1611). Sigogne's poetry
was certainly also influenced by the French coq-à-l'âne; one of
his poems is actually entitled 'Prophecy in the form of a coq-
à-l'âne' ('Prophetie en coq à l'âne'). Its opening lines give the
flavour of the work:

> Peuple malheur sur vous quand le sanglant Gerfaut
> Et le bleu limaçon mary de la limotte,
> Vers le Pole Antaricq s'en viendra d'un plain saut,
> Luisant comme un bonnet fait à la matelote . . .[58]

> Woe to you, people, when the bloody gerfalcon
> And the blue snail, husband of the slug,
> Will come towards the antarctic pole in a flat jump,
> Gleaming like a bonnet made sailor-fashion . . .

But other more densely fustian works, drawing heavily on the
terminology of medicine, alchemy and astrology, are in Burchiello's favourite form, the sonnet. The influence of Burchiello
and his Italian followers is more directly visible here:

> Vous qui Harpocratez un asne qui mordille
> En ce cloistre mondain de vieilles nations,
> Tremoussez-vous un peu en vos affections,
> Afin de luy donner chacun un coup d'estrille.
> Puis perclus de discours fracassez la vetille
> Par Philacteres poincts sufumigations,
> Car ces Paladiens en leurs opinions,
> Sincopent bien souvent sur un grain de lentille . . .[59]

> You who Harpocratize a donkey which nibbles
> In this worldly cloister of old nations,
> Bestir yourself a little in your affections,
> So that each of you may give it a stroke with a currying comb.
> Then, stiff-jointed in your speech, shatter the trifling thing,

---

58 *Le Cabinet satyrique, ou recueil parfaict des vers picquans & gaillards de ce temps*
(Paris, 1633), p. 587.
59 Ibid., p. 582. See also the 'Galimatias' by Sigogne, printed in Benayoun (ed.),
Anthologie du nonsense, pp. 51–2.

> By means of phylacteries, points and suffumigations;
> For these people, Palladians in their opinions,
> Often miss a beat when standing on a lentil.[60]

This brief history of nonsense poetry in medieval and Renaissance Europe has suggested that nonsense needs to be looked at in the same way as other literary genres: as something created, developed, re-worked and re-directed by individual writers. And this in turn implies that the occurrence of nonsense in successive periods, and in one country after another, should normally be looked at in terms of transmission, not spontaneous generation.

Which prompts the question: what knowledge did John Hoskyns have of these earlier forms of nonsense poetry when he penned his own nonsense verse in 1611? To this there can be no certain answer. Hoskyns was a highly literary man, a scholar of Greek as well as Latin, and the composer of a treatise on rhetoric. As a lawyer he would have had a good knowledge of Norman French: a reading knowledge of later French can therefore be presumed. But the nonsense fatrasies or fatras of the French Middle Ages were unavailable in printed texts at this time. Most of Sigogne's nonsense poetry seems also to have been published only after the author's death, which took place in the very year of Hoskyns's nonsense composition. Although Hoskyns never travelled to Italy or Spain, it would have been quite normal for a literary Englishman of his type to have a good reading knowledge of Italian, and possibly Spanish as well. In his treatise on rhetoric he made reference to popular works by Jacopo Sannazaro and Jorge de Montemayor, though it is not clear from his reference whether he had read them in the original.[61] The widespread popularity and frequent reprintings of Burchiello's verses throughout the sixteenth century make him – and his well-known imitators, such as Croce – by far the

---

60 Harpocrates was the Greek god of silence; suffumigations are fumigations from below; 'Palladians' means probably followers of Athene Pallas, the goddess of wisdom (rather than imitators of the Italian architect Palladio).
61 Osborn, *Life of Hoskyns*, p. 155.

most likely model for Hoskyns's own poem; so too does the very Burchiellesque density of absolute nonsense which Hoskyns achieved. The case for transmission from Italy to England is very strong, although direct proof is lacking.

Yet one final qualification must also be added. If a spark of nonsense was indeed transmitted in this way, that one spark was sufficient, and no further influence from Burchiello's works was needed: for it is quite certain that the person who caught the flame from Hoskyns and developed the nonsense genre to its full glory in seventeenth-century English poetry, John Taylor, was a monoglot whose knowledge of foreign literature came only from published translations.[62] And of Burchiello's nonsense poetry, not surprisingly, no translation into English was ever attempted.

---

62 The only works of foreign literature mentioned by Taylor were all works available in translation. See also his own defence of English poetry in *Workes*, sig. Bbb6ᵛ: 'Then I whose Artlesse studies are but weake, / Who never could, nor will but English speake'.

CHAPTER 4

The sources and resources of nonsense: literary conventions, parodic forms and related genres

THE PREVIOUS CHAPTERS of this Introduction have discussed the particular history of the nonsense genre developed by Hoskyns, Taylor and Corbet; the conjuncture of stylistic forces in Elizabethan and Jacobean literature which made it possible; and the earlier history of European nonsense poetry which probably supplied, through the 'Burchiellesque' tradition, a model for Hoskyns to imitate. But there is a still wider background of literary forms and devices which needs also to be considered, the most important of them being the tradition of 'impossibilia' (briefly mentioned in Chapter 3), which supplied so much of the substance of nonsense poetry, and the various types of parodic writing which provided the precedent of a literary form which is both meta-literary (in the sense that it takes literature as its object) and anti-literary. None of these genres, forms or devices could be described as having directly caused nonsense poetry to exist. But together they make up a large part of the range of sources and resources on which literary nonsense drew.

Impossibilia

The literary device which presents reversals of the natural order of things (known as 'impossibilia' in Latin and 'adynata' in Greek) has a very long history. It can be found in early Greek poets such as Archilochus, in Roman poets such as Virgil, Horace and Ovid, and indeed in some of the best-known prophetic verses of the Bible: 'The wolf also shall dwell with the lamb, and the leopard shall lie down with the kid; . . . and the lion shall eat straw like the ox.'[1] In the Middle Ages the device was widely used to comic effect, as we have already seen; in addition to its literary expressions, it also provided the subject of innumerable carvings, paintings and drawings which depicted impossible natural phenomena, inversions of animal behaviour or reversals of the relation between animals and men.[2] The most concentrated use of impossibilia in medieval literature was made by the courtly poets of the Provençal tradition, writers such as Raimbaut de Vaqueiras and Arnaut Daniel.[3] And from their works the device was taken over and developed further by Petrarch and his followers, becoming popular among writers influenced by Petrarchism such as Lope de Vega in Spain and the Pléiade school in France.[4]

1 Isaiah II: 6–7. On the classical authors see H. V. Canter, 'The Figure of Adynaton in Greek and Latin Poetry', *American Journal of Philology*, li (1930), pp. 32–41; E. Dutoit, *Le Thème de l'adynaton dans la poésie antique* (Paris, 1936); and the discussion in G. Cocchiara, *Il mondo alla rovescia* (Turin, 1963), pp. 71–93. The classical adynata are also discussed, in relation to modern Greek proverbs, in N. P. Andriotes, *Glossike laographia* (Athens, 1940).

2 For a rich bibliography covering the medieval and Renaissance iconography, see O. Odenius, 'Mundus inversus: några inledande bibliografiska anteckningar kring tre mellansvenska bildvarianter', *Arv: tidskrift för nordisk folkminneforskning*, x (1954), pp. 142–70. On the presentation of this theme in early modern broadsheets see D. Kunzle, 'World Upside Down: The Iconography of a European Broadsheet Type', in B. A. Babcock (ed.), *The Reversible World: Symbolic Inversion in Art and Society* (Ithaca, NY, 1978), pp. 39–94. For further visual examples, from the 15th century to the 19th, see G. Böhmer (ed.), *Die verkehrte Welt: Le Monde renversé: The Topsy-Turvy World*, catalogue of an exhibition held by the Goethe-Institut, Amsterdam, Paris, London and New York, 1985.

3 See O. Schultz-Gora, 'Das Adynaton in der altfranzösischen und provenzalischen Dichtung nebst Dazugehörigen', *Archiv für das Studium der neueren Sprachen*, year 87, clxi (n.s., lxi) (1932), pp. 196–209; Crocioni, 'Il "Menzionero" di Baldassare da Fossombrone', p. 239; and Cocchiara, *Il mondo alla rovescia*, p. 115. For a brief account of medieval impossibilia in relation to the classical tradition see Curtius, *European Literature and the Latin Middle Ages*, pp. 94–7.

4 See J. G. Fucilla, 'Petrarchism and the Modern Vogue of the figure Adynaton', *Zeitschrift für Romanische Philologie*, lvi (1936), pp. 671–81. Fucilla notes (p. 675) that the 'longest string of ornate *impossibilia* on record' was written by the minor Italian Renaissance poet Traiano Bordoni, occupying six pages of *Rime di diversi autori . . . libro nono* (Cremona, 1560) (pp. 130–35).

Taking the long history of this literary device as a whole, it is possible to divide the uses which were made of impossibilia into three broad categories: the dystopian, the utopian and the hyperbolic. Of these, the dystopian might seem to be the most obvious application for a trope which involves the overturning of the natural order. Certainly it furnishes one of the earliest examples of all, a speech of warning about tyranny given by Herodotus: 'Verily the heaven shall be beneath the earth and the earth high above the heaven, and the sea shall be a dwelling-place for men and fish shall dwell in the place of men now that of all people you, men of Lacedaemon, talk of ending equality and bringing back tyrants to the cities!'[5] Similarly Ovid, lamenting the reversal in his own fortune during his period of exile on the Black Sea coast, included a classic account of the world out of joint in his *Tristia*.[6] The trope often takes on cosmic overtones in the Latin poetry of the Middle Ages: thus the twelfth-century beast epic *Ysengrimus* includes the lament,

> Transsumpsere suas elementa ac tempora leges,
> Deseruitque prior non loca pauca situs.
> Estiue transiuit hyemps, hyemaliter estas . . .
> Piscibus accessit campus, harena satis.

> The elements and the seasons have transposed their laws,
> And many places have abandoned their old positions.
> Winter has turned summery, and summer wintry . . .
> The field has given way to fish, and the beach to crops.[7]

Such imagery was of course used to express the teachings of apocalyptic theology. Other inversions of order were similarly invoked to symbolize the breakdown of harmony or authority in the human world: thus the *Carmina Burana* poem previously

---

5 *Histories*, trans. H. Carter (London, 1962), p. 334 (V. 92).
6 *Tristia* I. 7, lines 1–10; e.g. lines 3–4: 'terra feret stellas, caelum findetur aratro, / unda dabit flammas, et dabit ignis aquas' ('The earth shall support stars, and the sky shall be cloven by the plough; water shall produce flame and flame water').
7 *Ysengrimus*, ed. and trans. J. Mann, Mittellateinische Studien und Texte, xii (Leiden, 1987), pp. 548, 550 (VII, lines 620–22, 632).

mentioned uses asses playing the lute as images of a world in which the unlearned have usurped the place of their masters.[8] Impossibilia therefore became a standard tool of satire, of criticism and denunciation. We find them being used, for example, by Luther in his attacks on the Papacy, and by writers such as John Taylor (as already mentioned) to denounce the unnatural rebellion of British subjects against their King.[9] The invention of elaborate and arresting (and in some cases shocking or revolting) inversions of nature was thus a very well-established theme in European literature; but so long as this device was used in a form that was subject to the controlling purpose of satire, criticism or theological teaching, it could never be properly described as nonsense writing.

The utopian use of impossibilia also goes back to some of the earliest known examples. The passage from Isaiah, already quoted, is one; another famous and influential text was the description of the Golden Age in Ovid's *Metamorphoses*.[10] Such sources were combined by early Christian theologians who set out to describe the Golden Age which, as the Sybilline prophecies foretold, would precede the coming of Christ: according to Lactantius, the mountains would drip with honey, the rivers would run with milk and wine, and the sheep mingle safely with the wolf.[11] Such images of cosmic plenty must have resonated powerfully in medieval Europe, where crop failures and famines were common experiences; so it is not surprising that the dominant form of utopian impossibilism in the medieval period was a vision in which the basic physical features of the world had become transmuted into foodstuffs.[12] The classic example of this

---

8 'Florebat olim studium', referred to above, ch. 3, n. 7.

9 For Luther (who pictured the Pope interpreting Scripture as an ass playing the lyre) see Böhmer (ed.), *Die verkehrte Welt*, pp. 5, 8. For Taylor see above, pp. 24–5 and poem 16.

10 Bk. I, lines 107–15.

11 *Divinae institutiones*, VII. 24–6.

12 For a powerful (but perhaps exaggerated) statement of the dominance of hunger in medieval and Renaissance European culture see P. Camporesi, *Bread of Dreams: Food and Fantasy in Early Modern Europe*, trans. D. Gentilcore (Cambridge, 1989).

was the medieval English poem 'The Land of Cockaygne',
describing an abbey on an island in the Atlantic where

> Ther beth rivers gret and fine
> Of oile, melk, honi and wine

> There are rivers great and fine
> Of oil, milk, honey and wine

and where

> The gees irostid on the spitte
> Fleeth to that abbai, god hit wot,
> And gredith 'gees al hote, al hote!'

> The geese roasted on the spit
> Fly to that abbey, God knows this to be true,
> And call out, 'Hot geese, hot geese!'[13]

The idea of roast geese advertising themselves is reminiscent of
one of the favourite *impossibilia* of the classical tradition, that
of oxen yoking themselves to the plough. For the vision of
Cockayne appealed to laziness as well as greed: what many of
the favourite images played on was not just the abundance of
things to eat, but the lack of effort required to produce them.
In the German tradition, Cockayne was known as 'Schlaraffenland': originally 'Schluderaffenland', this word came from 'schlu-
dern', meaning to work lazily, a verb related to the English
'slattern' and 'slut'.[14] Accordingly, one fourteenth-century Catalan description of the land of Cockayne includes trees which

---

13 Mätzner, *Altenglische Sprachproben*, 1, pp. 149, 151.
14 See Böhme, *Altdeutsches Liederbuch*, pp. 364–5. Schlaraffenland is discussed
also in Müller-Fraureuth, *Die deutschen Lügendichtungen*, pp. 14–15, 96–9, and in J.
Poeschel, 'Das Märchen vom Schlaraffenlande', *Beiträge zur Geschichte der deutschen
Sprache und Literatur*, v (1878), pp. 389–427. The connotation of idleness is also
conveyed by an English term for the Land of Cockayne, 'Lubberland': see for
example the late 17th-century ballad 'An Invitation to Lubberland', reprinted in
Ashton (ed.), *Humour, Wit and Satire*, pp. 34–7. For a more general account of
the Land of Cockayne, concentrating on Italian versions of the myth, see G.
Cocchiara, *Il paese di Cuccagna e altri studi di folklore* (Turin, 1956), pp. 159–87.

bear not only fruit but also fine articles of clothing.[15] In the Italian tradition this comic utopia was known also as 'Balordìa' (literally 'folly') and portrayed as a kingdom of the idle; it was also described by Boccaccio as 'Bengodi' (meaning 'enjoy-well'), a country in which the mountains were made of Parmesan cheese.[16]

The more bizarre of these utopian fantasies, like those of the dystopias, did furnish some of what might be called the materials of a nonsense universe. But so long as the description of a land of Cockayne was dominated by a controlling theme (that of effortless consumption), it would always have an overall consistency which worked against the creation of true nonsense: fantasy which makes sense, however fantastic, is not nonsense. A more wide-ranging and free-floating exercise of the imagination would be required to produce a description of a nonsense world.

One strong impulse in this direction came from the rediscovery in the Renaissance period of the works of the Greek writer Lucian, whose 'True Story' described a whole succession of fantasy worlds: one in which soldiers ride to battle on giant fleas, one in which infantry use asparagus as spears and mushrooms as shields, another in which people are clothed in glass and feed only on the smoke made by cooking flying frogs, and another, known as 'Lamp-town' (Lychnopolis), populated entirely by animate lanterns.[17] Since Lucian's work was intended as a parody of the boastful or fabulous travel narratives of his own day, it naturally struck a chord in the Renaissance period, when writings by explorers and travellers formed one of the boom industries of contemporary publishing. Lucian's influence can clearly be seen in, for example, the account of the voyages of

15 Bernat Metge, 'Llibre de fortuna e prudència', in his *Obra completa*, ed. L. Badia and X. Lamuela, 2nd edn. (Barcelona, 1975), p. 78.

16 Camporesi, *Bread of Dreams*, p. 79; Boccaccio, *Decamerone*, VIII. 3.

17 *Verae historiae* in Lucian, *Works*, ed. and trans. A. M. Harmon, 8 vols. (Cambridge, Mass., 1961), i, pp. 247–357. On the nature of Lucian's invention here see J. A. Dane, *Parody: Critical Concepts versus Literary Practices, Aristophanes to Sterne* (Norman, Oklahoma, 1988), pp. 75–82. On his influence during the Renaissance see C. Robinson, *Lucian and his Influence in Europe* (London, 1979).

Pantagruel in Rabelias's *Quart Livre*, which also parodies the contemporary genre. And yet even with someone as inexhaustibly inventive as Rabelais, the free play of imagination becomes quickly curtailed, being harnessed in several cases (notably the description of the land of the 'Papimanes' or pope-worshippers) to a satirical purpose. Another influential account of an imaginary world, Thomas Artus's *Relation de l'isle des hermaphrodites* (published in 1605), turns out similarly to be little more than an elaborate satire on the contemporary French court.[18] Also essentially satirical was a more wide-ranging and Lucianic work (written in the late 1590s and published in 1605) by an author close to the milieux from which English seventeenth-century nonsense poetry developed, *Mundus alter et idem*, by Joseph Hall.[19] Satire seems to have taken over in the case of many – perhaps most – of the descriptions of fantasy worlds between More's *Utopia* and Swift's *Gulliver's Travels*; that, indeed, is the reason why the boundaries between utopia and dystopia are so often blurred in these works. But so long as the satirical purpose is clearly visible, the blurring of other categories can never really amount to the anarchic category-mixing of nonsense.

It is the third type of impossibilia, the hyperbolic, which brings us closest to the origins of literary nonsense. This is the one type which is essentially rhetorical: that is, it makes reference to impossible things not because it is trying to describe an impossible world (whether unpleasant or pleasant), but as a rhetorical figure, to emphasize and dramatize impossibility itself. Instead of simply saying 'I will never cease to love you', for example, it forms a hyperbole with a physical image: 'Rivers will run uphill before I cease to love you'. The device is emphatic by nature, and the only way to add more emphasis is to pile on more impossibilia: rivers will run uphill, fish will sing in the trees, chickens will hunt hawks, blind men will see, and so on.

18 On this work see G. Atkinson, *The Extraordinary Voyage in French Literature before 1700* (New York, 1920), pp. 13–17.
19 Hall, *Another World and Yet the Same*, trans. J. M. Wands (New Haven, Conn., 1981).

This device was used in love poetry by classical poets such as Horace and Propertius, and was developed in a very similar way by Petrarch and his many imitators.[20] And it is, of course, a device which comes loaded with a kind of inherent instability: reversals of nature often present the sort of incongruity which we find comic, and yet they were used in this tradition for highly serious expressions of emotional states, such as pledges of love or statements of despair. The more extreme the state, the more exorbitant the expression of it, and the more comical and absurd that expression would then seem to be if one ceased for a moment to take the whole rhetorical enterprise seriously. In addition, the only way in which this trope could be extended was by compiling ever longer lists of impossibilia, which usually had little or no inherent connection one with another: this too strengthened the potentially comic effect, emphasizing the qualities of randomness and disjunction which are frequently found in comic genres and almost always found in nonsense.

We have already seen how intimately involved this rhetorical device was with the creation of nonsense among the German Minnesingers. It continued to enjoy close connections with nonsense literature until well into the seventeenth century. A poem such as the following, for example, which retains the form (while reversing the meaning) of a traditional 'impossibilia' love poem, displays a sense of the comic potential of the device which borders on the nonsensical:

> When in the month of *January*,
> Ripe apples grow on Trees,
> When butter doth in *February*
> At once both thaw and freeze,
> When Horses flie, beasts headless walk,
> When chairs and stools do move,

---

20 For examples from Horace and Propertius see Cocchiara, *Il mondo alla rovescia*, pp. 86–7; on Petrarch see Fucilla, 'Petrarchism'. For a study of Petrarch's influence, emphasizing his cultivation of paradox, antithesis and hyperbole, but not discussing this particular rhetorical device, see L. Forster, *The Icy Fire: Five Studies in European Petrarchism* (Cambridge, 1969).

When mutes as fast as women talk,
Then I will fall in love.

When Cherries in the month of *March*
As ripe are as in *June*,
When men instead of Corn sow Starch,
When Bears do sing in tune,
When Fishes on the Trees do chatter,
When womens tongues ne're move,
When men forbear to life and flatter,
Then will I fall in love.[21]

But this is comic-satirical, rather than nonsensical. Similarly, John Donne's 'Goe, and catch a falling starre' is a satirical reversal (though a less light-hearted one) of another traditional type of 'impossibilia' love poem, the type in which a lover promises (or his loved one demands) that he will perform all kinds of impossible tasks in order to prove his love.[22]

The shift from satire to nonsense might not involve any great change in the contents of the imagery; all that was required was an abandonment of any overall satirical purpose. In a few cases we can see this shift happen virtually before our eyes. One example is the quasi-nonsensical 'Interrogativa Cantilena' (poem 27), beginning 'If all the world were Paper, / And all the Sea were Inke', which looks like a sequence of satirical images from which the satirical purpose has just been drained away, leaving only a series of whimsical questions as the residue. (Possibly the opening image is derived from a powerfully satirical passage in a work by Thomas Dekker, which piles up impossibilia in a description of the endless stratagems adopted by a bankrupt: 'If all the water in the Thames were inke, and all the fethers upon

21 *The Oxford Drollery* (Oxford, 1671), pp. 78–9 (entitled 'A Mock-song to Love'); reprinted in W. Hicks (ed.), *Grammatical Drollery, consisting of Poems and Songs* (London, 1682), pp. 116–17 (entitled 'A positive Farewel to Love').
22 Donne's poem has been included, on questionable grounds, in a modern anthology of nonsense poetry: Haughton (ed.), *Chatto Book of Nonsense Poetry*, p. 91. For the tradition of impossible tasks see the classification in Dutoit, *Le Thème de l'adynaton*, pp. 171–2.

Swans backes were pens, and all the smoky sailes of western barges were white paper . . .')[23] Another example where the transition is clearly visible is that of a sequence of impossibilia in a satirical mock-prognostication (published under the title *Cobbes Prophecies* in 1614), which was adapted by a later writer into a nonsense poem, 'Newes'. (These two items are printed here as poems 28A and 28B.)

Two other directions in which impossibilia were taken to create nonsensical poetry can also be mentioned here. One was the cultivation of logical impossibilia: not reversals of the physical or biological order of nature, but contradictions in terms, such as midnight happening in the middle of the day, or children conceived before their parents. (Of course the boundary between physical and logical impossibilia is not clear-cut: a dumb man speaking is a logical contradiction, since 'dumb' means 'unable to speak', but it belongs too in the same realm of physical impossibilities as fish speaking or men flying.) One example of a nonsense poem devoted mainly to this kind of play of logical contradictions is the 'Bull Droll', printed here as poem 29. Another type of poem cultivated physical impossibilities of a particular sort: typically, flying through the air and traversing the globe at incredible speed. Such feats seem to derive originally from the impossible tasks demanded of (or promised by) lovers, as mentioned above. Impossibilia of this kind were concentrated in a sub-genre of absurd boasts, a latter-day version of the Lügendichtung, which seems eventually to have become attached to the genre of 'Bedlamite' or 'Poor Tom' verses, poems

23 'The Bankrouts Banquet' in Dekker, *The Non-dramatic Works*, ed. A. B. Grosart, 5 vols. (London, 1884–6), iii, p. 377. As several scholars have noticed, this imagery derives originally from the Talmud, and is common in rabbinical literature: see R. Köhler, *Kleinere Schriften zur neueren Litterateurgeschichte, Volkskunde und Wortforschung*, 3 vols. (Berlin, 1900), iii, pp. 293–4, and the summary in I. and P. Opie, (eds.), *The Oxford Dictionary of Nursery Rhymes*, rev. edn. (Oxford, 1980), p. 437. There is a fascinating discussion of this theme, in relation to a Spanish 'romancero' popular among the Jews of Sarajevo, in K. Vidaković-Petrov, *Kultura španskih jevreja na jugoslovenskom tlu: XVI–XX vek*, 2nd edn. (Sarajevo, 1990), pp. 212–19.

spoken by madmen. That this special kind of boasting poem was not originally connected with Bedlam is suggested by the two poems of this type printed here: in the later of the two, poem 31, the Bedlamite refrain looks as if it is merely tacked on to the poem and not essential to it, while the earlier of the two, poem 30, makes no Bedlamite references and is entitled simply 'Witley's lies'.

Parody

As the brief survey of impossibilia given above has suggested, it was possible to make a kind of nonsense poetry simply by describing, in poetry, absurd and impossible things. But there is a fundamental difference between making a straightforward use of narrative or descriptive literary forms to give an account of absurd events or things, and writing the kind of poetry which makes nonsense of the literary forms themselves. The first just presents a nonsense world to our imagination, through the vehicle of literature: the second presents us with nonsense litera-ture. One might say that the former, in describing a nonsense world, describes a parody of the world (though this is an extended and almost metaphorical use of the word 'parody'), while the latter *is* a parody – parody being, by its nature, a literary phenomenon.

This distinction, although fundamental, cannot be absolute or clear-cut. Even the plainest descriptive prose cannot be a purely transparent medium, merely conveying to us the world which is seen through it. Plain prose has its own literary conven-tions, and these too may be subject to a kind of parodic effect if the contents of the description are absurdly different from what such prose normally describes. Nevertheless, a basic differ-ence remains between nonsense writing in which the primary effect derives from the contents of the description (as in 'Witley's lies', poem 30), and writing in which the nonsense manipulation of a literary form is essential to its effect (as in the mock-Marlovian high rhetoric of John Taylor's finest nonsense poems). In most nonsense poetry – and, it can be said, in all the best nonsense poetry – the literary-parodic element plays an essential role. Readers can sense this difference if, for example, they compare the experience of reading the English translation of Burchiello's poem (given above, p. 71) with the experience of reading the original. In the form of a succession of lines of plain English prose, the poem is reduced, so to speak, to those contents which it describes: a succession of strange things, which may seem quaint or intriguing but which, with the literary structure dissolved away, can only be shapeless, forceless and ultimately uninteresting. There is none of the feeling of exhilaration there which comes from reading the original, where the whole effect depends on the overpowering sense of a literary form or a literary style (that of a grandiloquent mystical-rhetorical sonnet) making demands on the reader which are in the same instant cancelled by what the poem is actually saying.

So while the tradition of impossibilia may have provided, so to speak, much of the furniture of a nonsense world, that in itself was not sufficient to create proper nonsense literature. Static furniture or building-blocks were not enough. Also needed was a special kind of stylistic energy; and this came from the force of the parodic impulse.

The literature of the European Middle Ages contains few examples of parodies of individual authors, but many examples of styles, genres, literary forms and other types of speech and writing being subjected to ludicrous parody.[24] Particularly common, and sometimes startling to the modern eye, are the parodies of sacred hymns, sermons, readings from the gospels, and liturgical texts, including the mass itself: one Vatican manuscript of the fifteenth century includes a 'Missa potatorum' or

24 For general surveys see F. Novati, 'La Parodia sacra nelle letterature moderne', in his *Studi critici e letterari* (Turin, 1889), pp. 177–310; P. Lehmann, *Die Parodie im Mittelalter* (Munich, 1922); and S. L. Gilman, *The Parodic Sermon in European Perspective: Aspects of Liturgical Parody from the Middle Ages to the Twentieth Century*, Beiträge zur Literatur des XV. bis XVIII. Jahrhunderts, vi (Wiesbaden, 1974).

'Boozers' mass'.[25] Such texts have a socio-literary origin which is easily understood: parody flourishes among enclosed groups of people – in colleges, churches, monasteries, etc. – where certain standard texts or formulae are in habitual use. The formulaic texts of law, medicine and astrology were also common objects of parody, sometimes with satirical intent (as in the early medieval 'Testament of the Ass', in which the ass bequeaths his head to judges, voice to singers and tongue to preachers), and sometimes with a more free-ranging and nonsensical use of the imagination.[26] Rabelais's parody of legal argument in *Pantagruel*, Chapter 11 (which seems heavily influenced both by the French coq-à-l'âne and by the absolute nonsense of the Burchiellesque tradition), is the finest and by far the most nonsensical example of a legal parody. Mock-prognostications have already been mentioned, with the example of the prophecies of Pero Grulla in fifteenth-century Spain.[27] Again, Rabelais provides a particularly nonsensical example, with his parody of mystic-prophetic verses in *Gargantua*, Chapter 2:

> Mais l'an viendra, signé d'un arc turquoys,
> De v. fuseaulx et troys culz de marmite,
> Onquel le dos d'un roy trop peu courtoys
> Poyvré sera soubz un habit d'hermite ...

> But the year will come, marked by a Turkish bow,
> Five spindles and three cooking-pot bottoms,
> In which the back of a too uncourtly king
> Will be peppered beneath the cloak of a hermit ...[28]

In England, mock-prognostications enjoyed a particular vogue in the late sixteenth and early seventeenth centuries, with the

25 Novati, *Studi critici*, pp. 289–300. For parodies of religious services see also K. F. Flögel, *Geschichte des Burlesken* (Leipzig, 1794), pp. 200–203; and for a particularly fine late medieval English nonsense sermon see Wright and Halliwell (eds.), *Reliquiae antiquae*, i, pp. 82–4.
26 For translations of the 'Testament of the Ass' and the 'Testament of the Piglet' see Ziolkowski, *Talking Animals*, pp. 299–300.
27 See above, p. 74.
28 Rabelais, *Oeuvres complètes*, p. 33.

publication of works such as *A Wonderfull, strange and miraculous Astrologicall Prognostication* by 'Adam Fouleweather' (1591), *Platoes Cap* by 'Adam Evesdropper' (1604), *The Raven's Almanacke* by Thomas Dekker (1609), and *Cobbes Prophecies* (1614).[29] But these works were all essentially comic-satirical rather than nonsensical; as has already been suggested, a further adaptation was needed in order to convert ideas contained in the last of them into a genuine nonsense poem (see poems 28A and 28B).

Of the formulaic genres most frequently parodied, two deserve special mention: the medical prescription and the recipe. Good examples of nonsensical mock-prescriptions can be found in late fourteenth-century Catalonia and early fifteenth-century Germany.[30] A fifteenth-century English poem printed by Caxton, entitled 'A good medesyn yff a mayd have lost her madenhed to make her a mayd ageyn', also displays a rich stock of nonsensical conceits:

> She must have of the wyntyrs nyghte
> vii. myle of the mone-lyght
> Fast knyt in a bladder;
> She must medyl ther among
> vii. Wellsshemens song,
> And hang yt on a lader;
> She must have the left fot of an ele,
> Wyth the kreking of a cart-whele . . .[31]

> She must have of the winter's night
> Seven miles of the moonlight
> Tightly knitted in a bladder;

---

29 On this popular genre see H. Brown, *Rabelais in English Literature* (Cambridge, Mass., 1933), pp. 36–41; D. C. Allen, *The Star-Crossed Renaissance: The Quarrel about Astrology and its Influence in England* (Durham, NC, 1941), pp. 216–43; and F. P. Wilson (ed.), *Pantagruel's Prognostication*, Luttrell Reprints, no. 3 (Oxford, 1947).

30 Metge, 'Medecina', in his *Obra completa*, pp. 63–7; A Birlinger, 'Ein scherzhaftes Rezept', *Zeitschrift für deutsches Althertum*, xv (1872), pp. 510–12.

31 Printed (from the last page of Caxton's *Mirrour of the World* (London, 1481)) in Wright and Halliwell (eds.), *Reliquiae antiquae*, i, pp. 250–51; here p. 251.

> She must mix into it
> Seven Welshmen's songs
> And hang it on a ladder;
> She must have the left foot of an eel,
> With the creaking of a cart-wheel . . .

This type of mock-prescription had a perennial appeal, and it is possible to see some direct influence stemming from this particular poem (helped, no doubt, by its availability in a classic printed text) and bearing fruit in two mock-prescriptions of the seventeenth century, printed here as poems 32 and 33.

Mock-recipes or mock-menus also offered scope for nonsensical fantasy. Comic enumerations of endless varieties – and quantities – of foods (as in the fifteenth-century French *Nouveaux Sots de la joyeuse bande*, where the list takes up nearly forty lines of verse) parodied the lists of foods at official banquets, while nonsense recipes parodied elaborate instructions for preparing dishes with rare ingredients.[32] The minor poet and balladeer Martin Parker combined both elements in his 'Bill of Fare', a nonsensical (though tediously wordy) imitation of Jonson's satirical poem 'Cock-Lorell'. When Parker's publisher, Francis Grove, entered this ballad at the Stationers' Company on 4 October 1637, John Taylor was just completing a satirical prose-work on a gastronomic theme, *Taylors Feast*. Evidently Taylor read Parker's ballad just before the printing of his own work was completed (it was entered on 10 November); the nonsense elements in Parker's production naturally chimed with Taylor's own imagination, and on the final pages of *Taylors Feast* he gave a modified list of Parker's nonsense foods, adding some more of his own.[33] (These two items are printed here as poems 34A and 34B, though the second was not of course intended as poetry.)

---

32 For the passage from the *Nouveaux sots* see A. Montaiglon (ed.), *Recueil de poésies françaises des XVe et XVIe siècles*, 16 vols. (Paris, 1865–78), i, pp. 14–16.
33 For the Stationers' Company entries see E. Arber (ed.), *A Transcript of the Registers of the Company of Stationers of London, 1554–1640 AD*, 5 vols. (London, Birmingham, 1875–94), iv, pp. 394, 397. On Parker see H. E. Rollins, 'Martin Parker, Ballad-Monger', *Modern Philology*, xvi (1919), pp. 449–74.

Prose nonsense recipes of the seventeenth century include the following, entitled 'The Countess of *Kents* way of buttering *Turneps*', which, although consistent in its pursuit of the disgusting, has an overall inconsequentiality reminiscent of the nonsense recipes written three centuries later by Edward Lear:

> Take your *Hackney* Turneps, and put them into your pot unpar'd and as dirty as they come out of the ground, let your water but just cover them, 'tis no matter whether it be clean or no; so let them stew for a while, and when you feel them soft, put unto them an ounce of Rats-bane; so let them stew again till they are enough; then take your rankest hogs-grease, and *Jessimine* Butter, to give it a *Haut gout*; melt them together, and put them to your Turneps, then strew them with Tobacco, and so serve them.[34]

The nonsense recipe formula was also used for the purposes of political satire. One anonymous broadside published in 1659, entitled *An Excellent Recipe to make a Compleat Parliament or (if you please) a New Senate Fitted to the English-Man's Palate*, included the following ingredients:

> . . . one and fifty *Anabaptists, blanch't in fair river water*, threescore *Independents*, a quarter of a pound of *John Lilburn's bones beaten into a fine powder and sear'd*, the better to *unite* with the rest; whereunto add an ounce of *Oyle* of *Saint-John's-Wort*, a *drachme* of the scrapings of the Divell's *cloven foot*; five *spoon*-fulls of the *marrow* of old *Oliver's nose*; half a *Committee man*; two Gallons of *Aquafortis*, seventy *Scot's* haslets, together with a *Kidderkinfull of Hugh Peter's* sighs and tears, *evaporated* into *water* in an *Alembiqu'* made of an *Organ-pipe* . . .[35]

Recipes were particularly suitable for conversion into nonsense for one obvious reason: their structure, which is linear and additive, lends itself to the stringing together of more and more incongruous and disjunct ideas. List-making (as Rabelais demonstrated) is one of the most basic and effective routines of

34 *Wits Interpreter: The English Parnassus*, ed. J. C[otgrave] (London, 1671), p. 389.
35 *An Excellent Recipe*, BL Thomason 669. f. 21. 82.

comedy. Another genre which used this principle was the mock-booklist – of which Rabelais also gave a classic example with his listing of the library of St Victor in *Pantagruel*, Chapter 7. Rabelais's example was widely imitated, by writers such as John Donne (whose 'Catalogus aulicorum' was directly modelled on the library of St Victor) and Sir Thomas Browne, whose list of 'Rare and generally unknown Books' included 'Epicurus *De piet-ate*' and 'An exact account of the Life and Death of Avicenna, confirming the account of his death by taking nine clysters together in a fit of the cholic'.[36] Browne's list was part of a larger collection of improbable objects, parodying the 'cabinets of curiosities' of his day. A similar listing was provided by one of Rabelais's most talented followers in France, Adrien de Montluc, comte de Cramail, in a book filled with bizarre fantasy-lists and extended conceits; his lists of rare objects included

> Un traicté composé par Lantisparron, qui monstre l'invention de dresser les oyseaux de proye, à voler les estoilles errantes, sans qu'ils bruslent leur plumes dans le feu elementaire.
> Un vomitoire d'essence de chanure, pour faire rendre aux fourmis de Peru l'or qu'elles ont avallées.[37]

> A treatise written by Lantisparron, which shows how to train birds of prey to catch falling stars, without burning their feathers in the elemental fire.
> An emetic made from the essence of hemp, to make the ants of Peru vomit up the gold which they have swallowed.

The parodic book-lists of the sixteenth and seventeenth centuries belonged to the humanist world's comic sub-culture of mock-scholarship. Just as the churches and monasteries of the

---

36 Browne, *Works*, ed. S. Wilkin, 3 vols. (London, 1910), vol. 3, pp. 268–70. On Donne's 'Catalogus' see R. Colie, *Paradoxia epidemica: The Renaissance Tradition of Paradox* (Princeton, NJ, 1966), p. 227.
37 'De Vaux' [pseudonym of A. de Montluc, comte de Cramail], *Les Jeux de l'inconnu, augmenté de plusieurs pièces en ceste dernière edition* (Rouen, 1645), pp. 318–19.

Middle Ages had produced parodic versions of liturgical texts, so too the universities and the learned world of the Renaissance produced parodic imitations of humanist scholarship, with its cumbersome apparatuses of learned notes referring to ancient authors. Good examples of this technique can be found in Sanford's 'versi sciolti' (poem 3) and in James Smith's 'Ad Johannuelem Leporem' (poem 25), which comes from a similar milieu of university and Inns of Court-trained wits and scholars.

In addition to parodying the techniques of scholarship, writers also played with the techniques of classical rhetoric, the mastery of which formed such an important part of a Renaissance education. The most popular genre here was the mock-encomium, which used all the resources of rhetoric to pile up arguments in favour of some absurdly unsuitable thing. This type of parody was not unknown in the Middle Ages (there are medieval poems in praise of 'Nemo' (nobody), and a ninth-century encomium on baldness by the coincidentally named Hucbald), but it did undergo an explosion in popularity during the Renaissance period, helped not only by the renewed interest in classical rhetoric but also by the rediscovery of Lucian's works, which included mock-encomia of flies and parasites.[38] Thus we have rhetorical exercises in praise of the ant by Melanchthon, the louse by Daniel Heinsius, the flea by Calcagnini, and the egg by Puteanus; the *Paradossi* of Ortensio Landi in praise of indebtedness and prison, and the brilliant argumentation of Panurge in favour of debt in Rabelais's *Tiers Livre*, Chapters 3–4; and, of course, the *Praise of Folly* of Erasmus.[39] In Germany the genre underwent a special vogue in the early seventeenth century: one ponderous collection published in 1619 included items in praise of fleas, lice, spiders, geese, dogs, nothing, some-

38 See Dane, *Parody: Critical Concepts*, p. 84.
39 See A. Hauffen, 'Zur Litteratur der ironischen Enkomien', *Vierteljahrschrift für Litteraturgeschichte*, vol. 6 (1893), pp. 161–85; H. K. Miller, 'The Paradoxical Encomium with Special Reference to its Vogue in England, 1600–1800', *Modern Philology*, liii (1956), pp. 145–78, esp. pp. 151–3; and Colie, *Paradoxia epidemica*, esp. pp. 3–5.

thing and everything.[40] It flourished in England at the same time, with the publication of such works as Sir William Cornwallis's *Essayes of Certaine Paradoxes* (1616), which included encomia of debt, nothing and syphilis; Sir John Harington used all the devices of mock-encomium to add comic mock-dignity to his treatise on the construction of lavatories, *A New Discourse of a Stale Subject, Called the Metamorphosis of Ajax* (1596); and the influence of this literary tradition can be seen too in the various writings in praise of jail, hemp-seed and beggary which crop up in the works of John Taylor.[41]

None of these mock-encomia produced what could be called absolute nonsense, but they did powerfully reinforce one of the fundamental devices of literary comedy, a device which played a large role, as we have already seen, in the nonsense poetry of the seventeenth century: the inappropriate mingling of 'high' and 'low'. Nonsense mixed together high and low subject-matter and diction; the mock-encomium combined a low subject with the rhetorical techniques appropriate to a high one. The other popular parodic forms which operated on this principle were the mock-heroic and the travesty, both generally known as 'burlesque'. In mock-heroic poetry, known as 'high burlesque', a low subject-matter is given a high, heroic treatment: this type of humour had a long history, beginning with the pseudo-Homeric *Batrachomyomachia*, the 'Battle of the Frogs and the Mice', and extending also to the medieval *Roman de Renart*, which treats farmyard animals as if they were heroes of courtly romance. Travesty, on the other hand (also known as 'low burlesque'), takes a heroic subject-matter and gives it a low treatment, describing, for example, characters from the *Aeneid* performing

---

40 C. Dornavius (ed.), *Amphitheatrum sapientiae socraticae joco-seriae* (Hanover, 1619). Similar items of academic humour can also be found in another very Germanic production of the same period, *Facetiae facetiarum, hoc est, joco-seriorum fasciculus*, 2 vols. (Frankfurt, 1615), which includes a learned treatise on farting (i, pp. 73–98).

41 See Miller, 'The Paradoxical Encomium', p. 160. As Miller points out (pp. 163–5), Rochester's famous poem 'Of Nothing' was merely a late example of this long-established tradition.

the everyday actions of milkmaids and washerwomen. This was a modern invention, made popular by Scarron's *Typhon* (1644) and *L'Énéide travestie* (1648), the second of which was adapted for English readers by Charles Cotton as *Scarronides: Or, Virgile Travestie* (1664).[42] The sudden vogue for low burlesque in the mid seventeenth century caused a revulsion of taste among high-minded literary critics. Boileau, who was not against either mock-heroic poetry or parody in general (his own *Le Lutrin*, a *Clochemerle*-like story of a dispute in a provincial church recounted in ringing Alexandrines, was intended as an acceptable example of the mock-heroic), mounted a famous attack on low burlesque in his *L'Art poétique* (1674):

> Au mépris du Bon sens, le Burlesque effronté
> Trompa les yeux d'abord, plut par sa nouveauté.
> On ne vit plus en vers que pointes triviales.
> Le Parnasse parla le langage des Hales.

> The dull Burlesque appear'd with impudence,
> And pleas'd by Novelty, in Spite of Sense.
> All, except trivial points, grew out of date;
> *Parnassus* spoke the Cant of *Billingsgate*.[43]

And another influential critical work, by François Vavasseur, decreed that parodic humour was permissible only when it produced rare inventions, showed respect for decorum and served the purposes of utility, truth or elegance.[44] Such demands for

---

42 See J. Jump, *Burlesque* (London, 1972); G. Kitchin, *A Survey of Burlesque and Parody in English* (Edinburgh, 1931), pp. 90−95; R. P. Bond, *English Burlesque Poetry 1700−1750* (Cambridge, Mass., 1932), pp. 138−42; J. Rohou, 'Le Burlesque et les avatars de l'écriture discordante (1635−1655)', in I. Landy-Houillon and M. Menard (eds.), *Burlesque et formes parodiques* (Seattle, 1987), pp. 349−65; U. Broich, *The Eighteenth-Century Mock-Heroic Poem* (Cambridge, 1990), pp. 7−14.

43 N. Boileau, *Oeuvres complètes*, ed. F. Escal (Paris, 1966), p. 159; English translation by Sir William Soame quoted in Broich, *Eighteenth-Century Mock-Heroic Poem*, p. 15. On Boileau's other parodic works see Dane, *Parody: Critical Concepts*, pp. 135−6. For a good discussion of Boileau's theory of parody and burlesque see W. Karrer, *Parodie, Travestie, Pastiche* (Munich, 1977), pp. 54−7, 186−9.

44 F. Vavasseur, *De ludicra dictione liber in quo tota jocandi ratio ex veterum scriptis aestimatur* (Paris, 1658), pp. 449−50.

decorum and 'bon sens' played a part in the alteration of taste in England as well as France, an alteration which must have helped to ensure the decline of nonsense poetry as well as that of low burlesque.[45]

But although the mock-heroic and travesty might, in their most extreme forms, come close to nonsense, there remains a basic difference in the principles on which burlesque and non-sense work. Both forms of burlesque operate by confronting and reversing our ideas of 'appropriateness', our normal assumption that there is a 'high' subject-matter in real life, with a 'high' style appropriate to its description in literature, and a 'low' sub-ject-matter with a 'low' style. Good mock-heroic suggests that style may in fact play the primary role – that style can itself be a method of constituting a subject-matter. In this way it raises questions about the relation between the literary world and real life. A successful mock-heroic poem functions rather like the ambiguous duck-rabbit picture: we can shift between seeing the style as guyed and seeing the low subject-matter as energized. But nonsense functions more like a kaleidoscope: we can see a different pattern every time, because there is no inherent pat-tern there at all. Mock-heroic plays on a tension between the literary world and real life; good literary nonsense destroys this, by dissolving everything into different kinds of literary con-ventions.

Another parodic genre which enjoyed a continuous history from the Middle Ages to the seventeenth century was the mock-love poem. Here too a 'high' style, involving the use of rich metaphors to celebrate the beauty of the loved one, is applied to a 'low' subject – an ugly woman (or man). The genre was of course a direct parodic inversion of love poetry, and was particu-larly popular in literary cultures where courtly love songs flourished. Many French examples of this type of poem, known

45 For a valuable discussion of the change of taste which took place in England in the late 17th century, see K. Thomas, 'The Place of Laughter in Tudor and Stuart England', *The Times Literary Supplement*, no. 3906 (21 Jan. 1977), pp. 77–81.

as the 'sotte-chanson', survive from the late thirteenth and early fourteenth centuries; a typical verse from one poem declares:

> Dame vaillans, vermeille con serisse,
> Saige en dormant, sans mauvais vent geter,
> Noire en son vis, brune soz la chemise,
> Vos ne daigniés les traïson porter . . . [46]

> Valiant lady, red as a cherry,
> Wise when you are asleep, without farting,
> Black in your face, brown under your blouse,
> You do not scorn to commit treachery . . .

In the fourteenth and fifteenth centuries mock-love poems became popular in England too. One example offers, in a pattern which was to become increasingly typical of the genre, not only a lover's description of his lady but also her own description of her lover:

> youre manly visage, shortly to declare,
>   your forehed, mouth, and nose so flatte,
> In short conclusyon, best lykened to an hare
> Of alle lyvyng thynges, save only a catte . . . [47]

The Elizabethan poet and playwright Robert Greene wrote one of the most famous examples, a mock-pastoral interlude, 'Doron's Eclogue', in which similar compliments are exchanged between a shepherd, Doron, and his lass, Carmela. As Doron puts it:

> Carmela dear, even as the golden ball
> That Venus got, such are thy goodly eyes;
> When cherries' juice is jumbled therewithal,
> Thy breath is like the steam of apple-pies.

---

46 Quoted in Zumthor, *Essai de poétique médiévale*, p. 260. For the fullest collection of such verse, See A. Långfors (ed.), *Deux recueils de sottes chansons*, Annales academiae scientiarum fennicae, ser. B, liii, no. 4 (Helsinki, 1945). Långfors comments that there are few passages of real nonsense in the sottes-chansons (pp. 12–13).
47 Robbins (ed.), *Secular Lyrics*, pp. 219–20 (no. 208).

> Thy lips resemble two cucumbers fair;
> Thy teeth like to the tusks of fattest swine;
> Thy speech is like the thunder in the air;
> Would God, thy toes, thy lips, and all were mine![48]

Similar mock-love poems continued to be composed, with varying degrees of absurdity and obscenity, throughout the seventeenth century.[49] Although they never crossed the threshold of nonsense, they must have helped to whet the appetite for ludicrous anti-poetic imagery; and it is worth noting that one very popular work in a similar style, a whimsical parody of a love poem, was credited to the pen of the inventor of high literary nonsense poetry in seventeenth-century England, John Hoskyns.[50]

Finally, one peculiar type of parody of a poetic form remains to be mentioned: the 'medley', which took up the form of a popular song or ballad and turned it into nonsense by stringing together a series of unconnected lines or couplets. This is a type of poem which seems to have sprung up quite suddenly in England in the mid sixteenth century. One of the earliest English examples, which appeared in a collection printed between 1546 and 1552, includes the following stanzas:

> My lady went to Canterbury,
>   The saint to be her boot;
> She met with Kate of Malmesbury:
> Why sleepest thou in an apple root?
>
> Nine mile to Michaelmas,
>   Our dame began to brew;
> Michael set his mare to grass,
>   Lord, so fast it snew!
>
> For you, love, I brake my glass,
>   Your gown is furred with blue;

48 R. Bell (ed.), *Poems of Robert Greene and Christopher Marlowe* (London, 1856), p. 46.
49 See, for example, the poem 'In Praise of his Mistress's Beauty' in Wardroper (ed.), *Love and Drollery*, pp. 216–18.
50 The poem is printed in Osborn, *Life of Hoskyns*, p. 301.

The devil is dead, for there I was;
I wis it is full true.[51]

Similar medley verses appear as a soliloquy-song in a play published in 1568:

And now will I dance, and now will I prance,
For why, I have none other work:
Snip snap, butter is no bone meat:
Knave's flesh is no pork.

Hey tisty-toisty, an owl is a bird,
Jackanapes hath an old face;
You may believe me at one bare word,
How like you this merry case?[52]

The basic principle on which these poems work is clear: they guy the inconsequentiality of popular songs and ballads, suggesting that it makes little difference which order the lines come in, or from which different songs they are derived. (Such a device might be described as an inversion of the literary device of the 'cento', in which different lines from classical authors were put together in such a way as to make a new, connected, sense.)[53] This parodic method seems to have been invented not in England but, a little earlier in the sixteenth century, in Normandy, where medleys made out of the first lines or refrains of popular songs, and known as 'fricassées', had enjoyed a sudden vogue. Since the fricassées were often recited as part of the 'sotties' of the French popular stage, they were probably influenced too by the tradition of literary nonsense which stemmed from the medieval fatrasies, and which was also present on the

51 Chambers and Sidgwick (eds.), *Early English Lyrics*, pp. 254–5 (no. 151).
52 Ulpian Fulwell, *Dramatic Writings*, ed. J. S. Farmer (London, 1906), p. 27 (sung by the character Nichol Newfangle in the play *Like Will to Like*).
53 This method, which itself has classical origins, was traditionally used by Christian writers to convert words taken from classical texts into statements of Christian doctrine: see, for example, Alexander Ross, *Virgilius evangelisans* (London, 1634). There is one classic study of the cento: O. Delepierre, *Tableau de la littérature du centon chez les anciens et chez les modernes*, 2 vols. (London, 1875).

fifteenth- and sixteenth-century stage in the genre known as 'menus propos'.[54]

In England, however, the nonsense medley underwent one further transformation. It was taken up and used for a particular musical form, the 'catch', which, being a canon for three or more voices, had the effect of breaking a poem into separate lines and transposing those lines by means of the delays which the canon imposed. In the words of one modern summary, 'A judicious placing of rests in the parts ensured that words which had no connection in the written text would be heard in a new association which could give rise to more than one interpretation.'[55] One popular collection of 'rounds or catches', Thomas Ravenscroft's *Pammelia: Musicks Miscellanie* (1609), adapted several lines from the mid sixteenth-century example quoted above:

> My Ladies gone to Canterbury,
> S. Thomas be her boote.
> Shee met with Kate of Malmsbury,
> Why weepst thou maple roote:
> O sleepst thou or wakst thou Jeffery,
> Cooke, the rost it burnes,
> turne round about about,
> turne round about about,
> turne round about about.[56]

The long-lasting popularity of such catches, in circles of amateur singers such as those to which Samuel Pepys belonged, must also have strengthened the genre of nonsensical ballad-medleys which continued to be produced in England from the 1630s to

---

54 On the 'menus propos' see above, pp. 65–6. On the fricassée see Picot, 'La Sottie en France', esp. p. 238; and Kinch, *La Poésie satirique de Marot*, p. 158. The Elizabethan English medleys are briefly discussed in C. R. Baskervill, *The Elizabethan Jig and Related Song Drama* (Chicago, 1929), p. 83; but Baskervill seems unaware of this probable connection with the French fricassées.

55 *The New Grove Dictionary of Music and Musicians*, ed. S. Sadie, 20 vols. (London, 1980), s.v. 'Catch'.

56 *Pammelia*, sigs. C3^v–C4^r.

the final decades of the seventeenth century. Poems 35, 36, 37
and 38 are examples of the genre; the last two of these are from
Pepys's own collection.

Macaronics, word-coining, gibberish and canting

Various types of trans-linguistic foolery were part of the heritage
of European literature. The more elaborate kinds, naturally,
were developed in circumstances where linguistic self-
consciousness was at a premium: in schools and universities
where Latin was taught (and spoken), and in courtly literary
circles where the command of more than one modern language
was expected. Thus in popular literature there is the tradition
of 'dog-Latin' or 'kitchen-Latin', in which a comically minimal
Latin surface layer is added to a vernacular substratum; from
the travelling students of medieval Europe we have 'goliardic'
poems in which Latin and the vernacular intermingle; and from
courtly Provençal poets we have multi-linguistic oddities such
as the famous 'descort' in five languages by Raimbaut de
Vaqueiras. This last type of writing was not necessarily comic;
on the contrary, it could be highly serious, and was thought
especially appropriate for such functions as dedicatory poems,
where a special display of effort and skill was called for. Thus,
for example, the dedication of Abraham France's *The Arcadian
Rhetorike* (1588) to Mary, Countess of Pembroke, includes a
poem in a mixture of Latin, Italian, Spanish and English; and
the virtuoso Spanish poet Luis de Góngora was not striving for
comic effect when he wrote a sonnet in alternating lines of
Spanish, Latin, Italian and Portuguese.[57]

Nevertheless, the effects of incongruity and disjunction
tended always to shift such bi- or multi-linguistic works towards
a humorous effect. The term 'macaronic verse' or 'macaronics'

---

57 France, *The Arcadian Rhetorike* (London, 1588), title-page verso; for Góngora's
sonnet, written in 1600, see E. K. Kane, *Gongorism and the Golden Age: A Study
of Exuberance and Unrestraint in the Arts* (Chapel Hill, NC, 1928), p. 76.

is generally used to cover all comic poetry of this kind; but the term itself has a narrower meaning and a more specific literary history. Strictly speaking, macaronics involve not the juxtaposition of phrases or lines in different languages, but the comic latinization of the vernacular (mainly by adding Latin endings to vernacular words). As a humorous genre, this type of poetry was first popularized by an Italian, Teofilo Folengo (1491–1544); the name itself seems to have been derived from a famous poem by one of his followers, Tifi degli Odassi, which had a macaroni-maker as its hero.[58] The genre enjoyed a huge international vogue during the sixteenth and seventeenth centuries, with examples being published in most western European countries. It achieved its strongest comic effect, naturally enough, where the vernacular was least Latinate: an early seventeenth-century German poem about fleas (by 'Gripholdus Knickknakius') may serve as an example of the combination of linguistic energy and ponderous schoolroom humour which characterizes these works.

> Floia cortum versicale de flois swartibus,
> illis deiriculis, quae omnes fere Minsshos Mannos,
> Weibras, Jungfras, &c. behüppere & spiezibus
> Schnaflis steckere & bitere solent . . .[59]

In the case of Romance languages such as Italian and French, the linguistic effect was of course less intrinsically bizarre. But we should not forget that this vogue for macaronics took place at the same time as the great expansion of Latinate vocabulary – abstractions, technical terms and other 'inkhorn' words – which

58 On macaronics see Flögel, *Geschichte der Burlesken*, pp. 115–34; F. Lalanne, *Curiosités littéraires* (Paris, 1845), pp. 74–9; O. Delepierre, *Macaronéana, ou mélanges de littérature macaronique* (Paris, 1852) and his *De la Littérature macaronique, et de quelques raretés bibliographiques de ce genre*, Miscellanies of the Philobiblion Society, ii, no. 14 (London, 1856), which reprints Odassi's 'La Macharonea' on pp. 18–42; T. Wright, *A History of Caricature and Grotesque in Literature and Art* (London, 1875), pp. 315–23; and W. T. Dobson, *Poetical Ingenuities and Eccentricities* (London, 1882), pp. 59–114. On Folengo see also C. Previtera, *La poesia giocosa*, pp. 373–400.
59 *Facetiae facetiarum*, i, p. 443.

occurred in those languages just as it did in English; the comic latinization of the macaronics must have tapped into a vein of satire about this phenomenon too.

That was the vein from which Rabelais drew in his own fantastical word-coinages, such as the term 'désincornifistibulé', which one early English translator ingeniously adapted as 'dezinkhornifistibulated'.[60] Comic neologisms were a stock-in-trade of learned humorous authors, of course, and writers did not need to have read Rabelais in order to indulge in them. But the peculiar extravagance of Rabelais's own coinages did exert a powerful influence: in a work published in 1599 by one of his followers, for example, we find words such as 'raminagrobicontenance', 'archimarmitonerastique' and 'circonvolubilipatnoterization'.[61] The basic strategy of such neologisms is the same as that of macaronics: it makes use of our assumption that the more Latinate and formal-looking a word is in our language, the more rationally abstract its meaning must be. But while macaronics just play with this assumption by latinizing the kitchen vernacular, comic word-coinages go further and threaten, through a process of apparent elaboration of sense, to destroy sense altogether. In both cases, there is a comic effect of linguistic alienation, in which words are reduced (partially or wholly) to objects.

The end product of such a process is sheer linguistic nonsense or gibberish. This too was a literary form with a history of its own. Classical literature included some well-known examples of 'barbarian' speech, such as the ten lines in 'Phoenician' in Plautus' *Poenulus* which begin: 'Ythalonim ualon uth sicorathisyma comsyth'.[62] Whether such fragments were authentic specimens of foreign languages or not was perhaps unimportant:

---

60 Brown, *Rabelais in English Literature*, p. 45; the translator was John Eliot. On Rabelais's coinages see the classic study by L. Sainéan, *La Langue de Rabelais*, 2 vols. (Paris, 1922–3).

61 L. Sainéan, *L'Influence et la réputation de Rabelais: interprètes, lecteurs et imitateurs. Un rabelaisien (Marnix de Sainte-Aldegonde)* (Paris, 1930), pp. 276, 295.

62 See L.-E. Chevaldin, *Les Jargons de la farce de Pathelin* (Paris, 1903), pp. 43–6.

what mattered was the dramatic or comic effect of their sheer outlandishness. (The influence of Plautus' Phoenician can be seen in the mock-Turkish of the last two acts of Molière's *Bourgeois gentilhomme*.) In medieval literature, fantasy-imitations of foreign languages were used to explore the boundaries between the comic and the sinister: typically, such speech was put in the mouths of pagans or devils, or used in conjurations to summon up the latter. Thus the thirteenth-century *Miracle de Théophile* by Rutebeuf includes the splendid conjuration:

> Bagahi laca bachahé
> Lamac cahi achabahé
> Karryelos
> Lamac lamec bachalyos
> Cabahagi sabalyos
> Baryolas
> Lagozatha cabyolas
> Samahac et famyolas
> Harrahya

and the fourteenth-century *Miracle de Robert le Diable* has lines chanted by Saracens:

> Sabaudo bahe fuzaille
> Draquitone baraquita
> Arabium malaquita
> Hermes zalo[63]

As this last example illustrates, however, there was always a tendency for meaning of some kind to re-assert itself: thus we have 'Arabium', the god 'Hermes' and the Spanish term 'mala-quita' (malachite). The temptation to infiltrate meaning into apparent gibberish was usually stronger than the mere pleasure of creating exotic linguistic noise: John Taylor's 'Utopian' (poem 5), as already noted above, illustrates this point. One classic example of this tendency is the sequence of gibberish speeches

---

63 Garapon, *La Fantaisie verbale*, pp. 19–20, 29.

spoken by Rabelais's Panurge. A modern scholar has ingeniously demonstrated that each of these speeches can be translated into sense: the 'lanternois' on the basis of fragments of German and English, the 'antipodean' using Hebrew and Arabic, and the 'Utopian' with words taken from southern French dialects and Italian.[64] Even the original 'Utopian' language invented by Thomas More can be shown, by the same methods, to be heavily indebted to Persian.[65]

The sixteenth and seventeenth centuries were an age of galloping linguistic self-consciousness: of growing interest in the vernacular (in all its forms, including slang), of the investigation of hitherto unknown languages (such as those of the American Indians), of theorizing about the origins and nature of language itself, and of attempts to construct an artificial 'universal language' which would map out systematically the real essences of all existing things in the world. Out of this huge range of intellectual activities, one or two deserve mention here for their tangential connections with nonsense poetry.

The study of slang, especially the secret 'canting' terms used by thieves or gypsies, seems to have begun in earnest in the mid sixteenth century, with the publication in Venice of a guide entitled *Il modo novo da intendere la lingua zerga cioè parlar furbesco*.[66] Other such guides to canting terms were published in Italy, Spain and England, and the words themselves were soon being incorporated into literary works such as picaresque novels and 'coney-catching' tales. From there it was only a short step to the composition of 'canting songs'. (Occasional experiments in slang poetry had been attempted in the past, the most famous being Villon's extraordinary 'jargon ballads'; but canting songs could become a genre only when there was a whole body of

64 E. Pons, 'Les Langues imaginaires dans le voyage utopique: les "jargons" de Panurge dans Rabelais', *Revue de littérature comparée*, xi (1931), pp. 185–218.
65 E. Pons, 'Les Langues imaginaires dans le voyage utopique: un précurseur: Thomas Morus', *Revue de littérature comparée*, x (1930), pp. 589–607.
66 The work is anonymous; it was published in 1549 and reprinted in 1582, 1584 and 1628. See L. Sainéan, *L'Argot ancien (1455–1850)* (Paris, 1907), p. 12.

low-life literature for them to inhabit.)[67] A typical poem by
Thomas Dekker begins:

> Bing out, bien Morts, and toure, and toure,
>   bing out, bien Morts, and toure;
> For all your Duds are bingd awaste,
>   the bien coue hath the loure.[68]

> (Go out, good women, and look around,
>   Go out, good women, and look;
> For all your clothes have been stolen,
>   And the clever thief has the money.)

Like riddles, such poems are essentially the opposite of nonsense: they appear to lack meaning, but the meaning is only
hidden, not non-existent. Nevertheless, the poem depends for
its effect on setting up an initial barricade of sheer bafflement
to the reader's understanding. Momentarily at least, the reader
must undergo the experience of reading a kind of nonsense
poem, one whose form is recognizably poetic but whose verbal
contents defy comprehension. And the fact that those verbal
contents were drawn from the lowest form of low life must
have contributed also to that sense of the incongruous mingling
of high and low which, as we have seen, was one of the stylistic
preconditions of nonsense poetry during this period. In some
tangential way, therefore, these canting poems may have contributed to the creation of a literary *ambience* in which nonsense
poetry could flourish.

The other way in which early modern investigations into
language may have helped to foster literary nonsense was
altogether more fortuitous: the cultivation of mnemonic verses.
Two examples are printed in this collection. The first (poem
39) is of verses written by an earnest schoolmaster, Joseph

---

67 For an exceptionally elaborate investigation of Villon's jargon, attributing three
separate layers of meaning to each poem, see P. Guiraud, *Le Jargon de Villon ou
le gai savoir de la Coquille* (Paris, 1968).
68 From *O per se O* (1612); printed in J. S. Farmer (ed.), *Musa pedestris: Three
Centuries of Canting Songs and Slang Rhymes (1536–1896)* (New York, 1964), p. 11.

Brookesbank, whose idea it was to list all the monosyllabic words in the English language and teach them systematically to children by means of such mnemonics. The second is from a much more abstruse publication, George Dalgarno's *Ars signorum* (1661), which was one of the many seventeenth-century attempts to construct a 'real character' – that is, a method of representing things or qualities in writing which would be equally valid for all languages, because based on a systematic classification of all fundamental human concepts.[69] Dalgarno divided the 'simple notions' of human thought into seventeen different classes; to assist the reader, he arranged examples of such concepts in a series of mnemonic verses, a selection from which is printed here as poem 40. Of course it was not his purpose to write nonsense poetry as such (nor is it even clear whether these irregular and non-rhyming verses were intended to be read as anything similar to poetry at all). Nevertheless, it is pleasing to think of Dalgarno, a dour Aberdonian working as a schoolmaster in Oxford, penning such lines as 'When I *sit down* upon a *hie place*, I'm *sick* with *light* and *heat*'; and the association of sheer bizarrerie with mnemonic purposes (by both Dalgarno and Brookesbank) furnishes a rare link between seventeenth-century nonsense writing and the nonsense didacticism which is so much better known to us from the nineteenth century.

Dreams, madness, folklore and carnival

The main aim of this Introduction has been to show that nonsense poetry was a highly literary phenomenon: it was the product of particular literary milieux, subject to development and transmission just like other literary genres, and intimately related (above all through the procedures of parody) to other literary

---

69 See J. Knowlson, *Universal Language Schemes in England and France 1600–1800* (Toronto, 1975), and V. Salmon, *The Works of Francis Lodwick: A Study of his Writings in the Intellectual Context of the Seventeenth Century* (London, 1972), esp. pp 28–31.

forms and conventions. Nonsense poetry is not, in other words, something spontaneously produced by anarchic forces bubbling up from below – whether in the subconscious (dreams, madness) or in society and popular culture (folklore, carnival). In this final section, each of these rival explanations will be considered briefly.

The best account of the difference between nonsense literature and dreams or madness was given more than forty years ago by Elizabeth Sewell, whose little book *The Field of Nonsense* remains one of the most thoughtful and stimulating studies of nonsense literature. Sewell distinguishes persuasively between the dissolution of logic and reality which takes place in dreams, and the kind of playing with logic and reality (and literary convention) which we find in nonsense literature. 'Dream vision is essentially fluid; nothing is reliable, anything may change into anything else . . . The result is that dreams cannot be controlled and cannot be played with.' Romantic poetry, she argues, may have some kinship with dreams, if we follow Coleridge's dictum that poetry is at its best when it is only imperfectly understood; but 'There is nothing of this in Nonsense verse. Far from being ambiguous, shifting and dreamlike, it is concrete, clear and wholly comprehensible . . . Nonsense verse . . . seems much nearer logic than dream.'[70] Although Sewell's examples are mainly drawn from the works of Lear and Carroll, the same point can be made with seventeenth-century nonsense. 'I grant indeed, that Rainbows layd to sleep, / Snort like a Woodknife in a Ladies eyes' is a very strange statement, but what it states is not shifting or ambiguous: it means what it says, and the reader's pleasure comes from sensing that this meaning

---

70 Sewell, *The Field of Nonsense*, pp. 36, 23. Similar insights into the game-like relation between nonsense writing and sense have been expressed in a number of more recent studies: see especially W. Steiner, *The Colors of Rhetoric: Problems in the Relation between Modern Literature and Painting* (Chicago, 1982), pp. 93, 108; P. Hutchinson, *Games Authors Play* (London, 1983), pp. 84–6; A. Riehe, *The Senses of Nonsense* (Iowa City, 1992), pp. 1–20; and J.-J. Lecercle, *Philosophy of Nonsense: The Intuitions of Victorian Nonsense Literature* (London, 1994).

(clear, but impossible) has been created by a game-like manipulation of the rules by which normal, admissible meanings are expressed.

To these literary-critical arguments about the difference between nonsense and dreams or madness, some literary-historical considerations can also be added. If nonsense literature were the direct product of dreams or madness, which are presumed to be universal, we would expect nonsense literature to be universal too. All the evidence of a specific literary history of nonsense, presented in this Introduction, suggests otherwise. The truth is that dreams and madness, far from automatically generating literary forms, require the existence of suitable literary conventions in order to gain any significant purchase on literature in the first place. Dreams do play an important role, for example, in medieval literature; but they do so as a vehicle for allegory or divine vision (*visio* rather than *somnium*), since that was the function reserved for them by the literary conventions and psychological theories of the time.[71] Throughout the medieval and early modern periods, two different types of dream-explanation were available. Dreams could either be supernaturally implanted visions, containing enigmatic truths – in which case they would be treated as riddles or allegories, the very opposite of nonsense. Or else they could be explained physiologically (disordered humours in the brain, arising from diet, illness, exertion, or whatever) – in which case their incongruity, far from being something to delight in, was merely a kind of defect, of no interest except to the investigator of its physical cause.

Madness, in theory, was subject to a similar dual scheme of explanation, being attributable to divine *afflatus* on the one hand and physiological disorder on the other. In practice, however, it was normal to view madness only as a defect; Neoplatonic or quasi-Romantic associations with wisdom, poetry or creativity were largely absent from the early modern treatment of madmen

71 See S. K. Kruger, *Dreaming in the Middle Ages* (Cambridge, 1992).

in literature and real life. As one modern study observes: 'Lunatics were not treated with superstitious reverence; nor was their privileged legal status the result of a belief that they were goofy sages, ever ready to utter a profundity . . . Real madmen were terrifying and disgusting.'[72] The popular view of madness in the seventeenth century associated it with rage, violence, hostility, destructiveness or self-destruction; Robert Burton defined it as 'a vehement dotage; or raving without a fever, far more violent than melancholy, full of anger and clamour, horrible looks, actions, gestures . . .'[73] In a society where spectator sports such as bull- and bear-baiting enjoyed immense popularity, the spectacle of madness was also thought interesting or even amusing; London's Bethlehem hospital ('Bedlam') was a popular tourist site throughout the seventeenth century, and by 1707 was receiving 96,000 visitors a year.[74] But the type of pleasure derived from such spectacles seems to have been quite different from the sort of delight in elaborate incongruity afforded by seventeenth-century nonsense poetry.

One way of testing this judgement is to look at the comic representations of madness in the literature of the period. At the turn of the sixteenth and seventeenth centuries a fashion grew up for introducing madmen, for comic relief, into English dramas. Nearly thirty plays from this period have madness as part of the plot.[75] Typically the madmen were used for clowning and buffoonery; one modern critic has described their function as 'vaudeville'.[76] And yet, although there is some verbal humour in the utterances of these mad characters, there is nothing resembling the concentrated bizarrerie of nonsense poetry. The

---

72 M. MacDonald, *Mystical Bedlam: Madness, Anxiety, and Healing in Seventeenth-Century England* (Cambridge, 1981), p. 147.

73 Ibid., pp. 122–32; Burton, *The Anatomy of Melancholy* (London, 1883), p. 88 (Part I, sect. iv, mem. 1, subs. 4).

74 MacDonald, *Mystical Bedlam*, pp. 121–2.

75 E. A. Peers, *Elizabethan Drama and its Mad Folks* (Cambridge, 1914), p. 30.

76 L. B. Wright, 'Madmen as Vaudeville Performers on the Elizabethan Stage', *Journal of English and Germanic Philology*, xxx (1931), pp. 48–54.

Bedlam scenes in *The Honest Whore* (by Dekker and Middleton, 1604) and *Northward Ho* (by Dekker and Webster, 1607) are fairly typical of the genre: the madmen's speeches and dialogues are mainly confined to expressing fantasies or obsessions, with one man imagining that he is fishing, another obsessed with jealousy for his wife, and so on. Their speech may be disjointed and repetitive, but it makes persistent sense; and the greatest source of comedy in these lines is not incongruity but bawdy.[77]

The representation of madness in the literature of this period did not give rise to nonsense literature. Certainly the one acknowledged madman to have published poetry in the seventeenth century (Pepys's clerk James Carkesse, who was confined first in a private madhouse in Finsbury, then at Bedlam, before publishing his *Lucida intervalla* in 1679) did not produce anything resembling nonsense poetry: his verses, though self-consciously florid, make perfect sense.[78] Only in two minor ways did the presentation of madness in literature show any connection with nonsense writing. The first was through the genre of the 'Bedlamite' or 'Poor Tom' poem; as already mentioned (above, pp. 87–8), this type of poetry drew on the stock of physical impossibilia developed by 'boasting' poems or Lügendichtungen.[79] The second was through the institution of the Fool – a dual-category concept which spanned lunatics and mental

77 T. Dekker, *The Dramatic Works*, ed. F. Bowers, 4 vols. (Cambridge, 1953–61), ii, pp. 99–102, 457–63. For a more extended Bedlam scene, constructed on the same principles, see F. Beaumont and J. Fletcher, *The Dramatic Works in the Beaumont and Fletcher Canon*, ed. F. Bowers, 9 vols. (Cambridge, 1966–94), vi, pp. 181–90 (*The Pilgrim*, IV. iii).
78 On Carkesse see R. Porter, 'Bedlam and Parnassus: Mad People's Writing in Georgian England', in G. Levine (ed.), *One Culture: Essays in Science and Literature* (Madison, Wisconsin, 1987), pp. 258–84; and A. Ingram, *The Madhouse of Language: Writing and Reading Madness in the Eighteenth Century* (London, 1991), pp. 162–7.
79 For a collection of such poems see J. Lindsay (ed.), *Loving Mad Tom: Bedlamite Verses of the XVI and XVII Centuries* (London, 1927). See also the comments in W. Chappell, *Old English Popular Music*, ed. H. E. Wooldridge, 2 vols. (London, 1893), i, pp. 175–8.

defectives on the one hand ('natural fools') and witty entertainers ('artificial fools') on the other.

Most instances of Fool-ish behaviour fell quite clearly into one or the other of these categories. If they were examples of mental incapacity they would be comical for reasons of unwitting buffoonery, having little in common with the elaborate ingenuity of nonsense writing. If, on the other hand, they were examples of puckish humour, they would usually make humorous sense, not nonsense – as in the popular 'jest-books' of the late sixteenth and early seventeenth centuries, with their practical jokes, comic escapades and specimens of witty repartee. (This latter version of the Fool's foolery was the predominant one in early seventeenth-century England, after the role of the Fool had been largely redefined by talented comedians such as Tarlton, Kemp, and Armin.)[80] However, the fact that the concept of the Fool spanned both natural idiocy and comic cleverness did encourage a certain kind of deliberate cultivation of absurdity: the typical comic mode of a court fool was that of a clever man pretending to be simple-minded. The bathetically absurd, the inconsequential and the mock-gnomic were thus all characteristics of Foolish humour, and such qualities – which are related to those of nonsense literature – sometimes do surface in the songs or pronouncements of Shakespeare's Fools (above all, in *Twelfth Night* and *King Lear*). More elaborate forms of burlesque seem to have been practised by court fools in Renaissance Italy and France.[81] Elaborate burlesque does indeed bring us closer to literary nonsense – but it does so by drawing us into precisely the sort of self-conscious literary or courtly milieu in which, as this Introduction has argued, the real origins of nonsense writing are to be located.

---

80 See E. Welsford, *The Fool: His Social and Literary History*, 2nd edn. (London, 1968), pp. 158–81; and S. Billington, *A Social History of the Fool* (Brighton, 1984), pp. 29–30.
81 Welsford, *The Fool*, pp. 128–57; see also K. F. Flögel, *Geschichte der Hofnarren* (Leipzig, 1789).

Similarly, the argument that nonsense poetry depended on the existence of a substratum of folk nonsense (nonsense nursery rhymes or other specimens of nonsensical folk poetry) seems to reverse the true order of transmission. This argument has often been put forward in studies of nonsense literature which concentrate on the writings of Edward Lear and Lewis Carroll.[82] The nonsense poetry of those two authors does indeed stand in a special relationship to children's rhymes; but it is for the most part a parodic relationship, which typically involves taking an approved and improving rhyme (which itself makes perfect sense), such as 'Star of the evening' or 'How doth the little busy bee', and rendering it absurd. Even this degree of kinship with nursery rhymes, however, can hardly be looked for in the literary nonsense poetry of the seventeenth century, most of which was very evidently adult in its references and its audience.

The idea that nursery rhymes represent some sort of age-old sub-culture of poetical folk-nonsense is, in any case, of doubtful validity. What we now call nursery rhymes consists of a very disparate assortment of materials, having little in common beyond the fact that they are all recited by or to children. Many of them have ordinary literary origins, as songs, ballads, riddles, political squibs, etc., written by adults for adults and only subsequently simplified or bowdlerized for nursery use.[83] Some seem to have entered the 'nursery' repertoire only because of the chance decisions of individual editors to include them in printed collections of verses for children: thus 'If all the world were paper' (poem 27 in this collection) is, given its satirical reference to 'projects' and its bawdy reference to nuns' 'dark cloysters', evidently an adult poem of the early seventeenth

---

82 See, for example, R. Hildebrandt, *Nonsense-Aspekte der englischen Kinderliteratur* (Hamburg, 1962); and Petzold, *Formen und Funktionen der Nonsense-Dichtung*, esp. pp. 80–84.
83 See the Introduction to I. and P. Opie, *Oxford Dictionary of Nursery Rhymes*, esp. pp. 3–6, 19–30.

century, but it became a 'nursery rhyme' by virtue of its inclusion in two popular early nineteenth-century collections.[84]

The antiquity of most English nursery rhymes is hard to establish, at least before the eighteenth- and nineteenth-century collections in which so many of them were first printed. Iona and Peter Opie have suggested that roughly seventeen per cent of the rhymes printed in their *Oxford Dictionary of Nursery Rhymes* 'probably' date from before 1700.[85] Most of these are unrelated to nonsense: they are riddles, lullabies, alphabet-songs, and so on. Indeed, apart from 'If all the world were paper', there seems to be only one rhyme with origins before 1700 which can plausibly be described as nonsense poetry: 'Hey diddle diddle, / The cat and the fiddle, / The cow jumped over the moon ...' Given the echoes in two sixteenth-century sources (cited by the Opies) which refer to dancing, and one other possibly related seventeenth-century verse which also refers to a type of country dance, it seems likely that this 'nursery rhyme' in its current, nonsensical form (first printed in 1765) is a distorted version of some earlier verse – not in itself nonsensical – which was originally associated with country dancing.[86] Such distortions, usually produced over time by the Chinese whispers of oral transmission, are quite frequently found in the history of folksong and folk-beliefs.[87] Common though they may be, they are thus by their very nature accidental: they are the chance consequences of unintended processes of elision, erosion and substitution. Of

---

84 Ibid., p. 438 (n).
85 Ibid., p. 7.
86 For the Opies' sources, see ibid., p. 203. The possibly cognate 17th-century verse was printed in one of the drolleries, *Sportive Wit* (1656), and is reprinted in Wardroper (ed.), *Love and Drollery*, p. 221; it begins: 'The first beginning was Sellinger's Round / Where the cow leapt over the moon, / And the goodwife shit in the pisspot, / And the cream ran into her shoon ...' This itself looks like a coarse parody of some earlier dancing verses. (Sellinger's Round was a popular country dance, also known as 'The Beginning of the World': see Chappell, *Old English Popular Music*, i, pp. 256–8.)
87 For some well-documented examples see L. Eckenstein, *Comparative Studies in Nursery Rhymes* (London, 1906), pp. 143–70.

course it may sometimes have happened that the end-products of such processes gave listeners or readers much the same kind of delight in absurdity that is afforded by nonsense literature. But no one who places the elaborate and very self-consciously literary nonsense poetry of Hoskyns, Taylor and Corbet alongside the small quantity of fortuitously created folk-nonsense can plausibly argue that the former owes its origin – or any essential aspect of its nature – to the latter.

Those who argue for the folk-origins of nonsense have a much more substantial body of material on which to base their case when they turn to the traditions of folk festivity and carnival. Here a mass of evidence is available, showing that all western European societies have engaged in feasts and festivals (mainly linked to the ritual calendar of the Church) involving parodic inversions of the established order – the most important being the festivities surrounding Christmas and the New Year, and the carnival which preceded Lent.[88] In recent decades the theme of carnival has loomed large in all critical discussion of Renaissance and early modern comedy, thanks to an influential study of Rabelais and popular culture by the Russian literary theorist Mikhail Bakhtin. According to Bakhtin, the comedy of this period expresses a 'carnivalesque perception of the world', involving radical ambiguity, the celebration of gross physicality and, above all, the overturning of established order.[89]

---

88 The best national study of carnival traditions is J. C. Baroja, *El carnaval (analisis historico-cultural)* (Madrid, 1965). See also C. Gaignebet, *Le Carnaval: essais de mythologie populaire* (Paris, 1974); S. Billington, *Mock Kings in Medieval Society and Renaissance Drama* (Oxford, 1991); N. Z. Davis, 'The Reasons of Misrule: Youth Groups and Charivaris in Sixteenth-Century France', *Past and Present*, no. 50 (1971), pp. 41–75; Y.-M. Bercé, *Fête et révolte: des mentalités populaires du XVIe au XVIIIe siècle* (Paris, 1976), pp. 1–92; E. Le Roy Ladurie, *Carnival in Romans. A People's Uprising at Romans 1579–1580*, trans. M. Feeney (London, 1980). On the ritual calendar see R. Hutton, *The Rise and Fall of Merry England: The Ritual Year, 1400–1700* (Oxford, 1994).

89 M. Bakhtin, *L'Oeuvre de François Rabelais et la culture populaire au moyen âge et sous la Renaissance*, trans. A. Robel (Paris, 1970).

Bakhtin's interpretation could, in theory, be expressed as a purely formal analysis of the techniques and mental categories of early modern comedy. In practice, however, it has acquired also a socio-political dimension, both in Bakhtin's own exposition and in the uses to which his ideas have been put by many of his followers. When he talked of parody being generated by the 'folk spirit', Bakhtin seemed to imply that carnivalesque comedy was somehow more vital and more valid because it came (in socio-political terms) from below, as a kind of cultural protest or revolution. According to one recent study, for example, carnivalesque comedy can be seen as 'a positive critique [of power], a celebration and reaffirmation of collective traditions lived out by ordinary people in their ordinary existence ... [a] critique, which articulates the capacity of popular culture to resist penetration and control by the power structure'.[90]

Against this line of argument, two large-scale objections arise. The first has been noted by many historians and anthropologists: it is that limited episodes of licensed disorder can more convincingly be seen as safety-valves which protect the established order, rather than as genuine revolts against it.[91] (Of course such festive occasions may from time to time have furnished the ideal pretext or opportunity for real social revolt; but those episodes were, by their very nature, exceptions rather than the rule.) This functionalist explanation refers specifically to social order; at the same time, the fact that carnival festivities occupied fixed places in the ritual calendar of the Church suggests that their celebration was also quite compatible with a sense of the metaphysical order which that calendar itself expressed.

The second objection to the Bakhtinian argument is, for the

90 M. D. Bristol, *Carnival and Theater: Plebeian Culture and the Structure of Authority in Renaissance England* (New York, 1985), p. 4.

91 For a discussion of this point with reference to modern anthropological research, see Barbara Babcock's Introduction to her *The Reversible World: Symbolic Inversion in Art and Society* (Ithaca, NY, 1978), p. 22.

purpose of understanding the origins of nonsense literature, more important. It is that Bakhtin's account of comic-parodic literary forms having arisen from the 'folk spirit' (or, as one more recent Bakhtinian study puts it, of 'the language of festivity' having 'welled up from the depths of popular culture') tends to confuse two different things: the social nature of a cultural event, and the origins of the literary, aesthetic or ritual forms which that cultural event makes use of.[92] The fact that certain types of parodic comedy flourished at popular festivities does not necessarily mean that they owed their origins to the spontaneous creativity of 'the people'. To jump to such a conclusion would be rather like assuming that nursery rhymes must have arisen from the spontaneous creativity of small children. Bakhtin notes that parodic inversions were popular in the fairground and the village green, and he also observes that similar forms of comedy were to be found in 'higher' cultural milieux such as monasteries, universities and courts: putting these two facts together, he suggests that it is the 'folk spirit' of the former which, bubbling up from below, has generated the latter. This assumption is both unproven, and contrary to what we do know about the nature of parodic routines in the 'higher' culture.

Parodic literary humour flourishes most of all in enclosed communities with their own formulae, rituals and literary conventions: hence the liturgical parodies in medieval monasteries, the mock-learning and absurd rhetorical exercises at Renaissance universities, the mock-legal formulae of the Inns of Court, and so on. Humour is generated in these cases not by an intrusion of 'folk spirit' from below, but by an intensification of self-consciousness within the institution itself: the parodies are in-jokes, playing on the participants' sophisticated knowledge of the relevant formulae and codes. Bakhtin writes of the monastic humour of the Middle Ages as something

---

92 The recent study is F. Laroque, *Shakespeare's Festive World: Elizabethan Seasonal Entertainment and the Festive Stage*, trans. J. Lloyd (Cambridge, 1991): here p. 46.

produced by folk influences penetrating the monasteries.[93] All the evidence suggests that the order of transmission was the opposite: such parodic humour was first generated within the self-conscious literary milieu of the monasteries, and then transmitted to the folk culture beyond the monastery walls.

Indeed, one of the most striking discoveries of modern historical research is that, across the whole range of celebratory folk customs, the characteristic pattern has been one of transmission from the 'higher' culture to the 'lower', and not vice-versa. Christmas entertainments, for example, seem to have begun as a fashion in aristocratic and gentry households in the late fourteenth and early fifteenth centuries, spreading thereafter into the English villages. Christmas carols began as a literary genre (invented by Franciscans in Italy) and only began to percolate downwards into English popular culture in the fourteenth century. The celebration of St Valentine's day may have begun as a courtly amusement in the fifteenth century, spreading out thereafter among the aristocracy. And while much is obscure about the origins of morris dancing, the records clearly indicate that it was fashionable at court some time before it moved out into the country towns.[94]

Some of the most striking examples of this general tendency concern just those customary practices which seem most closely to embody the so-called 'carnivalesque' vision of the world: feasts of fools, boy bishops, mock-kings, lords of misrule, and so on. The general pattern here is one of enclosed institutions (monasteries, monastic schools, universities) developing practices which then spread out into popular culture – not the other way round. The feast of fools seems to have originated in the abbeys and cathedrals of early medieval Germany, where the practice grew up of allowing three days' licence for unruly behaviour

93 *L'Oeuvre de Rabelais*, p. 22.
94 All these examples are discussed in Hutton, *Rise and Fall of Merry England*, pp. 55–61.

(or the parodic inversion of rule) by the choirboys and the inferior clergy. Combined with the cult of St Nicholas, this practice gave rise to the institution of the 'boy bishop'; by the twelfth century this had become popular in French religious houses, and by the early thirteenth century it was spreading to English cathedrals, starting with York. Having percolated into English monastic houses too, this practice only began to spread out into parish churches in England in the fourteenth century.[95]

Another custom with very specific institutional origins was the selection of a 'bean king' to preside at Twelfth Night revels. (The bean was a hard lentil dropped into a cake mix; the title was then awarded to whoever found it in his portion of the cake.) This practice began at the French court in the thirteenth century, and was borrowed by the English court in the reigns of Edward II and Edward III. It was then imitated in the universities; a bean king is mentioned at Merton College, Oxford, in 1485. The title of 'bean king' seems to have been dropped at court, though it is possible that the practice itself continued there until the mid sixteenth century. What is more clear is that during the fifteenth century it was the universities which developed the idea of a mock-king to preside over Christmas and New Year revels, and endowed those kings with elaborate mock-titles: a 'Prester John' and a 'King Balthasar' are recorded in early fifteenth-century Oxford.[96]

At some time during the latter part of that century the general title 'Lord of Misrule' became the accepted term for such figures. There are two likely (and complementary) explanations for this development. The first is that, as Ronald Hutton has argued, this was a piece of 'self-conscious Renaissance classicism', given

---

95 Ibid., pp. 53–4. On the 'feast of fools' see also K. F. Flögel, *Geschichte der Groteskekomischen* (Leipzig, 1788), pp. 159–67.
96 Billington, *Mock Kings*, pp. 30–32; Hutton, *Rise and Fall of Merry England*, p. 60.

that such mock-rulers are mentioned by Tacitus and Lucian in their accounts of midwinter festivities in Rome.[97] The second is that the English academic celebrations had been influenced by similar secular festivities in France, where the organizers of urban festivals constituted themselves as 'Abbeys of Misrule'. (These practices seem to have become entrenched in secular society in France after a determined campaign by the Church to banish the 'feast of fools' from French cathedrals during the fifteenth century.) The mock-abbots of these French festive groups acquired retinues and courts of mock-dignitaries: Rouen's Abbot of Cornards, for example, was accompanied by the Prince of Improvidence, the Cardinal of Bad Measure, Bishop Flat-Purse, Duke Kick-arse and the Great Patriarch of Syphilitics, among others.[98]

By the turn of the fifteenth and sixteenth centuries, the Lords of Misrule had spread out from the English universities and were being adopted by aristocratic households; thereafter they were taken up by ordinary parishes and urban corporations.[99] They also became popular in the Inns of Court; and, from the 1480s onwards, Lords of Misrule were chosen to preside over the seasonal festivities at the royal court itself. Given the proximity of the court and the Inns in London, and the constant flow and interchange of wits and lawyers between them, it is not surprising that the courtly festivities and the lawyerly ones were often closely intertwined. For the royal Christmas celebrations of 1551, for example, the dignified lawyer George Ferrers was chosen as 'Lord of Misrule'; his parodic imitation of courtly ritual included a mock-embassy to the King, with an 'Irisheman' and an 'Irishewoman' wearing wigs of black flax. 'Uppon Christmas daie', he announced, 'I send a solempne ambassade to the Kings Majestie by an herrald, a trumpet, an orator speaking in a straunge language, an interpreter or truchman with

---

97 Hutton, *Rise and Fall of Merry England*, p. 60.
98 Davis, 'Reasons of Misrule', pp. 42−4.
99 Hutton, *Rise and Fall of Merry England*, pp. 60−61.

hym . . .'[100] One modern scholar has suggested that Ferrers's orator spoke 'nonsense'; his speech may well have consisted of a gibberish version of mock-Irish, though no details of its contents are recorded.[101] Visual extravagance and mock-ceremonial seem, at this stage, to have been more important than verbal humour.

During the second half of the sixteenth century, however, verbal humour and rhetorical parody gradually took on a more and more important role in the Christmas festivities of the Inns of Court. Increasingly, these occasions were used as opportunities to practise, in a comically self-conscious manner, courtly and rhetorical skills; in this the lawyers were no doubt also influenced by the literary exercises and plays performed at Christmas in several of the Cambridge colleges.[102] Already in 1561, the Christmas revels at the Inner Temple seem to have been heavily dependent on parodies of courtly formulae. The Lord of Misrule's herald introduces him as 'The mighty *Pala-philos*, Prince of *Sophie*, high Constable Marshall of the Knights Templars, Patron of the honourable Order of *Pegasus*', and he himself lists the members of his court: 'Sir *Morgan Mumchaunce*, of *Much Monkery*, in the County of *Mad Mopery*; Sir *Bartholmew Baldbreech*, of *Buttocks-bury*, in the County of *Brekeneck*', and so on. And when the Lord of Misrule enters his domain on St Stephen's Day, he 'pronounceth an Oration of a quarter of an hours length, thereby declaring the purpose of his coming'.[103]

These mock-ceremonials of the latter part of the sixteenth century bring us back, finally, to those revels at the Elizabethan Inns of Court with which this Introduction began: they return

---

100 A. J. Kempe (ed.), *The Loseley Manuscripts* (London, 1835), pp. 33, 52.
101 Billington, *Mock Kings*, p. 39. My suggestion is based on the fact that the Irishman and Irishwoman are listed immediately after the 'orator' and his 'truch-man' (i.e. dragoman, interpreter) in the clothing accounts for the festivity (Kempe (ed.), *Loseley Manuscripts*, pp. 51–2).
102 Billington, *Mock Kings*, pp. 36–7.
103 Sir William Dugdale, *Origines juridiciales, or Historical Memorials of the English Laws* (London, 1666), pp. 152, 155–6.

us to the *Gesta Grayorum*, to the *Prince d'Amour*, to fustian and tufftaffeta and the fertile wit of John Hoskyns. English seventeenth-century nonsense poetry, as this Introduction has argued, was not solely a product of that background; it depended also on a special conjunction of stylistic forces in the dramatic and satirical poetry of the time. It is also true that the most important practitioner of the genre, John Taylor, stood some way outside the privileged socio-literary circles of his day, and may have used nonsense poetry partly as a way of ironizing from a distance at the expense of its more elaborate poetic conventions.[104] But without that special socio-literary background – a peculiar hothouse world of court wits, lawyers and poets engaged in mutual ridicule and emulation – this nonsense poetry might never have arisen at all. Literary nonsense is, by its very nature, a product of literary culture, not of folk culture. As one modern critic has written: 'The way of Nonsense is analytic: to detach the rituals of high poetry from their normal structures of meaning, and to draw more or less explicit attention to their self-sufficiency as rituals.'[105] The more familiar readers are, therefore, with the 'high poetry' of the seventeenth century, the more pleasure they will gain from its nonsense counterpart – and even, perhaps, vice-versa.

104 He hints as much, in a comically self-deprecatory way, in *Taylors Motto* (*Workes*, sig. Ee4ʳ).
105 H. Kenner, 'Seraphic Glitter: Stevens and Nonsense', *Parnassus: Poetry in Review*, 1976 (no. 2), pp. 153–9; here p. 157.

POEMS

JOHN HOSKYNS

Cabalistical Verses

*Cabalistical Verses, which by transposition of words, syllables,
and letters make excellent sense, otherwise none*

In laudem Authoris

Even as the waves of brainlesse butter'd fish,
With bugle horne writ in the Hebrew tongue,
Fuming up flounders like a chafing-dish,
That looks asquint upon a Three-mans song:
Or as your equinoctiall pasticrust
Projecting out a purple chariot wheele,
Doth squeeze the spheares, and intimate the dust,
The dust which force of argument doth feele:
Even so this Author, this Gymnosophist,*
Whom no delight of travels toyle dismaies,
Shall sympathize (thinke reader what thou list)
Crownd with a quinsill tipt with marble praise.

* This word gymnosophist is derived from two Greeke
words γυμνòς & σοφιστής, wch signifie a naked

Cabalistical] see Introduction, p. 16   In laudem Authoris] 'in praise of the
author'   Three-mans song] part-song for three male voices   Gymno-
sophist] ascetic naked philosopher   quinsill] quinsell, long rein (for horses)

sophister. And he therefore cals the Author so, because one day he went without a shirt at Basil, while it was washing.

Source: Coryate, *Coryats Crudities*, sig. e6ʳ.

Basil] Basel, Basle (Switzerland)

HENRY PEACHAM

In the Utopian tongue

NY thalonin ythsi *Coryate* lachmah babowans
O *ASIAM* Europam Americ-werowans
Poph-himgi Savoya, Hessen, Rhetia, Ragousie
France, Germanien dove Anda-louzie
Not A-rag-on ô *Coryate*, ô hone vilascar.
Einen tronk Od-combe ny Venice Berga-mascar.

Source: Coryate, *Coryats Crudities*, sig. lr.

Rhetia] Rhaetia, Roman province corresponding to part of modern
Switzerland   Ragousie] probably meaning Ragusa (modern Dubrovnik),
though Coryate did not go there   Od-combe] Odcombe, Somerset,
Coryate's native village   Berga-mascar] from Bergamask, a rustic dance,
named after the allegedly clownish people of the Venetian province of Bergamo

JOHN SANFORD ('GLAREANUS VADIANUS')

Punctures and Junctures of Coryate

A Sceleton or bare Anatomie of the Punctures and Junctures of *Mr.* Thomas Coryate *of* Odcombe, *in loose verse called by the Italians,* versi sciolti, *because they go like Tom-boyes,* scalciati *without hose or shoe, bootlesse and footlesse: Perused this last quarter of the Moone, and illustrated with the Commentaries of Mr.* Primrose Silkeworme, student in Gastrologia and Tuff-moccado.

Beauclerke[a] of [b]*Odcombe*, Bellamy of Fame,
   Learnings quicke Atome, wits glosse on Natures text,
   [c]Sembriefe of time, the five finger of game,
   Ambs-ace of blots, sweep-stake of what comes next.
March-pane of Mirth, the [d]Genova past of love,

Odcombe] Coryate's native village in Somerset   versi sciolti] a type of blank
verse of irregular metre   scalciati] with shoes removed   Gastrologia]
title of a Greek poem on the science of catering for the stomach (gastrology),
cited by the Greek writer Athenaeus   Tuff-moccado] a tufted version of
mockado, a piled cloth of silk or wool, often called 'mock-velvet'
Beauclerke] beauclerk, learned man   Odcombe] Coryate's native village in
Somerset   Bellamy] belamy, good friend   Sembriefe] semibreve, musical
note   five finger] in card-playing, the five of trumps   Abms-ace] at
dice, a throw of double aces; hence the nadir of one's fortunes   blots] apart
from 'disgrace', etc., 'blot' also meant an exposed piece at backgammon
March-pane] marzipan   Genova past] paste of Genoa, a spiced
quince pie

The Graces ^egallipot, ^fMusicks fiddle-sticke,
The ^gspout of sport, and follies turtle Dove,
^hNoddie turn'd up, all made, yet lose the tricke.
Thou Chesse-board pawne, who on one paire of shoes,
Hast trode the foote-ball of this worlds Center,
Discovering placesⁱ couch'd between the poles,
Where honest vertue never yet durst enter.
How should I sing thy worth in fitting layes,
With starveling verses of an hide bound Muse,
And crowne thy head with mistletoe for bayes,
Unlesse thy ^jknapsacke did new thoughts infuse?
Such Gallo-Belgicke *Mercuries* are not chipt
From every billet, nor each axle-tree:
Nature her selfe in thee herselfe out-script
When she produc'd this vagrant Humble-Bee,
Whose buzze hath fild this worlds circled round,
Hing'd on the Articke and Antarticke starre,
And whose great fame now finds no other bound
Then from the Magellan strait to Gibraltar.
Whose glorious deeds out-face and fiercely daunt
^k*Guzman* of Spaine, and *Amadis* of France,
Uterpendragon, *Urson*, and *Termagant*,
Great *Don Quixote*, and *Joane of Orleance*.
Ludgate the floud-gate of great Londons people,
With double dores receives a wight so dapper:

gallipot] small glazed pot   fiddle-sticke] bow (of a fiddle); also meaning
something insignificant, absurd   Noddie] in card-playing, the knave
Gallo-Belgicke Mercuries] from *Mercurius Gallo-Belgicus*, a famous early
newspaper   billet] thick piece of fire-wood   Humble-Bee]
bumble-bee   Artick and Antartick] Arctic and Antarctic   Guzman]
Guzman d'Alfarache, hero of a Spanish romance of roguery   Amadis]
Amadis of Gaul, hero of famous French and Spanish prose romance of
chivalry   Uterpendragon] Uther, pendragon (warlord) of the Britons, father
of King Arthur   Urson] Orson: Valentine and Orson were legendary twin
brothers, brought up by a king and a she-bear respectively (see Dickson, *Valentine
and Orson*)   Termagant] imaginary deity supposed to be worshipped by
Muslims, and characterized by a very violent temper   Joane of Orleance]
Joan of Arc, known as the Maid of Orléans   Ludgate] fortified gate on
western side of the City of London

Bell-man and knell-man gentrie of the steeple,
    Do peale thy praise with Rousse & Bow-bell clapper.
Whiles I thy goodly frame do seeke to scanne,
    How part to part doth mortise, knit, and linke,
    I boulted have my spirits to the branne,
    And left my wits fast fettred in the Clinke.
For *Tom's* a [l]cap-stone, and a turne-spit jacke,
    A skrewed engine Mathematicall,
    To draw up words that make the welkin cracke
    Out of a wit strangly dogmaticall.
Tom[m] is an Irish Harpe, whose heart-strings tune
    As fancies wrest doth straine or slacke his cord,
    Sometimes he warbleth sweet as a stewd prune,
    And sometimes jarres out of a crackt sound-board.
Tom[n] is the padlocke of all secrecie,
    Whose tongue the tell-tale of whats done and more,
    Vents out the barmy froth of surquedrie,
    By thirteene to the dozen, thirtie to the skore.
Tom's a [o]Bologna sawcidge lovely fat,
    Stuft with the flesh of a Westphalian sow,
    The shoing-horne of wine, that serveth pat
    To make the feeble strong, the strong to bow.
Tom is a [p]twinne, and yet an Odde, and both,
    Twinne shoes, odde shirt, and both by combination:
    Which Odde-twinne-triple-one, to speaken troth,
    Hath runne a wild-goose race, a pilgrims station:
This, and all this, is *Tom*, and yet [q]much more,
    A Mandrake growne under some [r]*Heavie-tree*,

Rousse] rous, a bang or crash   Bow-bell] famous bell-peal of
St Mary-le-Bow, in the centre of the City of London   boulted . . . to the
branne] to bolt flour is to separate the pure flour from the bran by sifting
Clinke] debtors' prison in London   turne-spit jacke] clockwork mechanism
for turning a roasting-spit; wound up by raising a weight on a rope, the descent
of which powered the mechanism   stewd prune] jocular phrase for a whore
(playing on 'stews', i.e. brothels)   barmy froth] froth or 'barm' which forms
on fermenting beer   surquedrie] arrogance   Heavie-tree] gallows (*OED*
does not record this phrase, though it notes 'heavy hill', meaning the way to
the gallows)

There where *S. Nicolas* knights not long before
Had dropt their fat *axungia* to the lee.
The ⁵neck-weed-gallow-grasses sapling plant,
  A Mushrum startled with a thunder-clap,
  Which without noble stocke or such like vaunt
  In one nights space grew out of *Floraes* lap.
Yet for all this, *Tom*, thou hadst proved soone
  Abortive, and a fondling worth but little,
  Had not thy sire the man that's in the Moone,
  Oft fed thee in thy youth with ᶜCuckow spittle.
Then treade the steps of th'Author of thy birth,
Whoe once doth every Moneth surround the earth.

ᵃ A shrunke word of two into one, such as are, Hardy-
knowt, or Hogsnout, the name of Pope *Sergius*. So Atome
for *Ah Tom*.

ᵇ The Arpinum of this second Cicero. A village before
Ignoble. Now by him raissed to tenne rials of plate, and
of which himselfe is the Chorographicall Mappe.

ᶜ A musicall note containing foure odde humored crotch-
ets, and sixteene semiquavers as madde as March hares.

ᵈ He meaneth a pantrie coffin made of paste, in which the
white Blackmoore (as *Gusman de Alpharach* calleth the
Genovesi Moros blancos) stew certaine powerfull words

S. Nicolas knights] highwaymen   axungia] axunge, grease, lard
neck-weed-gallow-grasses] 'neckweed' and 'gallowgrass' were both jocular terms
for hemp (from which the hangman's ropes were made)   Floraes] Flora's
(the goddess of flowers)   Cuckow spittle] cuckoo-spit, frothy secretion left
by insects on plants   Hardyknowt] Hardicanute, Knut II of Denmark, who
ruled England from 1039 to 1042   Pope Sergius] there have been four Popes
called Sergius   Arpinum] Cicero's birthplace   rials of plate] a 'real de
plata' was a small Spanish silver coin worth roughly six English pence
Chorographicall] chorography is local geography, the description of places or
regions   Gusman de Alpharach] Guzman d'Alfarache, hero of a Spanish
romance of roguery   Genovesi] Genoese   moros blancos] white Moors

called *parole intoineate* to charme Bridegroomes points *nouer L'esquillette.*

[e] It is a vessell into which womens teares blended with loves sighs are distilled through a Serpentine or Crusible into a pure elixir, to cure *Junoes* kibe-heele.

[f] The Augures lituus or bended staffe, wherewith in the scale of Musicke men take the Altitude and elevation of a flat from the sharpe in Chromatique Symphonie.

[g] The spout of sport as a chimney is of smoake.

[h] Noddy *ego*, being Anagrammatized is *Don Diego*, who was a famous reader in the Bay of Mexico, where in steed of the seven liberall sciences, the seven deadly sinnes are publikely read and professed.

[i] He meaneth the Gallery of *Donna Amorosa* the old Countess of Orgueil in *Arabia deserta*, which is a meere magazin of verdugals, whither those courteous Dames called cortesans (as M. *Thomas* himselfe hath elegantly unshaled the word unto us) that doe enter to barter or chaffer, *elles perdent la vertu, mais la galle leur demeur.*

[j] He meaneth a soldiers or a travellers trusse or fardle or budget, which the old Romans called *mulos Marianos.*

---

parole intoineate] 'parole' is 'words' in Italian; 'intoineate' is perhaps mock-Italian for 'intoned'   nouer L'Esquillette] 'to stiffen the little splinter'   Serpentine] coiled pipe of a distilling apparatus   kibe-heele] chilblain on the heel   lituus] crooked wand or staff carried by a Roman augur   in steed] instead   Donna Amorosa] 'amorous woman'   Orgueil] 'pride'   Arabia deserta] the uninhabited or desert lands of Arabia   verdugals] verdingales, farthingales, hooped frameworks worn beneath skirts   unshaled] taken the husk off, expounded   chaffer] exchange, barter   elles perdent la vertu, mais la galle leur demeur] 'they lose their virtue, but retain their gall'   trusse] bundle or pack   fardle] fardel, bundle or pack   budget] purse or bag   mulos Marianos] muli Mariani (Marius's mules) was a nickname given to Roman soldiers commanded by Marius, who made them carry their baggage on their backs like mules

ᵏ These stories are found written in the Annales of the ebs & flouds of the Capsian sea, & in the third Tome of the wars between the Milt and the Splene. *Tit. Diaphragma, cap de Rumbis*; whither for brevities sake I remit the Reader. For to set tales upon Fables is as directly against the Pragmaticks of Spaine, as to weare *seda sobre seda*, satten upon silke, or creame upon milke.

ˡ This is a terme in the Art Trochelicke or Hydraulick water-works, according to which *Quintilian* saith of an old man that he doth *pituitam trochlea educere*: He pulleth up his tough fleame with a Crane and a Pulley.

ᵐ D. *Stapleton* hath written a book *de Tribus Thomis*. This is a Tom fit to be comprised in *tribus Tomis*.

ⁿ I reade in *Thomas de Combis* of one *Thomas* surnamed the sage, sapient the eight of that name, who for speciall merite was chosen Tribune of the wether-cocks of Ipswich, a man nobly and lineally descended from great *Solon*, because on one paire of soles he footed it to Venice.

ᵒ A French *Quelque chose* farced with oilet holes, and tergiversations, and the first blossoms of Candid Phlebotomie.

ᵖ *Tom* in Hebrew signifieth a twinne.

ᑫ He is the *Retracian* side of Fortunes title Page, who is said *utranq: paginam implere*.

the Milt and the Splene] 'milt' is another word for the spleen in mammals Tit. Diaphragma, cap de Rumbis] 'under the title "Diaphragm", the chapter on flatfishes' (Rhombis)   Pragmaticks] imperial degrees   seda sobre seda] 'silk upon silk'   Trochelicke] trochleic, pertaining to pulleys fleame] phlegm   Stapleton hath written a book de Tribus Thomis] Thomas Stapleton (d. 1598), a prolific Catholic controversial theologian, published *Tres Thomae*, a biographical study of St Thomas the Apostle, St Thomas of Canterbury and Sir Thomas More, in 1588   Solon] early Greek law-giver   Quelque chose] kickshaw, dainty dish   oilet] eyelet, hole in clothes for fastening   Retracian] not in *OED*, but in this context evidently meaning 'reverse'   utranq: paginam implere] 'to fill both pages'

^r A land-mark neere Excester, disterminating life and death to those Pilgrims that upon the high waies bid men stand, in steed of bidding them good-morrow.

^s The herbe knot-grasse, called in Greeke *Throtbolarios*, or *Stopp-wind-pippion*, wherewith they were wont to give the Commonwealth a vomit, *vide Aristoxenum de foraminibus tibiarum. Pag. 44000 paulo post finem.*

^t May it please thee Reader to be advertised out of Germany, that this is nothing else but honie dew, called *syderum saliva.*

Source: Coryate, *Coryats Crudities*, sigs. li^v–2.

<hr>

disterminating] marking the division between   knot-grasse] various types of weed with knotted stems were known as knot-grass, but the term is used jocularly for a hangman's rope   Throtbolarios] invented word, based perhaps on 'throat' and 'bolos' (Greek for the throw of a casting-net), meaning 'throat-catcher'   vide Aristoxenum de foraminibus tibiarum. Pag. 44000 paulo post finem] 'see Aristoxenus on the holes in shin-bones, p. 44,000, a little after the end': Aristoxenus was a pupil of Aristotle, author of treatises on many subjects, of which three books on music survive   syderum saliva] 'the spittle of the heavens', a term used for the phenomena of St Elmo's fire (electrical discharges on a ship) or will o' the wisp (marsh-gas flames)

JOHN TAYLOR

Cabalistical, or Horse verse (response to poem 1)

Johannes Hoskins, Cabalisticall, or Horse verse.

Hold, holla, holla, weehee, stand, I say,
Here's one with horse-verse doth thy praise display:
Without all sence, or reason, forme, or hue,
He kicks and flings, and winces thee thy due.
He maketh shift in speeches mysticall,
To write strange verses Cabalisticall;
Much like thy booke and thee, in wit, and shape,
Whilst I in imitation am his Ape.

Mount *Malvorn* swimming on a big-limb'd gnat,
And *Titan* tilting with a flaming Swanne,
Great *Atlas* flying on a winged Sprat,
Arm'd with the Hemispheares huge warming pan.
Or like the triple Urchins of the Ash,
That lie and flie through *Morpheus* sweet-fac'd doore,

Cabalisticall] see Introduction, p. 16   Mount Malvorn] the Malvern Hills,
range of hills in Herefordshire and Worcestershire; Howell recorded a
proverbial saying addressed to a henpecked husband, 'Go dig at *Mavorn* hill'
(*Paroimiographia*, p. 20), which suggests that the term carried obscure bawdy
overtones   Titan] general name for gigantic early gods who warred against
Saturn   Atlas] titan who carried heavens on his shoulders   Morpheus]
god of dreams

Doth drowne the starres with a Poledavies flash,
And make the smooth-heel'd ambling rocks to rore:
Even so this tall Columbrum Pigmy steeple,
That bores the Butterflie above the spheare;
Puls *Aeolus* taile, and *Neptunes* mountaines tipple,
Whilst *Coloquintida* his fame shall reare.
Loe thus my Muse, in stumbling jadish verse,
On horse-backe and on foot thy praise rehearse.

Source: Taylor, *Workes*, sig. Gg2ᵛ (collated with Taylor, *Laugh, and be Fat* (London, 1612), pp. 22–3).

Poledavies] poldavy, a coarse type of canvas   flash] sudden movement of a body of water   *Columbrum*] Colombrum *Workes*; Columbrum *Laugh, and be Fat*: perhaps 'columbarium', a dovecote or a Roman sepulchral building Aeolus] god of winds   Coloquintida] colocynth, plant used as a purgative

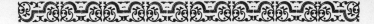

JOHN TAYLOR

Poem in the Utopian Tongue
(response to poem 2)

The Utopian Tongue

Thoytom Asse Coria Tushrump codsheadirustie,
Mungrellimo whish whap ragge dicete tottrie,
Mangelusquem verminets nipsem barelybittimsore
Culliandolt travellerebumque, graiphone trutchmore.
Pusse per mew (Odcomb) gul abelgik foppery shig shag
Cock a peps Comb sottishamp, Idioshte momulus tag
 rag.

Source: Taylor, *Workes*, sig. Gg4ʳ (collated with *Laugh, and be Fat*,
p. 38).

dicete] dicote *Laugh, and be Fat*   *travellerebumque*] travelleribumque *Laugh,*
and be Fat   (Odcomb)] Odcombe, Somerset, Coryate's native village

JOHN TAYLOR

Epitaph in the Barmooda *tongue*

Epitaph in the Barmooda *tongue, which must be pronounced* with the accent of the grunting *of a hogge.*

Hough gruntough wough Thomough Coriatough,
    Odcough robunquogh
Warawough bogh Tomitogh sogh wogh
    termonatogrough,
Callimogh gogh whobogh Raga-magh demagorgogh
    palemogh,
Lomerogh nogh Tottertogh illemortogh eagh
    Allaquemquogh,
Teracominogh Jagogh Jamerogh mogh Carnogh
    pelepsogh,
Animogh trogh deradrogh maramogh hogh Flandragh
    calepsagh.

Source: Taylor, *Workes*, sig. Ff2 (collated with Taylor, *Odcombs Complaint*, sig. B2ᵛ).

Tomitogh sogh] Tomitogh segh *Odcombs Complaint*   *Raga-magh*] Raga-mogh *Odcombs Complaint*   *Flandragh calepsagh*] Flandrogh calepsogh *Odcombs Complaint*

JOHN TAYLOR

Epitaph on Coryate

Epitaph in the Utopian *tongue*

Nortumblum callimumquash omystoliton quashte
  burashte,
Scribuke washtay solushay perambulatushte;
Grekay sons Turkay Paphay zums Jerusalushte.
Neptus esht Ealors Interremoy diz Dolorushte,
Confabuloy Odcumbay Prozeugmolliton tymorumynoy,
Omulus oratushte paralescus tolliton umbroy.

The same in English, translated by Caleb Quishquash,
an Utopian borne, and principall Secretary to the great
Adelontado of Barmoodoes.

Here lies the wonder of the English Nation,
Involv'd in *Neptunes* brinish vasty maw:

Paphay] probably from Paphos, a town on the west coast of Cyprus
Odcumbay] from Odcombe, Somerset, Coryate's native village
Adelontado] Adelantado, Spanish grandee, governor of a province
Barmoodoes] Bermudas

For fruitlesse travell, and for strange relation,
He past and repast all that e'r eye saw.
Odcomb produc'd him; many Nations fed him,
And worlds of Writers, through the world have spred him.

Source: Taylor, *Workes*, sig. Ff2ᵛ (collated with Taylor, *Odcombs Complaint*, sig. B3).

8

JOHN TAYLOR

Certaine Sonnets

Certaine Sonnets, in praise of Mr Thomas the deceased; fashioned of divers stuffs, as mockado, fustian, stand-further-off, and Motly, all which the Author dedicates to the immortall memory of the famous Odcombian traveller.

Conglomerating *Ajax*, in a fogge
Constulted with *Ixion* for a tripe,
At which *Gargantua* tooke an Irish bogge,
And with the same gave *Sisiphus* a stripe,
That all the bumbast forrests 'gan to swell,
With Triple treble trouble and with joy,
That *Lucifer* kept holiday in hell,

Mr Thomas the deceased] Thomas Coryate   mockado] piled cloth of silk
or wool, often called 'mock velvet'   fustian] type of cloth (see Introduction,
pp. 30–41)   stand-further-off] type of cloth described by Thomas Fuller
as follows in 1662: 'In my childhood there was one [stuff] called *Stand-far-of* . . .,
which seemed pretty at competent distance, but discovered its coarseness, when
nearer to the eye' (cited in *OED*, 'stand' VIII. 104)   Motly] worsted cloth
of variegated colours (not the parti-coloured costume now associated with this
term)   Odcombian] from Odcombe, Somerset, Coryate's native
village   Ajax] Greek hero   constulted] played the fool together (this
word may have been invented by Taylor; the earliest citation in *OED* is from
a later work by him, dated 1630)   Ixion] King of the Lapiths, bound to a
wheel of fire in the underworld as a punishment for trying to imitate
thunder   Sisiphus] Sisyphus, morally flawed hero punished in Hades by
having to push a boulder repeatedly uphill   bumbast] bombast, cotton-wool
padding

'Cause *Cupid* would no more be cald a boy.
Delucitating *Flora's* painted hide,
Redeemes *Arion* from the hungry Wolfe,
And with conglutinating haughty pride,
Threw *Pander* in the damb'd Venetian gulfe,
The Mediterrane mountaines laught and smil'd,
And *Libra* wandred in the woods so wilde.

Bright *Cassia Fistula* was wondrous sad,
To heare *Zarzaparillas* great mis-hap,
And *Coloquintida* was raging mad,
When *Saxifrage* was set in *Rubarbs* lap;
Dame *Lickorish* was in a monstrous fume,
Against the lushious Reasons of the sunne,
And *Trinidado* smoake avoids the roome,
Whilst *Gum-armoniack* sweares she is undone;
Unguentum album is so pale and wan,
That *Paracelsus* plaister mournes in black.
The Spanish *Eleborus* strongly can

delucitating] dilucidating, making clear   Flora's] goddess of flowers
Arion] famous poet and musician, saved from drowning by a dolphin
conglutinating] cementing together, uniting   Pander] originally, Pandarus,
who fought against the Greeks at Troy; traditionally regarded as the
archetypal procurer for having procured Cressida's love for Troilus   damb'd]
'damb' is an obsolete form of both 'dam' and 'damn'   Libra] the Balance,
sign of the zodiac   Cassia Fistula] the pudding pipe tree, or its seed-pods
(used as a laxative); so called to distinguish it from cassia lignea, a type of
cinnamon   Zarzaparillas] sarsaparilla, a type of tropical plant from the
Americas; its root was used in preparations to treat syphilis   Coloquintida]
colocynth, plant used as a purgative   Saxifrage] small rock-plant, used in
treatments for gall-stones   Rubarbs] not the modern plant, but a root
imported from China, used as a purgative   Lickorish] liquorice, used for
many medicinal purposes   Trinidado] tobacco from Trinidad
Gum-armoniack] a common spelling of gum ammoniac (so called because
obtained from the 'Ammonia' region of Libya), the resin of an umbelliferous
plant, used in medicines   Unguentum album] 'white ointment', used to
treat sores of horses   Paracelsus] (1493–1541), chemical and medical
writer   Eleborus] hellebore, a poisonous plant used in medicine

Make *Lignum vita's* hide with neezing crack:
Lo, thus with unguents, plaisters, oyles, and drugges,
We conjure up the fierce infernall bugges.

The headstrong Torchlight of Cimerian waves
With fiery frozen wonder leaps and vaults:
And on th' *Atlantick* Ocean cuts and shaves,
Whilst thunder thwacking *Ossa* limps and halts,
Robustious *Aetna* drownes the *Artick* Pole,
And forked *Vulcan* hath forsooke his forge,
Apollo'es piebald mare hath cast her fole,
And *Mulley Mahomet* hath fild his gorge.
Don Belzebub sits fleaing of his breech,
And Marble *Proteus* dances, leaps and skips,
Belerophon hath pend an excellent speech,
And big-bound *Boreas* kist *Auroraes* lips;
The *Welkin* rumbles; *Argos* lies asleepe,
And *Tantalus* hath slaine a flocke of sheepe.

Lignum vita's] lignum vitae, a type of tree from which resin was obtained,
used in the treatment of syphilis   neezing] sneezing   bugges] more or less
imaginary objects of terror (bogeys, bugbears)   Cimerian] 'Cimmerian
darkness' was proverbial, from the Cimmerii, a people who lived in dark
caverns   Ossa] mountain in Thessaly   Artick] Arctic   fole] foal
Mulley] mullah   Belzebub] god of the flies, one of the gods of the Philistines;
popularly, the name of a devil   Proteus] shape-changing marine
demi-god   Belerophon] Bellerophon, monster-killing hero, rider of the
winged horse Pegasus   Boreas] north wind   Aurora] dawn-goddess
Argos] Argos had one hundred eyes   Tantalus] King of Lydia, punished
in Hades by food and water which constantly escape his reach

When flounder-flapping *Termagant* was slaine,
The smug-fac'd *Cerberus* did howle and yell,
And *Polyphemus* rid in *Charles* his Waine,
Whilst *Gorgons* head rung great *Alcides* knell,
The rip-rap-riffe-raffe, thwick thwack stout Baboon
Gripes in his downy clutch the spungy Oake,
And young *Andromeda* at night rings noone,
Whilst *Asdrubal* at *tick tack* lost his cloake.
Prometheus covering the *Umbranoes* head,
And *Typhon* tumbles through the solid Ayre:
Proud *Pegasus* on Cheese and Garlick fed,
And *Proserpina* went to Sturbidge faire.
Pope *Hildebrand* bade *Pluto* home to supper,
And *Don Diegoes* horse hath broke his crupper.

flownder-flapping] this term, not in *OED*, possibly refers to the way in which flounders (small flat-fish) can be flipped up and caught by hand in shallow water   Termagant] imaginary deity supposed to be worshipped by Muslims, and characterized by a very violent temper   smug-fac'd] smooth-skinned, clean-shaven (only beginning in the 17th century to gain its connotation of 'self-satisfied')   Cerberus] dog of underworld   Polyphemus] one-eyed Cyclops who captured Ulysses and was blinded by him   Charles his Waine] Charles's Wain, constellation of Ursa Major (the Great Bear)   Gorgon] serpent-haired monster   Alcides] Hercules   gripes] grips Andromeda] maiden rescued from sea-monster by Perseus   Asdrubal] Hasdrubal, Carthaginian general   tick tack] old variety of backgammon   Prometheus] bringer of fire to mankind, punished by Zeus with vulture pecking at his liver   Umbranoes] umbrina's, a type of fish Typhon] hundred-headed giant, trapped beneath Mount Etna   Pegasus] winged horse   Proserpina] Persephone, daughter of Zeus and Demeter, seized by god of underworld   Sturbidge faire] Stourbridge fair, famous annual fair held outside Cambridge   Hildebrand] Pope Gregory VII   Pluto] god of underworld   Don Diegoes] Don Diego, general name for a Spaniard

Dick Swash drew out his three-pil'd blunted blade,
And slasht in twaine the equinoctiall line:
Tom Thumb did through th' Arabian deserts wade,
Where *Castor* and his brother *Pollux* shine,
The threed-bare flap-Jacks of the westerne Iles,
Exasperate the Marble Sithian Snow,
Dame *Venus* traveld fifty thousand miles,
To see the bounds of *Nilus* ebbe and flow.
The Gormundizing Quagmires of the East,
Ingurgitate the Eremanthean Bull:
And rude rebounding *Sagitarius* Ceast
To pipe Levaltoes to Gonzagaes Trull,
The Adriaticke Polcats sate carousing,
And hidebound *Gogmagog* his shirt was lowsing.

Sweet *Semi-circled Cynthia* plaid at maw,
The whilst *Endimion* ran the wild-goose chase:
Great *Bacchus* with his Cros-bow kild a daw,
And sullen Saturne smil'd with pleasant face.
The nine-fold Bugbeares of the Caspian lake,
Sate whistling *Ebon* horne-pipes to their Ducks,

Dick Swash] see Longer Notes, pp. 289–90   three-pil'd] term describing
the most luxurious variety of plush velvet   Castor . . . Pollux] twin sons of
Jupiter, turned into the constellation of Gemini   threed-bare]
thread-bare   westerne Iles] Outer Hebrides   *Exasperate*] Exasperates
Odcombs Complaint   Sithian] Scythian   Nilus] the Nile   *Ingurgitate*]
Ingurgitates *Odcombs Complaint*: swallow greedily   Eremanthean Bull] the
Erymanthian boar was a wild boar killed by Hercules   Sagitarius] sign of
the zodiac   Levaltoes] lavoltas, a fast, energetic dance which involved
leaping in the air   Gonzagaes] the Gonzagas were dukes of Mantua; the
last duke died in 1627   trull] whore   Gogmagog] Gog and Magog were
two giants brought in chains to London by Brutus; in a later version of the
myth, 'Gogmagog' was a single giant, transformed into a hill near
Cambridge   Cynthia] Diana, the moon-goddess   maw] card-game
Endimion] Endymion, famously beautiful shepherd   daw] jackdaw

Madge-howlet straight for joy her Girdle brake,
And rugged Satyrs friskd like *Stagges* and *Bucks*.
The untam'd tumbling fifteene footed Goat,
With promulgation of the Lesbian shores,
Confronted *Hydra* in a sculler Boat,
At which the mighty mountaine *Taurus* rores,
Meane time great *Sultan Soliman* was borne,
And *Atlas* blew his rustick rumbling horne.

Source: *Workes*, sigs. Ff2ᵛ–3ʳ (collated with *Odcombs Complaint*, sigs.
B4–6ʳ).

Ebon] ebony   Madge-howlet] the barn-owl   Lesbian] of the island of
Lesbos in the Aegean   Hydra] many-headed monster killed by
Hercules   Taurus] largest mountain in Asia Minor   Sultan Soliman]
probably meaning Süleyman I, the Magnificent (ruled 1520–66)   Atlas] titan
who carried the heavens on his shoulders

9

JOHN TAYLOR

Barbarian verses

*Certaine verses written in the Barbarian tongue, dropt out of
a Negroes pocket, which I thought good to insert, because they
tend to the honour of Tobacco.*

Vaprosh fogh stinkquash slavorumques fie fominoshte
Spitterspawlimon, loatherso hem halkish spewriboshte
Mistrum fog smoakrash, choakerumques olife trish trash.
Dam durticun belchum, contagioshte vomarroshe:
Whifferum, puffe gulpum, allisnuff huff fleaminon odish,
Rewmite contaminosh diabollish dungish odorish.

Source: Taylor, *Workes*, sig. Cccc3ʳ (collated with *The Nipping and
Snipping of Abuses*, sig. D3ʳ).

10

JOHN TAYLOR

Great Jacke-a-Lent

*Certain Blanke Verses Written of purpose to no purpose, yet
so plainely contriv'd, that a Childe of two yeeres old may
understand them as well as a good Scholler of fifty.*

Great *Jacke-a-Lent*, clad in a Robe of Ayre,
Threw mountaines higher then *Alcides* beard:
Whilst Pancradge Church, arm'd with a Samphier blade,
Began to reason of the businesse thus:
You squandring Troglodites of Amsterdam,
How long shall *Cerberus* a Tapster be?
What though stout *Ajax* lay with *Proserpine*,
Shall men leave eating powdred Beefe for that?
I see no cause but men may picke their teeth,
Though *Brutus* with a Sword did kill himselfe.

Jacke-a-Lent] originally, a doll-like figure pelted with stones as an amusement
during Lent; more generally, a comic personification of Lent, figuring in
Carnival pageants   Alcides] Hercules   Pancradge church] St Pancras
Church, in Needlers Lane in the City of London   *Samphier*] Sapphire
Portland MS; samphire is an edible plant   Cerberus] dog guarding
underworld   *Cerberus a Tapster*] Cerberus Tapster *Workes*; Cerberus a
Tapster *Jack a Lent, Portland MS*: a tapster is a person who draws beer in a
tavern   Ajax] Greek hero of Trojan war   Proserpine] Persephone,
daughter of Zeus and Demeter, seized by god of underworld   powdred]
salted

Is Shooters-hill turn'd to an Oyster pie,
Or may a May-pole be a butterd Plaice?
Then let Saint Katherins saile to Bride-well Court,
And Chitterlings be worne for statute lace,
For if a Humble-bee should kill a Whale
With the butt-end of the Antarticke Pole,
'Tis nothing to the marke at which we ayme:
For in the commentaries of Tower Ditch,
A fat stew'd Bawd hath bin a dish of state.
More might be said, but then more must be spoke,
The weights fell downe because the *Jacke* rope broke.
And he that of these lines doth make a doubt,
Let him sit downe and picke the meaning out.

Source: Taylor, *Workes*, sig. L6ᵛ (collated with *Jack a Lent*, sig. C4ᵛ,
and Nottingham University Library, Portland MS Pw v 37, p. 179.
This MS version omits four lines, changes the order of some lines,
and was evidently written from memory. The only two significant
semantic changes are recorded in the notes.)

Shooters-hill] hill south of London, on the road to Dover; famous haunt of
highwaymen   Saint Katherins] hospital on north bank of Thames, close to
Tower of London   Bride-well Court] London prison   Chitterlings]
stomach or small intestines of pig, sheep or calf, eaten fried or boiled   statute
lace] woven lace (cheaper than lace made by bobbin or needle); the weight of
the yarn used was regulated by statute   Humble-bee] bumble-bee
Antarticke] antarctic   Tower Ditch] moat of the Tower of London
dish of state] dish of Stake *Portland MS*   Jacke rope] rope operating a
mechanical spit or other such device

11

JOHN TAYLOR

Sir Gregory Nonsence His Newes
from No Place

Sir Gregory Nonsence His Newes from No Place

Written on purpose, with much study to no end, plentifully stored with want of wit, learning, Judgement, Rime and Reason, and may seeme very fitly for the understanding of Nobody.

Toyte, Puncton, Ghemorah, Molushque, Kaycapepson.

To the (Sir Reverence) Rich Worshipped Mr Trim Tram Senceles, great Image of Authority and *Hedgborough* of the famous City of *Goteham*, and to the rest of that admired and unmatchable Senate, with their Corruptions and Families.

Sir Gregory Nonsence] this name possibly echoes a name for the spirit of Christmas revels, 'Gregory Christmas', used in Jonson's *Christmas, His Masque* (*Works*, vii, p. 437) and apparently referring to the new calendar imposed by Pope Gregory XIII in 1582   *Written ... Kaycapepson*] omitted in *Workes*   Toyte ... Kaycapepson] gibberish words imitating Latin, Greek and Hebrew   Trim-Tram] from the proverb 'Trimtram, like master, like man'. Tilley (*Dictionary of Proverbs*, T525) quotes a line by Middleton and Rowley: 'My name is Trimtram, forsooth; look, what my master does, I use to do the like'   Hedgborough] headborough, parish equivalent of mayor   Goteham] Gotham, Nottinghamshire village famous for idiocy

Most *Honorificicabilitudinitatibus*, I have studied the seven Lubberly Sciences (being nine by computation) out of which I gathered three conjunctions foure mile Asseunder, which with much labour, and great ease, to little or no purpose, I have noddicated to your gray, grave, and gravelled Prate ection. I doubt not but I might have had a Patron neere hand, as the Deane of Dunstable or the Beadle of Layton Buzzard, but that I know the Phrase, Methode and Stile, is not for every mans understanding, no my most renowned Pythagor-Asses, for you this Hogshead of invention was brewed and broched, for I am ignorantly perswaded, that your wisedome can picke as much matter out of this Booke in one day, as both the Universities can in twelve moneths, and thirteene Moones, with six times foure yeeres to boot. I know your bounties too exding, for as old mother *Baly* said, the wit of man was much, when she saw a dog muzzled. Every man is not borne to make a Monument for the Cuckoo; to send a Trifoote home alone, to drive sheepe before they have them, or to Trundle Cheeses downe a hill. So saluting you with more respect then the Mayor of *Loo* did the Queenes Ape, I take leave to leave you, and rest yours to bid you

Honorificicabilitudinitatibus] correctly, 'Honorificabilitudinitatibus', dative of 'honourablenesses', from a genuine but famously over-elaborate medieval Latin word, 'honorificabilitudo': used by Shakespeare (*Love's Labours Lost*), Nashe (*Lenten Stuffe*) and Marston (*Dutch Courtesan*)   Lubberly] coarse, stupid   noddicated] as made-up word, based perhaps on 'indicated' and 'notified' but using 'noddy' (a simpleton)   gravelled] non-plussed (originally, from the image of a ship on a sandbank)   Deane of Dunstable] proverbial figure symbolizing ignorance and provincial simplicity   Beadle of Layton Buzzard] a non-proverbial counterpart to the Dean of Dunstable (Leighton Buzzard, Bedfordshire, is a town six miles from Dunstable)   broched] broached   exding] exceeding   old mother Baly] unidentified Monument for the Cuckoo . . . Cheeses down a hill] these are references to the legendary exploits of the men of Gotham: see Boorde, *Merie Tales of Gotam*   Trifoote] trefoot, trivet, a three-footed object   Loo] Looe, town in Cornwall where (according to Taylor, *Wit and Mirth: Workes*, sigs. Rr3ᵛ–Rr4ʳ) a man with a performing monkey sent a 'warrant' to the Mayor, commanding him to pay his respects to 'the Queenes Ape', and the Mayor and citizens obeyed

welcome, if you came within a mile of my house to stay all night,

Yours *Rolihayton*.

To Nobody

Upon a Christmas Even, somwhat nigh Easter, anon after Whitsuntide, walking in a Coach from London to Lambeth by water, I overtooke a Man that met me in the morning before the Sun set, the wind being in *Capricorne*, the Signe *Southwest*, with silence I demanded many questions of him, and he with much pensiveness did answer me merrily to the full, with such ample and empty replications, that both our understandings being equally satisfied, we contentiously agreed to prosecute the narration of the Unknowne Knight Sir *Gregory Nonsence*: so sitting downe upon our shoulders, resting uneasily on a banke of Sicamors, under a tree of Odoriferous and contagious Camomile, after three sighs, smilingly uttered in the Hebrew Character, two grones from the Chaldean Dialect, five sobs from the Arabian Sinquapace, sixe dumps from the Germane Idiome, nine Moods of Melancholly from the Italian tongue, with one hub bub from the Hibernian outcry. And last he laughed in the Cambrian tongue, & began to declare in the Utopian speech, what I have here with most diligent negligence Translated into the English Language, in which if the Printer hath placed any line, letter or sillable, whereby this large volume may be made guilty to be understood by any man, I would have the Reader not to impute the fault to the Author, for it was farre from his purpose to write to any purpose, so ending

Rolihayton] unidentified   replications] replies   *narration*] narratio
Workes; narration *Sir Gregory*   Sinquapace] cinquepace, a lively dance,
perhaps identical with the galliard   dumps] mournful songs

at the beginning, I say as it is applawsefully written and commended to posterity in the Midsummer nights dreame. If we offend, it is with our good will, we came with no intent, but to offend, and show our simple skill.

Rolihayton.

The names of such Authors Alphabetically recited, as are simply mentioned in this Worke.

Amadis de Gaul.

Archy Arms.

Bevis of Hampton.

Boe to a Goose.

Charing Crosse.

Coakley.

Dunsmore Cow.

Davy Wager.

Ekanwich Muffe.

Frier and the boy.

Fubs his Travels.

Gargantua.

Gammon of Westphallia.

Grigs Granam.

Hundred merry tales.

applawsefully] ap plawsefully *Workes*; applawsefully *Sir Gregory*   if we offend . . . our simple skill] a parody of the prologue to *Pyramus and Thisbe*, the play within a play in Shakespeare's *A Midsummer-Night's Dream*, V. i   Amadis de Gaul] hero of romance   Archy Arms.] Archy Armstrong, court fool of James I (ridiculed in the dedication of Taylor's *Praise, Antiquity, and Commodity of Beggery* (1621))   Bevis of Hampton] hero of romance   Coakley] unidentified   Dunsmore Cow] the dun cow of Dunsmore was a mythical beast slain by Sir Guy of Warwick   Davy Wager] perhaps a personification of a wager which must be paid, by analogy with 'Davy Debet' (a debt)   Ekanwich Muffe] unidentified   Fubs his Travels] probably playing upon the verb 'to fub', meaning to cheat, to impose upon   Grigs Granam] 'grig' means a merry, jocular fellow, and 'granam' means grandam, grandmother; but the overall significance of this phrase is unclear   Hundred merry tales] a popular 16th-century jest-book (see Oesterley (ed.), *Shakespeare's Jest Book*)

Huon of Burdeux.
Jacke Drum.
Knight of the Sunne.
Knave of Diamonds.
Lanum.
Long Meg.
Mad Mawlin.
Nobody.
O toole.
Proofes of oooo.
Quinborough Oysters.
Ready money.
Shooters Hill.
Singer.
Sir Thomas Persons.
Tarleton.
Tom Derry.

Huon of Burdeux] Huon of Bordeaux, hero of romance   Jacke Drum] see
Longer Notes, p. 291   Knight of the Sunne] mock-title of Thomas Parsons
(see note on Parsons below), used by him in a famous piggy-back jousting
match against Archy Armstrong   Lanum] John Laneham, Elizabethan
actor, who performed with the Earl of Leicester's men in the 1570s and the
Queen's men in the 1580s (Nungezer, *Dictionary of Actors*; he is mentioned
by Taylor as a comic actor in *Workes*, sig. Ff1ᵛ)   Long Meg] Long Meg of
Westminster, a famous Elizabethan virago (see *The Life and Pranks of Long Meg
of Westminster* (London, 1582))   Mad Mawlin] unidentified; perhaps
'Mawlkin' or 'Mawkin', dimunitive of Maud, used as name of sluttish or
lower-class women in proverbial expressions   O toole] Captain Arthur
O'Toole, Irish ex-soldier and buffoonish figure at the court of James I,
ridiculed by Taylor in *The Great O'Toole* (London, 1622)   Quinborough]
Queenborough, on the Isle of Sheppey, Kent   Shooters Hill] hill south
of London, on the road to Dover; famous haunt of highwaymen   Singer]
John Singer (d. 1608), famous comic actor, member of Queen Elizabeth's
troupe in 1580s; Taylor knew him when he was a clown at the Fortune playhouse
(Nungezer, *Dictionary of Actors*)   Sir Thomas Persons] Thomas Parsons, a
big man from Shropshire, was employed as Porter of the King's Gate at the
court of James I and Charles I; the 'Sir' is a comic tribute by Taylor, like the
other titles he gave Parsons in a mock-encomium prefixed to *Taylors Goose*
(London, 1621) (*Workes*, sigs. K3ᵛ–K4ʳ)   Tarleton] Richard Tarlton (d. 1588),
famous comic actor and jester to Queen Elizabeth (see Nungezer, *Dictionary
of Actors*)   Tom Derry] a natural fool (i.e. simpleton) at the court of
James I

Tom Thumbe.
Unguentum Album.
Will Summers.
Wit whither wilt thou?
Woodcocke of our side.
Xampelloes Quiblines.
Yard of Ale.
Zany on tumbling.

It was in June the eight and thirtieth day,
That I imbarked was on Highgate Hill,
After discourteous friendly taking leave:
Of my young Father *Madge* and Mother *John*,
The Wind did ebbe, the tide flou'd North South-east,
We hoist our Sailes of Colloquintida,
And after 13. dayes and 17. nights,
(With certain Hiroglyphicke houres to boot)
We with tempestuous calmes, and friendly stormes,
Split our maine top-mast, close below the keele.
But I with a dull quicke congruity,
Tooke 19. ounces of the Westerne winde,
And with the pith of the pole Artichoke,
Saild by the flaming Coast of Trapezond,

Unguentum Album] 'white ointment', used for sores on horses   Will
Summers] Will Somers (d. 1560), court fool to Henry VIII   Wit whither
wilt thou?] popular 16th-century poem, by anonymous author (see Clark (ed.),
Shirburn Ballads, pp. 268–9, and Ault (ed.), *Elizabethan Lyrics*,
pp. 269–70)   Woodcocke of our side] woodcocks were easily caught; hence
used as a metaphor for dupes, simpletons   Xampelloes] unidentified
Quiblines] quiblins, quibbles, tricks or arguments   Zany on tumbling] 'zany'
is from 'Zanni', the Venetian form of 'Gianni' (Giovanni), traditional name
of a mountebank's or acrobat's assistant who performed comically incompetent
imitations of his master's actions: 'Hee's like a *Zani* to a tumbler, That tries
trickes after him to make men laugh' (Jonson, *Every Man out of his Humour*,
IV, 1)   Highgate hill] hill north of London   *Colloquintida*,]
Colloquintida. *Workes*; Colloquintida, *Sir Gregory*: Colocynth, plant used as a
purgative   pole Artichoke] a play on 'pole Artick' (i.e. arctic pole), perhaps
by analogy with 'pole-bean' (a climbing bean)

There in a Fort of melting Adamant,
Arm'd in a Crimson Robe, as blacke as Jet,
I saw *Alcides* with a Spiders thred,
Lead *Cerberus* to the Proponticke Sea,
Then cutting further through the marble Maine,
Mongst flying Buls, and 4. leg'd Turkicocks,
A dumbe faire spoken, welfac'd aged youth,
Sent to me from the stout Stimphalides,
With tonguelesse silence thus began his speech:
Illustrious flap-jacke, to thy hungry doome,
Low as the ground I elevate my cause,
As I upon a Gnat was riding late,
In quest to parley with the Pleiades,
I saw the Duke of Hounsditch gaping close,
In a greene Arbour made of yellow starch,
Betwixt two Brokers howling Madrigales,
A Banquet was served in of Lampraies bones,
Well pickel'd in the Tarbox of old time,
When *Demogorgon* saild to *Islington*;
Which I perceiving with nine chads of steele,
Straight flew unto the coast of Pimlico,
T'informe great *Prester John*, and the *Mogull*,
What exlent Oysters were at *Billingsgate*.

Trapezond] Trebizond, port on Black Sea coast of eastern Anatolia
Alcides] Hercules   Cerberus] dog of underworld   *Proponticke*]
Prononticke *Workes*; Propouticke *Sir Gregory*: the Bosphorus, which leads to
the Pontic Sea (the Black Sea)   Stimphalides] monstrous birds on the shores
of Lake Stymphalos, killed by Hercules as one of his labours   Pleiades]
seven daughters of Atlas, transformed into a constellation by Zeus
Hounsditch] Houndsditch, street in City of London   Brokers] retailers,
second-hand dealers or pawnbrokers; also, pimps   Tarbox] box used by
shepherds to hold tar (used as ointment for sheep)   Demogorgon]
mysterious deity of the underworld   Islington] village north of London
chads] shads (a type of fish)   Pimlico] a port in Honduras; or possibly an
area on the north bank of the Thames, upstream from Westminster, though
'the district is not mentioned by the name of Pimlico in any existing document
prior to the year 1628' (Kent (ed.), *Encyclopaedia of London*, p. 30)   Prester
John] legendary king of Ethiopia   Mogull] ruler of Muslim empire in
northern India

The *Mogull* (all inraged with these newes,)
Sent a blacke snaile post to *Tartaria*,
To tell the Irishmen in *Saxony*,
The dismall downefall of old Charing Crosse.
With that nine butter Firkins in a flame,
Did coldly rise to Arbitrate the cause:
Guessing by the Sinderesis of Wapping,
Saint *Thomas Watrings* is most ominous.
For though an *Andiron*, and a paire of Tongs,
May both have breeding from one teeming womb,
Yet by the Calculation of Pickt-hatch,
Milke must not be so deere as Muskadell.
First shall Melpomene in Cobweb Lawne
Adorne great *Memphis* in a Mussell boat,
And all the muses clad in Robes of Ayre,
Shall dance, Levoltoes with a Whirligig,
Faire *Pluto* shall descend from Brazen Dis,
And *Poliphemus* keepe a Seamsters shop,
The Ile of *Wight* shall like a dive-dapper,
Devoure the Egyptian proud *Piramides*,
Whilst *Cassia Fistula* shall gurmundize,

Billingsgate] London fish-market   Tartaria] Tartary, central Asia
Charing Crosse] memorial cross at western end of the Strand, London
Sinderesis] synderesis, in scholastic theories of the conscience the collection
of primary moral principles in each human intellect   Wapping] port on
eastern side of City of London   Saint Thomas Watrings] a place of
execution south of London (so called because it was a watering place on the
Kent road)   Andiron] fire-dog, used to support burning wood
Pickt-hatch] notorious tavern-brothel in Clerkenwell   Muskadell]
muscatel (sweet wine)   Melpomene] Muse of tragedy   Lawne] fine
linen   *Levoltoes*] Levoltons *Workes*; Levoltoes *Sir Gregory*: the lavolta was a
fast, energetic dance which involved leaping in the air   Whirligig] a rotary
toy, e.g. a top; also used of other rotating devices   Pluto] god of
underworld   Dis] Hades   Poliphemus] Polyphemus, Cyclops blinded by
Odysseus   dive-dapper] small diving waterfowl   Cassia Fistula] the
Pudding Pipe tree, or its seed-pods (cassia pods, used as a laxative); so called
to distinguish it from cassia lignea, a type of cinnamon   gurmundize]
gourmandize, eat gluttonously

Upon the flesh and blood of Croydon cole dust,
Then on the bankes of Shoreditch shall be seene,
What 'tis to serve the great Utopian Queene.
This fearefull period with great joyful care,
Was heard with acclamations, and in fine,
The whilst a lad of aged Nestors yeeres,
Stood sitting in a Throne of massy yeast:
(Not speaking any word) gave this reply:
Most conscript Umpire in this various Orbe,
I saw the Caedars of old *Lebanon*,
Read a sad Lecture unto *Clapham* heath,
At which time a strange vision did appeare,
His head was Buckrum, and his eyes were sedge,
His armes were blue bottles, his teeth were straw,
His legs were nine wel squar'd Tobacco Pipes,
Cloath'd in a garment all of Dolphins egges,
Then with a voyce erected to the ground,
Lifting aloft his hands unto his feet,
He thus beganne, Cease friendly cutting throtes,
Clamor the Promulgation of your tongues,
And yeeld to Demagorgons policy.
Stop the refulgent method of your moodes,
For should you live old *Paphlagonias* yeeres,
And with *Sardanapalus* match in vertue,
Yet *Atropos* will with a Marigold,
Runne through the Mountains of the Caspian Sea.
When you shall see above you and beneath,
That nothing kils a man so soone as death,

Croydon] village south of London   Shoreditch] district of City of
London   Nestor] elderly King of Pylos, who accompanied the Greeks to
Troy   *old Lebanon*] old, Lebanon *Workes*; old Lebanon *Sir Gregory*
Clapham] village south of London   Buckrum] buckram, stiffened
canvas   sedge] type of coarse reed, used for making matting
Demagorgon] mysterious deity of the underworld   Paphlagonias]
province of Asia Minor   Sardanapalus] king of Assyria famous for life of
luxury   *vertue,*] vertue. *Workes*; *Sir Gregory*   Atropos] the Fate who
cuts the thread of each human life

Aquarius joyn'd with *Pisces*, in firme league,
With Reasons and vindictive Arguments,
That pulveriz'd the King of Diamonds,
And with a diogoricall relapse,
Squeaz'd through the Sinders of a Butterflye,
Great *Oberon* was mounted on a Waspe,
To signifie this newes at Dunstable.
The Weathercock at Pancrage in a fume,
With Patience much distracted hearing this,
Repli'd thus briefly without feare or wit,
What madnesse doth thy Pericranion seaze,
Beyond the Dragons taile Artophilax.
Think'st thou a Wolfe thrust through a sheep-skin glove,
Can make me take this Gobling for a Lambe:
Or that a Crocadile in Barly broth,
Is not a dish to feast don Belzebub,
Give me a Medler in a field of blue,
Wrapt up stigmatically in a dreame,
And I will send him to the gates of Dis,
To cause him fetch a sword of massie Chalke,
With which he wan the fatall Theban field,
From Romes great mitred Metropolitan.
Much was the quoile this braving answere made,
When presently a German Conjurer,

diogoricall] possibly a misprint for 'diagonicall', from 'diagonic', meaning
diagonal; or more probably 'diagoricall', intended as an adjective from Diagoras,
an early Greek atheist (see Nashe, *Works*, iv, p. 237, and Schäfer, *Early
Lexicography*, ii, 'diagorize', correcting *OED*)   Oberon] king of the
fairies   Dunstable] town in Bedfordshire, used in proverbial sayings to
symbolize ignorance and provincial simplicity   Pancrage] St Pancras Church,
in Needlers Lane in the City of London   Pericranion] pericranium, used
loosely to mean brain, skull or head   *Artophilax*] Artyphilax *Workes*;
Artophilax, *Sir Gregory*: Arctophylax, a constellation at the tail of Ursa Major
(the Great Bear)   Gobling] goblin   Belzebub] god of the flies, one of the
gods of the Philistines; popularly, the name of a devil   Medler] medlar
(fruit-tree)   stigmatically] vilely, villainously (derived from the branding, i.e.
stigmatizing, of criminals)   Dis] Hades   Theban] of the city of Thebes,
in Boeotia (Greece)   Metropolitan] senior bishop (i.e., the Pope)
quoile] coil, disturbance, fuss

Did ope a learned Booke of Palmistry,
Cram'd full of mental reservations:
The which beginning with a loud low voyce,
With affable and kind discourtesie,
He spake what no man heard or understood,
Words tending unto this or no respect,
Spawne of a Tortoyse hold thy silent noyse,
For when the great Leviathan of Trumps,
Shall make a breach in *Sinons* Tennis Court,
Then shall the pigmey mighty *Hercules*,
Skip like a wildernesse in Woodstreet Counter,
Then *Taurus* shall in league with *Hanniball*,
Draw *Bacchus* dry, whilst *Boreas* in a heat,
Invellop'd in a Gowne of Isicles:
With much discretion and great want of wit,
Leave all as wisely as it was at first.
I mused much how those things could be done.
When straight a water Tankard answer'd me,
That it was made with a Parenthesis,
With thirteene yards of Kersie and a halfe,
Made of fine flaxe which grew on Goodwin sands,
Whereby we all perceiv'd the Hernshawe's breed,
Being trusted with a charitable doome,
Was neere Bunhill, when strait I might discry,
The Quintessence of Grubstreet, well distild

Leviathan] huge biblical sea-creature   Sinon] Greek who tricked the
Trojans into taking the wooden horse into their city   *Court*,] Court.
Workes; Sir Gregory   Woodstreet Counter] debtors' prison in the City of
London   Taurus] either the astrological sign, or the mountain in
Anatolia   Hanniball] Hannibal, Carthaginian commander who warred
against Rome   Boreas] north wind   Kersie] type of coarse woollen
cloth   Goodwin sands] area on coast of Kent, once owned by Earl Goodwin,
but later inundated by the sea; used in a proverbial saying for foolish projects:
'Let him sett up shop on Goodwins sands' (Howell, *Paroimiographia*, p. 14)
Hernshawe] heronshaw, young or small heron   Bunhill] marshy area north
of City of London   Grubstreet] Grub Street, near Moorfields in the City
of London: in 1598 it had 'a number of bowling-alleys and dicing-houses' (Stow,
Survey, pp. 382–3); its reputation as a place of hack-writers and printing-houses
arose only in the mid 17th century

Through Cripplegate in a contagious Map.
Bright *Phaeton* all angry at the sight,
Snacht a large Wool-packe from a pismires mouth.
And in a Taylors Thimble boyl'd a Cabbage.
Then all the standers by, most Reverend, Rude,
Judg'd the case was most obscure and cleere,
And that three salt Ennigmates well appli'd,
With fourescoare Pipers and *Arions* Harpe,
Might catch *Gargantua* through an augor-hole,
And twas no doubt but mulley *Mahamat*,
Would make a quaffing bowle of *Gorgons* skul,
Whilst gormundizing *Tantalus* would weepe,
That *Polipheme* should kisse *Auroraes* lips,
Tri-formed *Cinthia* in a Sinkefoile shape,
Met with the Dogstarre on Saint *Davids* day,
But said *Grimalkin* mumbling up the Alpes,
Made fifteene fustian fumes of Pasticrust.
This was no sooner knowne at *Amsterdam*,
But with an Ethiopian Argosey,
Man'd with Flap-dragons, drinking upsifreeze,
They past the purple gulfe of Basingstoke.
This being finisht, search to any end,
A full odde number of just sixteene dogs,
Drencht in a sulpher flame of scalding Ice,

Cripplegate] district of City of London   Phaeton] Phaethon, son of Helios,
the sun-god, who drove the chariot of the sun for a day, lost control, and was
killed by Zeus   Wool-packe] woolpack, large sack used for transporting
wool   pismire's] ant's   Ennigmates] enigmas (probably by association
with the Greco-Latin plural 'aenigmata')   Arion] legendary poet saved from
drowning by dolphin   mulley] mullah   Gorgon] monster with serpents
for hair   gormundizing] gourmandizing, eating gluttonously
Polipheme] Polyphemus, Cyclops blinded by Odysseus   Aurora]
dawn-goddess   Cinthia] Cynthia, Diana, the moon-goddess
Sinkefoile] cinquefoil, five-leaved   Grimalkin] name given to a cat,
especially an old she-cat   mumbling] eating slowly or biting softly
fustian fumes] rage giving rise to invective (see Introduction, pp. 40–41)
Argosey] large merchant-ship   Flap-dragons] flambéd raisins, quenched
when eaten   upsifreeze] deeply, to excess (used of drinking; from 'op sijn
Vriesch', in the Frisian fashion)

Sung the Besonian Whirlepooles of *Argeire*,
Mixt with pragmaticall potato Pies,
With that I turn'd my eares to see these things,
And on a Christall wall of Scarlet dye,
I with mine eyes began to heare and note,
What these succeeding Verses might portend,
Which furiously an Anabaptist squeak'd,
The audience deafly listning all the while.

*A most learned-Lye, and Illiterate Oration, in lame galloping
Rime, fustianly pronounced by* Nimshag, *a Gimno-*sophicall
Philosopher, in the presence of *Achitophel Smel-smocke,
Annani-Asse Aretine, Iscariot-Nabal, Franciscus Ra-viliaco,
Garnetto Jebusito, Guido Salpetro Favexit Pouderio,* and many
other grave Senators of Limbo. Translated out of the vulgar
Language, of Terra incognita, *and is as materiall as any part
of the Booke, the meaning where-*of a blind man may see
without Spectacles as well at midnight, as at noone day.

The Story of *Ricardo*, and of *Bindo*,
Appear'd like *Nylus* peeping through a windo:

Besonian] usually a noun, meaning low fellow, scoundrel   Argeire]
Algiers   pragmaticall] skilled in affairs   Nimshag] *'Nymshag* an ancient
Utopian Philosopher' (Taylor, *Jack a Lent: Workes,* sig. L3')
Gimnosophicall] adjective from 'gymnosophist', a naked philosopher or
ascetic   Achittophel] Achitophel, Ahithophel, counsellor with false
reputation for wisdom who advised Absalom to rebel against David (2 Samuel
16–18)   Annani-asse] Ananias, struck dead for dishonesty (Acts 5: 1–5)
Aretine] Pietro Aretino (1492–1556), famous comic and obscene writer
Iscariot] Judas Iscariot, betrayer of Christ   Nabal] rich but churlish man
who refused assistance to the followers of David: 'Nabal is his name, and
folly is with him' (1 Samuel 25: 25)   Fransiscus Ra-viliaco] François Ravaillac,
who assassinated Henri IV of France in 1610   Garnetto] Thomas Garnett,
English Jesuit, accused of involvement in Gunpowder Plot and executed for
high treason in 1608   Jebusito] Jebusite, of tribe expelled by Israelites
Guido Salpetro Favexit Pouderio] referring to Guy Fawkes, with 'Favexit'
(spelt 'Fauexit'), a Latin word from the Dies Irae, for 'Fawkes', and italianized
forms of 'saltpetre' (an ingredient of gunpowder) and 'powder'   terra
incognita] unknown land   Ricardo, Bindo] unidentified   Nylus] the Nile

Which put the wandring Jew in much amazement,
In seeing such a voyce without the Cazement,
When loe a Bull, (long nourish'd in *Cocitus*),
With sulphure hornes, sent by the Emp'rour *Titus*,
Ask'd a stigmatike *Paracelsian* question,
If *Alexander* ever lov'd *Ephestion*.
   I seeing each to other were much adverse,
In mirth and sport set down their minds in sad verse.
Which as my brains with care have coin'd & minted,
With plenteous want of judgment here tis printed,
But if *Grimalkine* take my line in dudgion,
The case is plaine, I pray good Readers judge ye on,
That *Esop* that old fabulisticke *Phrygian*,
From the Nocturnall floud or lake cal'd *Stigian*,
Came to the Court at *Creete*, clad like a Legate,
The Porter kindly to him open'd the-Gate,
He past through *Plutoes* Hall in Hell most horrid,
Where gnashing cold mixt with cumbustious torid,
Where all things that are good & goodnes wanted,
Where plants of mans perdition still are planted,
Where Ghosts and Goblings all in sulphure suted,
And all the fiends like Cuckolds were cornuted.
At last he audience got in *Plutoes* presence,
And of his whole Embassage this was the sence:
To thee Tartarian Monarch now my Rime-is,
And therefore marke my Prologue, or *Imprimis*,

---

without the Cazement] outside the casement (window-frame)   *Cocitus*),]
Cocytus, *Workes*: Cocytus, river of the underworld   Titus] famously virtuous
Roman Emperor (d. AD 81)   stigmatike] vile, villainous (derived from the
branding, i.e. stigmatizing, of criminals)   Paracelsian] adjective from Paracelsus
(1493–1541), chemical and medical writer   Ephestion] Hephaestion, general
and friend of Alexander the Great   Grimalkine] name given to a cat,
especially an old she-cat   dudgion] dudgeon, resentment   Esop . . .
Phrygian] the philosopher and fable-writer Aesop was from Phrygia
Stigian] Stygian, of the river Styx   Plutoes] god of underworld
Goblings] goblins   cornuted] made to wear horns, i.e. cuckolded
Embassage] embassy   Tartarian] of Tartary, central Asia   Imprimis] in
the first place (word used at start of documents, e.g. inventories)

Thou that in *Limbo* art as 'twere *Rex Regnant*
Beare with my wit, which is not sharp or pregnant,
I come from Houndsditch, Long-laine, & from Bridewel,
Where all that have liv'd ill, have all not dide well,
Where as the Vices shew like Vertues Cardinall,
Where's mony store and conscience very hard in al,
Through thy protection they are monstrous thrivers,
Not like the Dutchmen in base Doyts and Stivers,
For there you may see many a greedy grout-head,
Without or wit, or sence, almost without-head,
Held and esteem'd a man whose zeal is fervent,
And makes a shew as he were not your servant.
To tell this newes I came from many a mile hence,
For we do know ther's ods twixt talke and silence.
With that the smug-fac'd *Pluto* shook his vestment,
Deep ruminating what the weighty Jest ment,
Calling to mind old *Dodonaeus* Hearball,
With Taciturnity and Actions verball,
Quoth he, I care for neither Friend or Kinsman,
Nor doe I value honesty two pinnes man:
But 'tis a Maxime Mortals cannot hinder,
The doughty deeds of Wakefields huffe cap Pinder,
Are not so pleasant as the faire *Aurora*,
When *Nimrod* rudely plaid on his Bandora.

Rex Regnant] ruling king   Houndsditch] street in City of London
Long-laine] Long Lane, street in City of London   Bridewell] London
prison   Doyts] small Dutch coins, worth one eighth of a stuiver   Stivers]
stuiver, Dutch coin worth between 1*d* and 2*d*   grout-head] dunce,
blockhead   smug-fac'd] smooth-skinned, clean-shaven (only beginning in
the 17th century to gain its connotation of 'self-satisfied')   Pluto] god of
underworld   Dodonaeus] name for Zeus (Jupiter), from his oracle at
Dodona   Actions verball] legal prosecutions enacted orally in court, not in
writing   Wakefields ... Pinder] Pinder (i.e. impounder of stray animals)
of Wakefield, character in Robin Hood ballads   huffe cap] blustering,
swashbuckling (originally referring to liquor which goes to the head)
Aurora] dawn-goddess   Nimrod] great-grandson of Noah, 'a mighty
hunter before the Lord' (Genesis 10: 9)   Bandora] musical instrument
similar to guitar or lute

For 'tis not fit that any Turke or Persian,
Should in a Cloke-bag hide a feaver Tertian,
Because the Dog-starre in his cold Meridian,
Might arme himself in fury most quotidian.
With that, most quick a Pettifoggers tongue went,
(Well oild with *Aurum, Argent,* or such *Unguent*)
Is't fit (quoth he) here should be such incroachment,
By such whose fathers ne'r knew what a Coach ment;
Or shal their Scutchions fairly be indorsed,
Who riding backward jadishly were horsed;
For though in *India* it be rare and frequent,
Where to the wall most commonly the weak went,
Yet neither can the *Soldan* or the *Sophy,*
Shew any Presidents for such a Trophy.
By Rules of Logicke, he's a kind of Cative,
And makes no reckoning of his Country native,
That doth with feeble strength, love with derision.
And without bloodshed makes a deepe incision,
Why should a man lay either life or lim ny,
To be endangered by a falling Chimney:
For though the prosecution may be quaintly,
Yet may the execution end but faintly,
Let's call to mind the famous acts of *Hector,*
When aged *Ganymede* carousing *Nectar,*
Did leave the Greekes much matter to repine on;
Untill the Woodden Horse of trusty *Sinon,*
Foald a whole litter of mad Colts in Harnesse,

feaver Tertian] tertain fever or ague, characterized by high temperature every
other day   Pettifogger] pejorative term for lawyer dealing in minor
actions   Arum, Argent] gold, silver   *incroachment*] innroachment
Workes; incroachment *Sir Gregory*   whose fathers . . . Coach ment] coaches
were introduced to London only in the late 16th century   Soldan] Sultan,
ruler of Ottoman Empire   Sophy] ruler of Persia   Presidents]
precedents   cative] caitiff, wretched person (originally, a captive)   ny]
nigh   Hector] hero of Trojan War   Ganymede] cup-bearer to the
gods   Sinon] Greek who tricked the Trojans into taking the wooden horse
into their city

As furious as the host of *Holophernes*.
But to the purpose here's the long and short on't,
All that is said hath not beene much important,
Nor can it be that what is spoke is meant all,
Of any thing that happens accidentall.
We will examine wisely what the Foe sent,
And whether he be innocent or nocent.
In weighty matters let's not be too serious,
Ther's many an Eunuch hath bin thought venerious,
And 'tis a thing which often hath bin heard on,
That he that labours, doth deserve his Guerdon.
Let us the first precadent time examine,
Youle find that hunger is the cause of famine,
The Birds in Summer that have sweetly chirped,
Ere winter hath beene done, have beene extirped.
He may wear Robes, that nere knew what a Rag ment,
And he that feasts, may fast without a fragment,
The end proves all, I care not for the Interim,
Time now that summers him, will one day winter him.
To outward view, and Senses all exterier,
Amongst all fooles I never saw a verier,
Then he that doth his liberty prohibit,
To fall in danger of a fatall Jibbit.
Nor for this purpose here to talke come I,
How silver may be mock't with Alcamy.
I oft have heard that many a Hawke hath muted,
Whereby the Faulkners Clothes have bin polluted.
This may be avoyded if the Knight *Sir Reverence*,
Be wary with a negligent perseverance:

Holophernes] mighty general of the Assyrians, killed by Judith (Apocrypha,
Book of Judith)   on't] ont *Workes*; *Sir Gregory*   venerious] lustful, given
to venery   Guerdon] reward   precadent] probably meaning
'precedent'   Jibbet] gibbet   Alcamy] alchemy   muted] excreted
bird-droppings   Faulkners] falconer's   Sir Reverence] phrase derived
from the respectful or apologetic formula 'save reverence', 'saving your reverence';
also a slang term for human excrement

For men of Judgement never thinke it decent,
To love a stinking Pole-cat well for the sent.
But if a man should seriously consider,
Where Charity is fled or who hath hid her,
He in the end would give this worthy sentence,
The earth hath beene accursed since she went hence.
The times are biting, and the dayes Caniculer,
And mischiefe girds about the Globes orbiculer,
How from the Countrey all the plaine Rusticity,
Lives by deceit, exiling plaine simplicity.
A face like Rubies mix'd with Alabaster,
Wastes much in Physicke, and her water-caster,
That whosoe'r perceives which way the stink went
May sent and censure she's a great delinquent.
Why should a Bawd be furr'd with Budge & Miniver,
As if she were a Lady, or Queene *Guiniver*,
When as perhaps there's many a modest Matron,
Hath scarcely meat, or money, clothes, or patron?
And wherefore should a man be growne so stupid:
To be a slave to *Venus* or to *Cupid*?
Hee's but a foole that hoping for a vaine prize,
Being captived can have no baile or maine prize.
For he that hath no shift let him determine,
He shall be bitten with Fleas, Lice, or vermine.
This being all his speeches, *Pia Mater*,
He call'd a Sculler, and would goe by water:
When straite the Stygian Ferriman a rare one,
Old amiable currish curteous *Caron*,

Caniculer] canicular, adjective referring to the hot 'dog-days' of summer
orbiculer] orbicular, circular   *Alabaster*] Alablaster *Workes*; Alabaster *Sir
Gregory*   water-caster] medical diagnostician who inspected the patient's
urine   Budge] lamb's skin with the wool dressed outwards; used on Oxford
BA hood   Miniver] white fur used as trimming on ceremonial costumes
(probably Siberian squirrel); used on Oxford MA hood   Guiniver]
Guinevere, wife of King Arthur   maine prize] mainprize, legal surety to
secure the release of a prisoner   Pia Mater] innermost membrane surrounding
the brain   Stygian Ferriman . . . Caron] Charon, boatman of the
underworld, who ferried people across the river Styx

Row'd with a whirl-wind through the *Acheron* ticke,
And thence unto the Azure Sea proponticke,
There *Neptune* in a burning blue Pavilion,
In state did entertaine this slow Postillion,
There *Proteus* in a Robe of twisted Camphire,
With a grave beard of monumentall Samphire,
Quoth he, shall we whose Ancestors were war-like,
Whose rich Perfumes were only Leeks and Garlike,
Whose noble deeds nocturnall and diurnall,
Great Towns and Towers did topsie turvy turne al,
Shall all their valour be in us extinguish'd?
Great *Jove* forbid, there should be such a thing wish'd,
Though *Cleopatra* was *Octavian's* rivall.
It is a thing that we may well connive all,
Amongst the Ancient it is undisputable,
That women and the winds were ever mutable,
And 'tis approv'd where people are litigious,
There every Epicure is not religious,
Old *Occamus* knowing what they ment all,
Brought *Zephirus* unto the Orientall,
And he by Argument would prove that love is
A thing that makes a wise man oft a Novice:
For 'tis approv'd, a Greyhound or a Beagle,
Were not ordain'd or made to hunt the Eagle,
Nor can the nimblest Cat that came from *Gottam*,
Search the profundity of *Neptunes* bottom.
Let roaring Cannons with the Welkin parley,
It's known, good liquor may be made with Barley,
And by experience many are assured,

Acheron] river of the underworld   ticke] perhaps a form of 'dick', itself a
variant form of 'dyke'   proponticke] the Bosphorus, which leads to the
Pontic Sea (the Black Sea)   Postillion] coach-boy   Proteus]
shape-changing marine demi-god   Camphire] camphor   Samphire]
edible plant   Octavian] Octavianus, name used by the Emperor Augustus
from 44 to 27 BC   Occamus] William of Ockham, English medieval
philosopher   Zephirus] the west wind   Gottam] Gotham,
Nottinghamshire village famous for idiocy

Some grounds are fruitfull, if they be manured.
For in the rudiments of health or sanity,
An arrant Whore is but a piece of vanity:
Some men with fury will procrastinate,
And some with leaden speed make haste in at,
But in conclusion many things impurely,
Die in the birth, and never end maturely.
The man that seeketh straying minds to weane all,
From veniall vices, or offences penall:
Had he the forces of the Turkish Navy,
He would ly downe at last and cry *peccavi*,
Of one thing I have oftentimes tooke notice,
The foole that's old, and rich, much apt to dote is;
And by the light of *Pollux* and of *Castor*,
A Woolfe in Shepheards weeds is no good Pastor.
Those that do live a Commicke life by Magicke,
Their Sceanes in their Catastrophes are tragick.
And he that ore the world would be chief Primat,
May give occasion for wise men to rime at.
Before men fell to wrangling disagreement,
A Lawyer understood not what a fee ment:
It was a time when Guilt did feare no censure,
But love, and peace, and charity was then sure.
Now fathers (for their bread) dig and delve it,
The whilst the Satten Sons are lin'd with Velvet.
Thus doe I make a hotch potch messe of *Nonsence*,
In darke Enigmaes, and strange sence upon sence:
It is not foolish all, nor is it wise all,
Nor is it true in all, nor is it lies all.
I have not shew'd my wits acute or fluent,
Nor told which way of late the wandring Jew went:
For mine owne part I never cared greatly,
(So fare I well) where those that dresse the meat lie.

peccavi] 'I have sinned'   Pollux . . . Castor] twin sons of Leda, transformed
by Zeus into the constellation Gemini   Satten] satin

A miserable Knave may be close fisted,
And prodigall expence may be resisted,
I neither care what *Tom*, or *Jacke*, or *Dicke* sed,
I am resolv'd and my mind is fixed,
The case is, not as he, or I, or you sed,
Truth must be found, and witnesses produced,
My care is, that no captious Reader beare hence,
My understanding, wit, or reason here-hence.
On purpose to no purpose did I write all,
And so at noone, I bid you here good night all.

Then with a tuchbox of transalpine tarre,
Turning thrice round, and stirring not a jot,
He threw five tunne of red hot purple Snow,
Into a Pigmeis mouth, nine inches square,
Which strait with melancholly mov'd,
Old *Bembus* Burgomaster of *Pickt-hatch*,
That plunging through the Sea of *Turnebull streete*,
He safely did arrive at *Smithfield Barres*.
Then did the Turntripes on the Coast of *France*,
Catch fifteene hundred thousand Grashoppers,
With fourteene Spanish Needles bumbasted,
Poach'd with the Egs of fourscore Flanders Mares,
Mounted upon the foote of *Caucasus*,
They whorld the football of conspiring fate,
And brake the shins of smugfac'd *Mulciber*.

tuchbox] touchbox, used by musketeers to keep their powder dry   Bembus]
Cardinal Pietro Bembo (1470–1547), famous as author of dialogues on the
nature of love   Pickt-hatch] notorious tavern-brothel in Clerkenwell
Turnebull streete] alternative name of Turnmill Street, street famous for taverns
and brothels (including Pickt-hatch) in Clerkenwell, London   Smithfield
Barres] barrier on northern edge of Smithfield, marking boundary between City
of London and Clerkenwell   Turntripes] probably by analogy with
'turnspit', the menial who turned the roasting-spit in a kitchen (hence also a
term of contempt)   Spanish Needles] famous as best-quality steel
needles   bumbasted] stuffed   smugfac'd] smooth-faced, clean-shaven
(only beginning in the 17th century to gain its connotation of
'self-satisfied')   Mulciber] the god Vulcan

With that grim *Pluto* all in Scarlet blue,
Gave faire *Proserpina* a kisse of brasse,
At which all Hell danc'd Trenchmore in a string,
Whilst *Acheron*, and *Termagant* did sing.
The Mold-warp all this while in white broth bath'd,
Did Carroll *Didoes* happinesse in love,
Upon a Gridiron made of whiting-mops,
Unto the tune of *John* come kisse me now,
At which *Avernus* Musicke gan to rore,
Inthron'd upon a seat of three-leav'd grasse,
Whilst all the Hibernian Kernes in multitudes,
Did feast with Shamerags stew'd in Usquebagh.
At which a banquet made of Monopolies,
Tooke great distaste, because the Pillory
Was hunger-starv'd for want of Villaines eares,
Whom to relieve, there was a Mittimus,
Sent from *Tartaria* in an Oyster Boate,
At which the King of *China* was amaz'd,
And with nine grains of Rewbarbe stellified,
As low as to the altitude of shame,
He thrust foure Onions in a Candle-case,
And spoild the meaning of the worlds misdoubt,
Thus with a Dialogue of crimson starch,

Proserpina] Persephone, daughter of Zeus and Demeter, seized by god of underworld   Trenchmore] boisterous old English dance   Acheron] river of the underworld   Termagant] imaginary deity supposed to be worshipped by Muslims and characterized by a very violent temper   Mold-warp] mole   Didoes] 'Queen Dido' was a popular ballad-tune (see Chappell, *Popular Music*, i, pp. 370–74)   whiting-mops] young whiting (fish)   John come kisse me now] popular song (see Chappell, *Popular Music*, i, p. 147)   Avernus] river of the underworld   Hibernian Kernes] Irish foot-soldiers   Shamerags] shamrocks (not a joke-spelling but a common variant, closer to Gaelic 'seamrag')   Usquebagh] whisky (Gaelic 'uisge beatha', 'water of life'); associated mainly with Ireland, not Scotland, in the 17th century   Mittimus] warrant sent by JP or judge to a prison, naming someone to be held in custody there   Tartaria] Tartary, central Asia   Rewbarbe] not the modern plant, but a root imported from China, used as a purgative   stellified] placed among the stars or transformed into a constellation; hence, extolled   Candle-case] container for candles

I was inflamed with a num-cold fire,
Upon the tenterhookes of *Charlemaine*,
The Dogstar howld, the Cat a Mountaine smilde,
And *Sisiphus* dranke Muskadell and Egges,
In the hornd hoofe of huge *Bucephalus*,
Time turn'd about, and shew'd me yesterday,
Clad in a Gowne of mourning had I wist,
The motion was almost too late they said,
Whilst sad despaire made all the World starke mad,
They all arose, and I put up my pen,
It makes no matter, where, why, how, or when.

Some Sence at last to the Learned.

You that in *Greeke* and *Latine* learned are,
And of the ancient *Hebrew* have a share,
You that most rarely oftentimes have sung
In the *French*, *Spanish*, or Italian tongue,
Here I in *English* have imployed my pen,
To be read by the learnedst Englishmen,
Wherein the meanest Scholler plaine may see,
I understand their tongues, as they doe mee.

Finis

---

tenterhookes] hooks used for holding or stretching cloth during its
manufacture   Cat a Mountaine] leopard or panther   Sisiphus] Sisyphus,
morally flawed hero punished in Hades by having to push a boulder repeatedly
uphill   Muskadell and Egges] muscatel (sweet wine) with raw egg was
regarded as an aphrodisiac   Bucephalus] horse of Alexander the Great

Faults escaped in the Printing, *which a wise Reader may mend when he sees them.*

In the 25. page 44. line, for a *Friers mouth* read a *Pudding.*
In the 170. page 53 line, for a *foole* read a *Bable.*
In the 90. page, 27 line, for a *friend* read *rare.*
In the 30 page 6. line 78. for a *Whore* read a *Bridewell.*
In the 100 page, line 40. for a *Bawd* reade a *Cart.*
In the 12. page 11 line, for *noone* read *dinner.*
In the 16. first, and all the Pages following for *Tobacco* read a *Witch.*
In the 40. page, and 80. line, for a *Calves head* read *Bacon.*
In the 37. page, and 1. line, for *vice* read *plenty.*
In the 000. page, and 3. line for *money* read *scarce.*
In the last Page, for *conscience,* read *none.*
In every page for *sence* read *nonsence.*

Source: Taylor, *Workes*, sigs. Aa1–4ʳ (collated with Taylor, *Sir Gregory Nonsence*).

Faults escaped . . . nonsence] these nonsense errata are omitted in *Workes*
Friers mouth . . . Pudding] this plays on a proverbial saying, 'As fit as a pudding for a friar's mouth' (Tilley, *Dictionary of Proverbs*, P620)   Bable] bauble
Bridewell] London prison   Bawd . . . Cart] 'carting' (being carried in an open cart through the streets, exposed to public ridicule) was a common punishment for bawds

12

MARTIN PARKER

Sir Leonard Lack-wit's speech to the Emperor of Utopia

To that most ignoble Icarion Idiot Mag pye among men, and a Bull-beggar among Birds and Beasts, Signior Anonimus Ignato, *Emperour of Utopia, great King of Fairy Land, Prince of the high and mighty Nation, called the Pygmies, Duke of Diomondo, Earle of Clapperdudgeon, Governor of Greenland, and all the inhabitable Ilands in that waste part of the Terrestrial Globe,* Sir Leonard Lack-wit *his Masterships most sublime vassall, greeteth in this manner.*

O thou who art the onely Dominator
Ore all these spacious bounds of Erra Pater,
Thou that dost rule even from the Wals of Bantam
Unto the very confines of Bizantam,
To thee great King of Crickets, geese & ganders,
I that was once one of thy chiefe commanders,
Now to such honour by that meanes am risen,

Icarion] perhaps Icarian, of Icarius, Athenian who was killed in revenge after making people drunk with wine   Ignoto] from Latin 'ignotus', unknown   Diomondo] meaning uncertain   Clapperdudgeon] cant name or term of reproach for a beggar   Erra Pater] legendary Jewish astrologer, reputed author of popular work, *A Prognostication for ever of Erra Pater, a Jewe . . . verie profitable to keepe the bodie in health* (London, 1606)   Bantam] city (and state) in Java   Bizantam] Byzantium

That I have leave to famish in thy prison.
I that lived like a Lord among thy Laquies,
Now know not at what rate a pint of Sacke is:
I that with Beefe and Bacon fed my Carkis,
Now hardly know what kind of meat a Lark is,
I that thy Gardner was to dig and delve it,
Have never a sute but sattin, plush or velvet.
I that was wont to keep frogs from thy trenches
Am now enjoyn'd to keep but just ten wenches.
I that have heretofore danc't many a merry Jig,
Am now constrained to weare a periwig:
Yet know, great mongril, that I do not feare thee,
Nor would I have thee think that I do jeer thee.
If thou tell me that I want understanding,
To have the Ile of dogs at my commanding,
I tell thee plainely I conceive great jelousie,
That thou thy selfe art but a foole as well as I,
Although my name be Lack-Wit, yet it may be,
That I have wit enough to please a Lady.
Ide have thee know that I a man of note am,
My father once was Alderman of Gotam.
I have observed by my neglective knowledge,
That al the wise men come not from the colledg,
And I have known a dunce (as was thy grandser)
Demand a thing which Doctors cannot answer,
And tis apparant both to good and bad men,
That those who have no wit are fools or madmen
Yet I have seen a drunkard oft goe reeling,
When yet his head hath hardly toucht the seeling.
The Proverbe sayes, Plain dealing is a jewell,
And I in Lent am glad of Watergrewell.
Wert thou as mercifull as was Busiris,

Gotam] Gotham, Nottinghamshire village famous for idiocy   *grandser)*]
grandser *The Legend of Sir Leonard*: grandsire, grandfather   Busiris] King
of Egypt who killed all strangers that visited his realm

Yet to have justice of thee my desire is.
Nay hadst thou as much ease as hath Ixion,
Yet may a Mouse run safely by a Lion;
Nay more, wert thou as true and just as Simon,
Yet may thy Table serve for men to dine on.
These things have oft tane up my contemplation
Me thinkes a Hangman's no good occupation:
And though my teeth within my bosom chatter
Be't known to thee, I came not here to flatter:
It glads me more to heare a Carman whistle,
Than to smell thee when thou dost fart & fistle.
The fals of great men through ambitious climing
To poore men oft occasion gives of riming,
Yet should blind Homer see what here I utter,
Tis ten to one but he'd against me mutter.
And Ile be sworne on Ciceroes Epistles,
One sheafe of wheat is worth a load of thistles.
There's many travellers find newes to brag on,
That are as true as Trundles Sussex Dragon:
But when the Wandring Jew comes to Westchester
He'l tell at Coventry what's done at Leister,
If I should say I was at Leipsitch battle,
I doubt some men would think 'twer idle prattle.
But thers rare wonders told in Kent street garison
Your weekly newes to that makes no comparison.
I oftentimes have heard my Grandam wonder,
Why sheep and wolves should live so far asunder

Ixion] King of the Lapiths, bound to a wheel of fire in the underworld as a
punishment for trying to imitate thunder   Simon] Simon Magus, regarded
as an archetype of corruption (hence 'simony') for having tried to purchase the
gifts of the Holy Spirit (see Acts 8)   tane] taken   fistle] fizzle, a silent
fart   Trundles Sussex Dragon] see Longer Notes, pp. 293–4   Leipsitch
battle] Battle of Breitenfeld, just north of Leipzig (1631): the first important
victory of Protestant forces (Swedish and Saxon) over the Catholic powers in
the Thirty Years' War   Kent street garison] Kent or Kentish Street, in
Southwark, contained a famous leper-house (perhaps humorously referred to
as the 'garison' here)

I did resolve her doubt, yet I said nothing
Wolves be not known from sheep clad in sheeps clothing.
Yet I confesse, tis more fit for King Priam,
To talke of these things than such fools as I am.
Wel though these lofty matters are past my sense
The proverbs saith, lovers may speak by licence.
And now great Monopoly having vented
My empty vessell, I am well contented,
What saist thou to me? Why didst thou convent me
To tel the news for which thou maist torment me?
Tush I regard thy spight lesse than a token,
For thou canst take no hold of what I've spoken:
I nonsence spoke on purpose to deceive thee,
Now farewell: as I found thee, so Ile leave thee.

Source: Parker, *The Legend of Sir Leonard Lack-Wit, sonne in law to Sir Gregory Nonesence* (London, 1633), sigs. B5^r–6^v.

---

torment me?] torment me *The Legend of Sir Leonard*

13

RICHARD CORBET

A Non Sequitur

Marke how the Lanterns clowd mine eyes
See where a moone drake ginnes to rise
Saturne craules much like an Iron Catt,
To see the naked moon in a slipshott hatt,
Thunder thumping toad stooles crock the pots
  To see the Meremaids tumble
Leather catt-a-mountaines shake their heeles
  To heare the gosh-hawke grumble
    The rustie threed,
    Begins to bleed,
  And cobwebs elbow itches
    The putrid skyes
    Eat mulsacke pies
  Backed up in logicke breeches

Munday trenchers make good hay
The Lobster weares no dagger
Meale-Mouth'd shee-peacockes powle the starres
And make the lowbell stagger
  Blew Crocodiles foame in the toe

slipshott] slipshod, i.e. wearing a slip-shoe or slipper   crock] make
dirty   catt-a-mountaines] leopards or panthers   gosh-hawke]
goshawk   threed] thread   elbow itches] see Longer Notes, p. 290
mulsacke] see Longer Notes, p. 292   *breeches*] brecehes *Wit Restor'd*
powle] poll, decapitate   lowbell] bell used in nocturnal bird-catching

Blind meal-bagges do follow the doe
A ribb of apple braine spice
Will follow the Lancasheire dice
Harke how the chime of *Plutoes* pispot cracks,
To see the rainbowes wheele ganne, made of flax.

Source: *Wit Restor'd* (London, 1658), p. 61.

ganne] bark like a fox

14

RICHARD CORBET

A mess of non-sense

Like to the silent tone of unspoke speeches
or like a lobster clad in logick breeches
or like the gray fleece of a crimson Catt
or like the Moonecalfe in a slipshooe-hatt
or like the shaddow when the sunne is gone
or like a thought that ne're was thought upon
    Even such is man, who never was begotten
    untill his children were both dead & rotten.

Like to the Ivory touchstone of a cabbadge
or like a crablouse with his bag and baggadge
or like the Fower square circle of a ring
or like the hay ding, ding, a ding, ding
or like the braineles braines of buttered fish
or like the garbidge of a chafing dishe
    Even such is man, whoe without doubt
    spake to small purpose when his tongue was out.

Like to the fresh fading withered rose
or like to Rythme and verse that runs in prose
or like the humbles of a tinder boxe

Moonecalfe] a congenital idiot   slipshooe] slip-shoe, slipper   Fower]
four   braineles . . . buttered fish] a borrowing from Hoskyns, poem 1, first
line   humbles] entrails

or like a man thats sound and hath the poxe
or like a hobnayle coyn'd in single pence
least it should want its preterperfect tence
    Even such is man who dyde and then did laugh
    to see theis strang lines set on his epitaph.

Source: Bodl. MS Rawl. poet. 160, fo. 156ʳ. This appears to be the earliest version of this poem; the MS which contains it is a collection of poetry mainly from the 1620s, including works by Jonson and Herrick. Slightly different versions are contained in many other MSS, most of which seem to have Oxford connections: see BL MS Egerton 2421, fos. 11ᵛ–12ʳ; and Bodl. MSS Ashmole 36, fo. 70ʳ; Ashmole 37 (bound with Ashmole 36), fo. 256ʳ; CCC 328, fo. 25ʳ; Eng. poet. e. 97, p. 166; Rawl. poet. 117, fo. 94ᵛ; Rawl. poet. 160, fo. 156ʳ; Tanner 465, fo. 83ʳ. In three of these (Bodl. MSS Ashmole 37, Tanner 465, and Rawl. poet. 117) the poem is attributed to 'Dʳ Corbett'. It was also printed in *Witt's Recreations Augmented* (London, 1641), sig. Y4ᵛ, under the title 'A mess of non-sense'; in *The Academy of Complements* (London, 1650), pp. 163–4, as 'Sense'; and in *Wit Restor'd* (London, 1658), pp. 137–8, as 'Epilogus Incerti Auctoris'.

preterperfect tence] past perfect tense, e.g. 'I have eaten'

JOHN TAYLOR

verses from Aqua-Musae

I can Rand words, and Rime as well as thou:
Speak and write Nonsence, even by thy example,
(Though not like thine Admir'd abroad so ample)
Like to the inundation of a flame,
Or like a Mad Lord, never out of frame,
Or like the Entrailes of a purple Snaile,
Or like the wagging of the Dog-starres Taile,
Or like the Frost and Snow that falls in *June*,
Or like sweet Musique, that was ne're in Tune:
Or like a Ship that wants sides, Stem and Keele,
Or like the Marrow-bones of Fortunes Wheele,
Even such is *Wither*, like all these or nothing,
Yet like himselfe, in every good mans Loathing.
And is not this rare Nonsence, prethee tell,
Much like thy writing, if men marke it well:
For Nonsence is Rebellion, and thy writing,
Is nothing but Rebellious Warres inciting.

Source: Taylor, *Aqua-Musae* (Oxford, 1644), sig. A2ʳ.

Rand] cut into slices   Wither] George Wither (1588–1667), poet and
pamphleteer, whom Taylor admired and befriended before the Civil War,
but bitterly attacked after Wither joined the parliamentary side in 1642

JOHN TAYLOR

verses from Mercurius Nonsensicus

Like to a whirle-wind in a Taylors thimble,
Or like a gouty Tumbler, quick and nimble,
Or like Hay making in a showre of raine,
Or like a Wedding where there are not twaine,
This booke compar'd, and uncompar'd you'l find,
As like as is the Water to the Winde.

Like to th' embroidered Meadowes of the Moone,
Or like the houres 'twixt six and seven at Noone,
Or like a Cock that wants Stones, Spurs, and Comb,
Or like a Traveller that's ne're from home,
Or like Tobacco that wants stink or smoake,
Or like the Devill in Religious Cloake;
Such is this Pamphlet, writ with such advisement,
As troubles not the State, or what the Wise meant.

Source: Taylor, *Mercurius Nonsensicus* (n.p. [London], 1648), title-page
and p. 7.

JOHN TAYLOR

The Essence of Nonsence upon Sence

The Essence, Quintessence, Insence, Innocence, Lyesence, & Magnifisence *of* Nonsense *upon* Sence: *Or, Sence upon Nonsence. The Third Part, the fourth Impression, the fifth Edition, the Sixth Addition, upon Condition, that (by Tradition) the Reader may laugh if he list. In Longitude, Latitude, Crassitude, Magnitude, and Amplitude, lengthened, widened, enlarged, augmented, encreased, made wider and sider, by the addition of Letters, Syllables, Words, Lines, and far fetch'd Sentences. And the lamentable Death and Buriall of a Scottish Gallaway Nagge. Written upon* White Paper, *in a* Brown Study, *betwixt* Lammas *Day and* Cambridge, *in the Yeare aforesayd. Beginning at the latter end, and written by* John Taylor *at the sign of the poor* Poets Head, *in* Phoenix Alley, *near the middle of* Long Acre, *or* Coven Garden. Anno, Millimo, Quillimo, Trillimo, Daffadillimo, Pulcher.

Gallaway Nagge] type of small horse from Galloway, in south-western Scotland   in a Brown Study] in a depressed mood   Lammas Day] 1 August   Long Acre] street adjoining Covent Garden, London   Anno, Millimo . . . Trillimo] this rigmarole phrase comes probably from Nashe, who took it from Wilson's *Art of Rhetorique* (see Nashe, *Works*, i, p. 101; iv, p. 64)   Pulcher] 'pretty, beautiful'

In Laudem Authoris

Must *Non-sence* fill up every Page?
  Is it to save th'expence
Of wit? or will not this dull Age
  Be at the Charge of sence?

But *(John)* though Fortune play the Whore,
  Let not the Vulgar know it;
Perhaps if you had not been poor,
  You had not been a Poet.

Your Estate's held in *Capite*,
  It lies upon *Pernassus*;
Complain not then of Poverty,
  You are as rich as *Crassus*.

                H.B.

Nonsense upon Sense, &c.

Mount meekly low, on blew presumptuous wings,
Relate the force of fiery water Springs,
Tell how the Artick, and Antartick Pole
Together met at Hockley in the Hole:
How Etna, and Vessuvius, in cold bloud,
Were both drown'd in the Adriatick floud.
Speak truth (like a Diurnall) let thy Pen

In laudem Authoris] 'In praise of the author'   in Capite] this plays on the literal meaning, 'in your head', and the legal meaning, 'as tenant-in-chief' Pernassus] Parnassus, mountain sacred to the Muses   Crassus] Roman of legendary riches   H.B.] unidentified   Artick, and Antartick] arctic and antarctic   Hockley in the Hole] public gardens in Clerkenwell, London, famous for bear-baiting and cock-fights   Diurnall] daily newspaper

Camelion like, rouze Lions from their Den,
Turne frantick Wolpacks into melting Rocks,
And put Olympus in a Tinder box:
Report how Ruffian Cats doe barke like dogs,
And Scithian Mountains are turnd Irish Bogs,
Feast Ariadne with Tartarian Tripes,
Transforme great Canons to Tobacco-pipes:
Make Venus like a Negro, white as jet,
And puffe-paste of the Tomb of Mahomet.
Then mounted on a Windmill presently
To Dunstable in Derbyshire I'le flie
From thence Ile take the Chariot of the Sun,
And swim to Scotland, and bring news what's done:
From thence I'le soare to silver Cinthia's lap,
And with Endimion take a nine years nap:
There Ile drinke healths with smug-face Mulciber,
At all the twelve signes in the Hemisphere.
Tush tell not me these things are past dispute,
I'le from th'Hesperides bring golden fruit:
Such as the Poets Palfrey Pegasus,
Fetch'd from the fertile Molehill Caucasus,
Tis not the Persian Gulph, or Epshams Well,
Nor Westminsters sweet Plum-broth (made in Hell)
Can change my resolution, I have vow'd,
To speake with silence and to write aloud,
That Bulls of Basan, and the Circean Swine,

Wolpacks] wool-packs, large bags used for transporting wool   Olympus]
mountain of the gods   Ariadne] daughter of Minos who married
Theseus   Tartarian] of Tartary, central Asia   Dunstable] town in
Bedfordshire, used in proverbial sayings to symbolize ignorance and provincial
simplicity   Cinthia] Cynthia, Diana, the moon-goddess   Endimion]
Endymion, famously beautiful shepherd, visited by the moon-goddess while
he slept   smug-face] smooth-skinned, clean-shaven (only beginning in the
17th century to gain its connotation of 'self-satisfied')   Mulciber] the god
Vulcan   Hesperides] nymphs who guarded golden apples (stolen by
Hercules)   Pegasus] winged horse   Epshams Well] Epsom's Well, spa at
Epsom, Surrey   Bulls of Basan] see Psalms 22: 12 ('Many bulls have
compassed me: strong bulls of Bashan have beset me round')   Circean
Swine] the witch Circe transformed Ulysses' crew into swine

Shall all dance Trenchmore at these words of mine.
Rowse up thou Ghost of Gusman, and apply
Thy selfe to me and let's write Tempe dry:
Be rul'd by me, we'le empty all Hellicon,
In scribling 'gainst the Whore of Babylon.
The Dunsmore Cows milke shall make Sillibubs,
And our Religion shall be brought in Tubs.
Make hast unto the faire call'd Bartholomew,
And thence from the Heroick Mungrell Crew,
Take the fine gugaw hobby horses all,
Which we will man, and then a Counsell call
And conquer Callice, Kent and Christendome,
Knock down the Turck, and bravely ransack Rome;
What can be done more? What more can be sed?
Let's play at Blind-man-buffe for Ginger-bread:
We'le have a dish of Dabs in Fish-street drest,
And with the Lobsters Ladies we will feast.
For as the Gowt is but a pleasing itch,
The best Bear-garden Bull-dog was a Bitch.
We have both eight and eighteen parts of speech,
Whereby I learn Ash burns as well as Beech,
Gargantua's scull is made a frying pan
To fry or follow the Leviathan,

Trenchmore] boisterous old English dance   Gusman] Guzman d'Alfarache,
hero of a Spanish romance of roguery   Tempe] famously beautiful
river-valley in Thessaly   Hellicon] Helicon, mountain sacred to the
Muses   Whore of Babylon] the scarlet whore of Babylon, a figure symbolizing
evil (in Rev. 17), applied by polemical Protestant writers to the Papacy
Dunsmore Cows] the dun cow of Dunsmore was a mythical beast slain by Sir
Guy of Warwick   Bartholomew] famous annual fair held in West
Smithfield, City of London   gugaw] gewgaw, a gaudy or paltry thing
Callice] Calais   Dabs] small flat-fish   Fish-street] Old Fish Street, in
the City of London   *Lobsters Ladies*] Lobsters Lady *Nonsence upon Sence*
Leviathan] huge Biblical sea-creature

That Gogmagog, Nick Wood, or Mariot,
Nor Creatan Miloe or Iscariot
Were not such valiant stomack'd men as those
That eat the Devils gowty petitoes.
Hark, hark, how from the South fierce Boreas rores
Give me a Sculler or a pair of Oares.
Ile make the Orient, and the Occident,
Both friends at Smithfield in the wild of Kent:
For now Tom Holders Mare hath broke her Crupper
Dresse me a dish of AE-dipthongs to supper.
The Dean of Dunstable hath bought and sold
Twelve lies new Printed, for two groats in gold.
Tis almost past the memory of man,
Since famous Arthur first in Court began:
Yet though King Lud did raign in Troynovaunt,
Will Summers was no kin to John of Gaunt.
What news from Tripoly? ware horns there ho:
The West-wind blows South-North at Jerico.
Steer well and steady, boyes look, look to th'Helme,
Fetch Goesberries that Grow upon the Elme:
Like Cormorants lets live upon the Ayre,
And of a Whirle-poole make a Marble Chair.

Gogmagog] Gog and Magog were two giants brought in chains to London
by Brutus; in a later version of the myth, 'Gogmagog' was a single giant,
transformed into a hill near Cambridge   Nick Wood] Nicholas Wood, of
Harrisom, Kent, a famous glutton, described by Taylor in a pamphlet entitled
The Great Eater (1630)   Mariot] John Marriott (d. 1653), corpulent lawyer,
also accused of gluttony in a scurrilous pamphlet entitled *The Great Eater of
Graye's-Inn* (1652)   Creatan Miloe] Creatan, Miloe *Nonsence upon Sence,
Essence of Nonsence*; Milo of Crete was a famous strong-man   Iscariot] Judas
Iscariot, betrayer of Christ   petitoes] a term usually referring to pigs'
trotters   Boreas] north wind   Smithfield] district containing cattle
market in City of London   wild of Kent] Weald of Kent, area between the
North and South Downs   Tom Holders Mare] unidentified; this line is
presumably from a popular song   Crupper] Cruppe *Essence of Nonsence*
Dean of Dunstable] proverbial figure symbolizing ignorance and provincial
simplicity   King Lud] mythical early King of England   Troynovaunt]
London (a name for it used in medieval romances)   Will Summers] Will
Somers (d. 1560), court fool to Henry VIII   John of Gaunt] third son of
Edward III

Blind men may see, and deafe men all shall hear
How dumb men talk, because Cow-hides are dear.
Go to th'Utopian Kingdome and relate,
That to their King these lines I dedicate:
Bid him take note of me, and understand
He hath not such a Poet in his Land.
Down by the dale with milk and cream that flows,
Upon a Hill (below the Valley) grows
Hungarian Peacocks white as crimson Geese,
There sate a Rat upon a Holland Cheese:
No sooner did blind Bayard see the sight,
Two beauteous ugly Witches took their flight
To tell the King of China wondrous news,
How all Scotch Knaves were hang'd and English Jews.
Th'Athenian Hidra, and the Bird Torpedo
Were catcht in France in Mouse-traps near Toledo.
A Scolopendra comming neare Pickthatch,
Made drunke a Constable and stole his watch.
Do what you can, Madge howlet is an Owle:
And Beans with Buttermilke is rare wilde Fowle.
The Coblers daughter, wee three both together,
Wee'le match, he'l give a thousand pieces with her;
Besides the smoake of Keinsam and Bell-Swagger,
Who oft at Mims did use his dudgeon Dagger:
Then shall the Perecranians of the East,
South, North, and West, with every Bird and Beast;
All knuckle deep in Paphlagonian Sands,

blind Bayard] mythical horse, subject of proverbial saying 'Who so bold as blind
Bayard?' (Tilley, *Dictionary of Proverbs*, B112)   Hidra] Hydra, many-headed
monster   Torpedo] electric ray (a fish)   Scolopendra] mythical fish
which, 'feeling himself taken with a hooke, casteth out his bowels, untill he
hath unloosed the hooke, and then swalloweth them up againe' (Bullokar,
English Expositor)   Pickthatch] Pickt-Hatch, notorious brothel-tavern in
Clerkenwell, London   Madge howlet] barn-owl   Keinsam] perhaps
Keynsham, in Somerset   Bell-Swagger . . . at Mims] see Longer Notes,
p. 289   dudgeon dagger] short dagger with handle made of dudgeon (root
of the box-tree)   Perecranians] pericraniums, used loosely to mean skulls,
brains or heads   Paphlagonian] of area in Anatolia (modern Turkey)

Inhabite Transylvanian Netherlands:
'Tis the onely gallant way to gaine promotion,
To squeese Oyle from the Cindars of Devotion,
Translate our Rownd head Turnips into Carrets,
And turne the lowest Cellars to high Garrets:
Let Neptune be a shepheard, and let Vulcan
Make hast to Greeneland, and there drinke his full Kan.
Titus Andronicus hath writ a Treatise,
Of Molehils in the Entrailes of Dame Theatis,
Wherein a man may learn before he looks
To catch mince-pies with neither nets nor hooks:
There policy with practise cut and dri'd
Were carted both in triumph through Cheapside.
If Monday hang himselfe no further seek.
Henceforward Tuesday shall begin the week.
No more of that I pray, I am afear'd
Ther's not one hair upon Diana's beard.
Great Agamemnon late combin'd with Hector,
To preach at Amsterdam an Irish Lector,
Which shall convert the Horse, the Asse, and Mule
And all the Beasts in Hipperborean Thule
If Sun-shine will with shaddowes but content
We'le make the winter of our discontent
To force fierce Crook-back into better tune,
And turne Decembers heat to frost in June.
When this externall substance of my soule
Did live at Liberty, I caught wild fowle,

Titus Andronicus . . . Theatis] text here from *Nonsence upon Sence*; *Essence of Nonsence* inverts the order of these lines, and prints 'entrance' for 'Entrailes'
Titus Andronicus] subject of Shakespeare's play   Theatis] Thetis, a
sea-goddess   Cheapside] street in City of London   If Monday hang
himselfe] see Longer Notes, p. 292   *Henceforward*] Henceforth *Essence of Nonsence*; Henceforward *Nonsence upon Sence*   Diana's] moon-goddess and
goddess of hunting   Agamemnon] commander of Greek forces in Trojan
War   Hector] commander of Trojan forces in Trojan War   Lector]
lecture   Hipperborean] Hyperborean, in the far north   Thule] island in
the far north   Crook-back] apparently a reference to Richard III

I was a Caitiffe in the Court of Spaine,
And playd at shuttle-cock with Charlemaine:
Then I did magnifie and mundifie,
Then I the Fairy Queen did putrifie,
And purifie againe, and dignifie,
All such as did her greatnesse deifie,
Females did edifie and fructifie,
And Amplifie and coldly gratifie.
The Lake of Lerna I did clarifie,
My Verse the Aethiop Queen did beautifie,
With rage my patience I would qualifie,
I can both certifie and testifie
How death did live, and life did mortifie:
Feare alwayes did my courage fortifie:
He's crafty that his wits can rectifie,
To villifie, make glad and terrifie,
And with coarse words old debts to satisfie,
That man Ile ratifie and notifie
To be one that himselfe will Justifie,
And fie, fo, fum, concludes him with O fie:
Thus from complexions I have Mineralls drawne,
Brave Captaine Fumble layd his sword to pawn
To ransome Jeffrey Chaucers Cipresse Gowne.
Thersitis with a Rush knockt Ajax downe
Imperious Momus wrote th'Atlantick story
Of wars betwixt Achilles and John Dory:
'Twas dedicated to the Isle of Lundy,
An Embleame right of *transit gloria mundi.*

Caitiffe] Caiftiffe *Essence of Nonsence*: a captive, or more generally a wretched
person   mundifie] mundify, purify, clean   Lake of Lerna]
dwelling-place of the Hydra   *coarse*] course *Essence of Nonsence*   Captaine
Fumble] unidentified   Cipresse] fine transparent cloth, used for veils
Thersitis] Thersites, ill-natured Greek soldier at Trojan War   Ajax] Greek
hero of Trojan War   Momus] god of satire   Achilles] Greek hero of
Trojan War   John Dory] French pirate, hero of popular ballad; also, a type
of fish   Isle of Lundy] island in Bristol Channel   transit gloria mundi]
'(so) passes the glory of the world'

Thus the great Amadis de Gal was able
With Nonsence (like sence) to endure a Fable.
Thus Mirmidons, upon the plains of Sarum
Did beat up Pompies quarters with alarum.
Let not the distances of place molest us,
Abidos is not forty miles from Sestus:
As Hero lov'd Leander, I'le agree,
Though he and she were mad, what's that to me?
Tis like Cleopatra and Antonius
Met, but saw not the Cardinal Baronius:
The Capitol, and silken Rock Tarpeyus
In a Seadan to Lichfield shall convey us;
And like a wheel-barrow we'l cut and curry,
And fetch good news from Shropshire and from Surry:
There is no Eunuch of the Race of Brutus,
That either can confute us, or cornute us.
Old Solon was no jester, nor no jyber,
And English Thames is better than Rome's Tyber:
I took a Camel, and to Naples went I,
Of pickled Sausedges I found great plenty:
The Gudgeon catcher there o'retop'd the Nobles,
And put the Vice Roy in a peck of troubles:
Brave rag tag multitude of Omnium Gatherum,

Thus the great . . . alarum] these four lines are not in *Nonsence upon Sence*
Amadis de Gal] Amadis of Gaul, hero of famous French and Spanish prose
romance of chivalry   Mirmidons] Myrmidons, industrious people on
southern borders of Thessaly   plains of Sarum] Salisbury plain
Pompies] Pompey's (Roman general who fought against Caesar in Civil
War)   Abidos . . . Sestus] cities on either side of the Hellespont
(Bosphorus)   Hero . . . Leander] Leander, youth from Abydos, was in love
with Hero, priestess of Sestos, and swam across the Hellespont to meet
her   Antonius] Marcus Antonius, who fell in love with Cleopatra
Cardinall Baronius] Caesar Baronius (1538–1607), influential Italian Cardinal
and prolific ecclesiastical historian   Tarpeyus] Tarpeius, precipice on edge
of Capitoline hill in Rome, where condemned men were thrown to their
deaths   Seadan] sedan chair   Race of Brutus] according to myth, Brutus
was the ancestor of British kings   cornute] give horns to (i.e. cuckold)
Solon] early Greek law-giver   jyber] jiber, maker of jibes   Omnium
Gatherum] confused medley

Shuffle 'um together, and the Devill father'um:
But now and then was squez'd a rich Delinquent,
By which good means away the precious chink went:
Renowned was the Raskall Massennello,
In fifteen dayes he was raw, ripe, and mellow.
Laugh, laugh, thou whining Foole Heraclitus,
And weep thou grinning Asse Democritus:
The grey Horse is the better Mare by halfe,
The Bull at Bear-Garden, and Walthams Calfe
Are reconcil'd, but not concluded fully
Who pleaded best, Demosthenes or Tully:
I am indifferent, fill the other Kan,
Logick hath art to make an Ape a man.
I weeping sing, to think upon the Quiblins
Twixt Romane, and Imperiall Guelphs and Giblins.
How Munsters John a Leide, and Knipperdoling
Were barbarous Barbers in the art of poling.
From Sence and Nonsence, I am wide, quoth Wallice,
But not so far as Oxford is from Callice:
Give me a Leash of merry blades, right Bilboes,
True tatter'd Rogues in Breech, Shirts, Skirts, and Elboes,

chink] cash, coins   Massennello] Mas' (Tommaso) Aniello, fisherman who led revolution in Naples in 1647 and ruled there for nine days   Heraclitus] melancholy Greek philosopher   Democritus] Greek philosopher famous for laughing at follies of mankind   Bull at Bear-Garden] tavern in Bear Garden, also known as Paris Garden, area on south bank of Thames famous for bear-baiting and brothels   Walthams Calfe] proverbial symbol of stupidity: 'As wise as *Walthams* calf, who went nine miles to suck a Bull, and came home as dry as he went' (Howell, *Paroimiographia*, p. 6; Tilley, *Dictionary of Proverbs*, W22)   Demosthenes] famous Greek orator   Tully] Marcus Tullius Cicero, famous Roman orator and philosopher   Quiblins] quibbles, tricks or arguments   Guelphs and Giblins] Guelphs and Ghibellines, pro-papal and pro-imperial factions in medieval Italy   Munsters John a Leide] John of Leiden (Jan Beukels), Anabaptist who led uprising in city of Münster in 1534   Knipperdoling] Bernhard Knipperdolling, German Anabaptist and supporter of John of Leiden, beheaded in 1536   poling] polling, beheading   Wallice] probably Sir William Wallace (1272–1305), leader of Scottish resistance to England and hero of epic poem   Callice] Calais   Leash] set of three   Bilboes] type of sword (of superior quality)

And each of them will make a fit Disciple
To ride up Holborn to the tree that's triple:
A man may think his purse is quite turn'd Round-head,
When all the crosses in it are confounded:
'Tis sayd that Poetry a thriving trade is,
And gets a world of wealth from Lords and Ladies;
The Devill they do, false shamefull Lown thou ly'st,
And when thou canst no longer live, thou dy'st.
Lend me Rhamnussnes Flanders blade, Ile lash
The sober Centaure, turn great Oaks to Ash:
A long Devils broath, be sure you bring a spoon,
Our mornings shall begin at afternoon;
And Minos, Eacus, nor Rhadamantus
May rore and rant, but never shall out rant us.
As we are Temporall, let's be Temporizers,
We scorn to be surpriz'd, we'l be surprizers:
Let's make grim Pluto stink, the welkin rumble,
And Hollophernes bluster, blow, and grumble,
Rending up mighty Thistles by the roots,
Because an Ostler stole away his boots:
Then with a multiplying Gally pot,
Ile know the projects of the crafty Scot;
And then he shall be forc'd to hide his head
In Tenebris, in Poland, or in Swead:
Fough, this Tobacco stinks; thou dirty Hag,

tree that's triple] gallows, at Tyburn (approached from City of London via
High Holborn)   Round-head ... crosses] coins had crosses on them, and
Puritans disapproved of making the sign of the cross (cf. Nashe, *Works*, ii,
p. 223: 'his purse was aged in emptines, and I think verily a puritane, for it kept
it selfe from any pollution of crosses')   Lown] offensive term used for
inferior or stupid people   Rhamnussnes] Rhamnus was the site of a famous
statue of Nemesis (goddess of divine retribution); hence Rhamnusia, a name
for Nemesis   Flanders blade] sword of superior quality, made in
Flanders   Minos ... Rhadamantus] the three judges of the underworld
Pluto] god of underworld   Hollophernes] Holophernes, mighty general
of the Assyrians, killed by Judith (see Apocrypha, Book of Judith)
multiplying] term used to describe telescopes and microscopes   Gally pot]
small glazed pot   In Tenebris] 'in darkness'   Swead] Sweden

Stand further near, Ile put thee in a bag.
Search Asia, Affrick and America,
To find the Goddesse Berecinthia,
And know how Pirramus and Thisbe fell
Together by the eares late in Bridewell.
Words are but wind in Terme time, but Vacations
Are fit to publish silent Proclamations.
There was a business never understood,
The woman's suit in Law was just and good:
She lost the day, this did her Cause disgrace,
The Lawyer put some ill into her Case.
Before Ile live this life, Ile take a knife,
And drown my selfe, and then what needs a Wife?
Strange things are done by Art and humane power,
Quinborow Castle landed neare the Tower.
Much like a Prodigy old time played Rex:
A Kentish Castle came to Middlesex.
May not a man cal'd Newgate dwell at Higate,
And wed a Widdow at the Pie at Algate?
Therefore let us like or dislike Presbytery,
It will worke finely if it once besquitter ye.
Bring me a Salamander from Surat in France,
The Alps and the Pirenian hils shall dance.
In Greenewich Parke there smiling Nioby

Stand further near] Abato fair *Nonsence upon Sence*   Berecinthia] Cybele,
fertility goddess   *Pirramus and Thisbe fell*] Pirramus and this befell, *Essence
of Nonsence*; Pirramus and Thisbe fell *Nonsence upon Sence*: Pyramus and Thisbe
were famous lovers in Babylon, who both died after a tragic
misunderstanding   *by the ears*] by the years *Essence of Nonsence*; by the eares
Nonsence upon Sence   Bridewell] London prison   case] probably a play
on both the legal meaning and the meaning 'clothes' or 'body'   Quinborow]
Queenborough, port on the Isle of Sheppey, Kent   Rex] 'king'   Newgate
. . . Higate] Newgate was also a district (with a prison) in the City of London;
Highgate was a village north of London   the Pie at Algate] famous tavern
(mentioned by Taylor in *Taylors Travels*, p. 47) at Aldgate, on eastern side of
City of London   besquitter] transitive verb coined from the intransitive
'to squitter', to have diarrhoea   Surat] town in India where Coryate
died   Pirenian] Pyrenean   Nioby] Niobe, boastful woman punished by
the gods

Shall laugh and lye downe like an Oyster Pye.
Fame is a lying slut, she told me tayles,
That in October Christmas came from Wales:
Believe it take the wings of Icarus,
And walke to Hounsditch, and to Erebus,
There tell them playnly how the case stands here,
And bring us word how matters do goe there.
Unto the Market Ile run presently,
And there a peck of troubles I will buy,
One told me they would multiply and grow:
All England with them I will plant and sow.
Which as they ripen dayly Ile take care
That every living soule shall have a share:
Ile serve myselfe first, and Ile have such store
In time of need to serve a thousand more.
But I forget my Theame. O foule offence!
This nonsence hath a taste of too much sence:
The Asse, Goos, Woodcock, Buzard, and the Gull,
Beat out their brains, and put them in my scull;
And tell the men of Gotham tis thought fit
The Wisemen there should lend me all their wit:
For Nonsence I will tax all Christendome,
Great Emperours and Kings shall pay me some,
And many a Major, or justice of the Peace
Will give me tribute and the Tax encrease
To such a height, that Cardinals from Rome,
Cuckolds, and Costables shall pay me some:
Strong Hull, with fatal Hell, and Hallifax,
Shall naturally bring me tole and tax:

Icarus] son of Daedalus who flew with artificial wings from Crete, fell, and
drowned in the sea   Hounsditch] Houndsditch, street in City of London
Erebus] part of underworld   Asse ... Gull] all proverbial symbols of
stupidity or credulity   Gotham] Nottinghamshire village famous for
idiocy   Major] mayor   Costables] constables   Hull ... Hallifax] a
proverbial beggar's litany began: 'From Hell, Hull, and Halifax' (Tilley,
Dictionary of Proverbs, H399); Kingston upon Hull and Halifax had strong
penal laws against begging   tole] toll

The mighty stock of Nonsence I will win
Shalbe the universal Magazine,
For Universities to worke upon
The Rich Philosophers admired Stone:
Then I make Poets rich, and Usurers poor;
And thus resolv'd at this time write no more.

This dedication is humbly directed to a living man, quartered into four Offices (*viz.*) a Scavenger, a Beadle, a Cobler, and halfe a Constable.

To the high and mighty *Davidius Vulcanus*, Duke and Dominator of the Dunghils, and absolute, resolute, dissolute, Scavenger of the Town and Territories of *Gravesend* in *Norfolk*, great Master and Baron of the Wheel-barrow, the only Farmer, Transporter, Lord of the Soyle, and Privy searcher of all Mixens, and Muckhils, simple or compound, in the Liberties aforesaid. Cleanser, Clearer, and avoyder of the most Turpitudinous, Merdurinous, excrementall offals, Muck, and Garbage. Refiner, Purger, Clarifier, Purifier, Mundifier, Excluder, and Expulser of the Putrifactious and Pestiferous Contagions; the *Potentissimo, Excellentissimo*, Invader, Scatterer, Disperser, Consumer, and Confounder of offensive and unsavoury savours, smels, scents, and Vapours: Great Soldan, Sultan, and Grand Signiour over all varieties of stinks, and stinkards; most Triumphant Termigant, unresistable Conqueror and Commander of the major and minor (the great and the less) Turditarians, chief Corrigidor & Beadle of all the Precinct, sole Transplanter,

write no more] write more *Nonsence upon Sence*   Davidius Vulcanus] invented name   Gravesend] town in Kent   Mixens] middens, dung-hills   avoyder] voider, emptyer   Merdurinous] consisting of dung and urine   Mundifier] purifier   Potentissimo, Excellentissimo] 'most powerful, most excellent'   Soldan] sultan   Termigant] imaginary deity, supposed to be worshipped by Muslims and characterized by a very violent temper   Turditarians] invented name   Corrigidor] corregidor, Spanish magistrate

Terrifier, Controller, and Corrector of Beggers and Vaga-
bonds. The terrible Hue and Cry, Cryer, chiefe Court-
Cryer, Jayle Keeper, and only Confiner of the Hogs; chiefe
and most frequent vigilant Watchman, demy-Constable,
and Image of Authority, the most accomplished Cobler,
exquisite Translator, and exact Reformer of oppressed,
decayed, wicked, & oppressed soals: And the only judiciary
rectifier, underlayer, and setter upright of such Brethren
and Sisters as doe goe aside, and tread their foot awry in
these dayes of Vanity, and paths of Iniquity: In hope (Great
Sir) I have not abated you of the least tittle of your title,
your Honorable stile being so high, that no Christian,
Pagan, Heathen, Turk, Jew, Infidell, Cuckold, or Canni-
ball, can never climb to the top of it, there being a late
report that your multiplicity and many affaires of State
have disturbed your rest, & impaired your health, inso-
much as it is thought your pericranion is crazed or cracked,
and you thereby in danger to fall into a Callenturian disease, which is to be doubted may produce a Vertigo in
your head, wherby your wit may be troubled with a
superfluous flux, which may prove a molestation to your
selfe, and the whole Town, that hath in it selfe, and in
every place round about it, more trouble then they can
well bear. But if their hard fortune should be, that when
you are working to your own Ends, and that you should
call for your Aule, and death should mistake and bring
you your Last, whereby such a privy member as your selfe
might be publickely lost; it is feared, griefe would overflow
the whole town, and that some of the Townesmen (with
the help of their Wives) would run starke horne mad: To
prevent this great detriment of such a losse as that Town
may undergo in this time of scarcity of wit, wisedome, and

pericranion] pericranium, used loosely to mean skull, brain or head
Callenturian disease] calenture, tropical disease characterized by fever and
delirium   Aule] awl   bring you your Last] a common pun   horne
mad] enraged; often with implication of having been cuckolded

wise men; for feare you should fall into the dangerous
diseases of the Mubble-fubbles, or the grumbling of the
Gizzard: Therefore to drive away dumps, and to give you
some Recreation, I have made bold to present your greatnesse with this Dedication, which if you will vouchsafe
but to read and understand, and in so doing you shall do
more for the Author, then he ever was or shall do himselfe.

J.T.

Allandro pasqueto Valatrumpa entangrino livroe.

Il vento Chioli, Mauritambull Teda fulgare,
Antro della campo il Danto Corda sublima
Pantathos, streno standina eschine vandri
Bene in shendo, tircia, penthe dissadi.
Mecrops Sans fida vocifera Randa Bavinea,
Allatendrea quanto, Eltrada Pizminoy venta,
Mega Pollimunton, Theorba quasi quicunque
Tripolina Tiphon, Quabacondono sapho.
Terra tragmus sophye, sunt diacalcitheo Geata.
Avostre Obserdandi Zhean De Fistye Cankie De Sallamanca
Andalowsia.

Or thus you may English it, in the transcending prayse of
the Authour and his Booke.

Till PHOEBUS blustring blasts shall cease to blow,
And AEOLUS shall hide his radiant Rayes

Mubble-fubbles] nervous depression   Allandro . . . Geata] these nonsense
macaronics contain some genuine French, Italian, Latin and Greek words, as
well as invented words, but make no overall sense; the 'English' which follows
is not a translation   *Valatrumpa*] Mallatrumpa *Nonsence upon Sence*
Zhean De Fistye Cankie] invented name, suggesting 'fistula' and 'canker'
Sallamanca Andalowsia] Salamanca is in Castile   Phoebus] Phoebus Apollo,
the sun   Aeolus] god of winds

Till VULCANS Forge be fram'd of Scithian Snow,
And NEPTUNE like a Shepheard spend his dayes;
When SATURNE shall sell Mouse traps and allow
MARS to sing Madrigals, and round delayes:
The shall thy Book and thee be out of Date,
And scorn the envy of consuming Fate.
To your Worthinesse in all observance Devoted, John
Defistie Cankie of Sallamanca in *Andalusia.*

The Second Part to the same Sence.

When as a Woodcock did a Phoenix hatch,
Once in the Raigne of Julian the Apostate,
When Spiders Nets an Elephant did catch,
The Alehouse had no fire to make a Toast at;
Then in those merry lamentable dayes,
Upon a Christmas Eve near Michaelmas,
New Market heath did hoarsly sing the praise
Of Apuleius, or the Golden Asse.
The Adamantine fall of seven fold Nile,
Had boyled Musk-Millions from the Mount Pernassus,
Whereas the sing song wanton Crocodile
Made Romane Cressus smile, and Lidian Crassus,
When Charing Crosse the Sun of Summers Leg,
Had Kitned in the eyelids of a Nowne,

round delayes] roundelays, a type of song   envy] fury *Nonsence upon*
Sence   John Defistie Cankie] invented name, suggesting 'fistula' and
'canker'   Julian the Apostate] Julian, nephew of Constantine the Great,
became Roman Emperor in 261 and abjured Christianity   New Market heath]
area outside Newmarket, Suffolk, used for hunting and horse-racing
Apuleius . . . Golden Asse] Apuleius (b. 125), author of picaresque tale, 'The
Golden Ass' (*Metamorphoses*)   Musk-Millions] musk-melons, i.e. the
common melon   Pernassus] Parnassus, mountain sacred to the
Muses   Cressus . . . Crassus] there was no Roman of note called 'Cressus';
perhaps a confused reference to the famously rich Roman politician and
general, Crassus, and the famously rich king of Lydia, Croesus   Charing
Crosse] memorial cross at western end of the Strand, London

And Christmas Carrols played at Mumble peg,
With the Buls pizzel of a Market Towne;
Then shall a Pronowne and a Participle
Fight doggedly for wagging of a straw,
And then Tom Thum with Gogmagog shall tipple,
And shew the Learnedst Lawyers what is Law.
Then Ghastly flesh of shillings fry'd in steaks,
And Oyntments drawn from warm ingratitude
Did draw the teeth of two and forty weeks
From out the heels of sqemish magnitude.
But yet (O yet) a new laid Madrigall
Had bak'd the haunches of a Spanish child,
And matcht 'em to Sir Guy the Seneschall,
Who liv'd Adulterously with Bosworth field,
Whilest this was doing, all undone, and Done,
As men undoe a Trout to make a Loach,
For as with spoons a Lord may eat the Sun,
So layes a Bitch her Litter in a Coach.
The Times have beene, (but Time is turn'd to pap)
That men might speake like Sea-crabs with a Quill,
And old Devotion wore a corner'd Cap
Upon the Stomack of a Water-mill.
But as a Bag pipe flying through the Ayre,
Doth water all the Earth with Scottish Jigs,
So Times to change their turns at Sturbridge Faire;

Mumble peg] game in which players take turns to throw a knife at the ground;
the player who fails to make it stick there has to draw out of the ground with
his teeth a peg driven in by blows of the knife's handle   pizzel] pizzle,
penis; a bull's pizzle was used as a flogging instrument   Tom Thum] Tom
Thumb, tiny hero of popular ballad   Gogmagog] Gog and Magog were
two giants brought in chains to London by Brutus; in a later version of the
myth, 'Gogmagog' was a single giant, transformed into a hill near
Cambridge   sqemish] squeamish   Sir Guy the Seneschall] Guy of
Warwick, hero of popular romance   Bosworth field] site (in Leicestershire)
of battle in which Henry Tudor defeated Richard III (1485)   Sturbridge
Faire] famous annual fair, held outside Cambridge

For all the World now rides on Ale and Wigs.
O that my wings could bleat like butter'd pease,
But bleating and my Lungs have caught the itch,
Which are as musty as the Irish Seas,
Which in their left side now have both the Stich.
I grant indeed, that Rainbows layd to sleep,
Snort like a Woodknife in a Ladies eyes,
Which makes her bark to see a Pudding creep,
For creeping puddings alwayes please the Wise.
The force of custome makes a man to pisse
A cast of Merlins in King Dido's mouth:
Hence comes the squint ey'd Proverb, which is this,
All men are borne their backsides to the South.
A Letter late came from the Stygian Lake
That told me Cerberus himselfe had choak'd:
He took a Milstone for a butter'd Cake,
When first red Herrings were at Yarmouth smoak'd:
The Orientall Chilblains of the West
Flew like a Colliflower in Chequer broath,
And then the Fairy Queen in Buckrum drest,
Rod through the Ayre well mounted on a Moth.
Man as he is a Cloakbag, is a fish,

Wigs] a type of bread roll or bap, often eaten with ale; cf. Taylor, *Workes*, sig.
L5ᵛ: 'round halfe-penny loaves are transform'd into square wigges, (which
wigges like drunkards are drown'd in their Ale)'. The whole phrase plays on
the saying 'All the world now runs on wheels', a popular complaint (by watermen,
among others) against the introduction of coaches to Elizabethan London
butter'd pease] apart from its literal meaning, this may possibly refer to
'Buttered Peas', a popular English country dance (see Walpole, *Letters*, i,
p. 32)   Snort] snore   Woodknife] dagger, used by huntsmen for cutting
up game   to see a pudding creep] see Longer Notes, p. 293   cast of
Merlins] in hawking, a cast is more than one bird (usually, a couple) cast off
the hand simultaneously; merlins are a type of small hawk. This phrase may
have bawdy overtones: Ray recorded 'He keeps a cast of Merlins' as a
proverbial phrase for a 'wencher' (*Collection of English Proverbs*, p. 89)
King Dido's] Dido was Queen of Carthage   Stygian Lake] lake formed by
river Styx, in underworld   Cerberus] dog guarding underworld
Yarmouth] port in Norfolk, famous for smoked herrings   Chequer broath]
broth made from chequers, the fruit of the wild Service tree   Buckrum]
buckram, stiffened canvas   *Man*] Min *Essence of Nonsense*

But as a humane Creature he's a Cock:
Which boyld with pindust in a Chafing dish,
Eats like stew'd Mustard made in Vulcans smock.
Once in an evening when the morning Sun
Did hotly speak with cold Meridian splendor;
There was a jolly Frier told a Nun
That Feminine was Masculine Male Gender.
Things have their times, as Oysters have their wool:
Dogs have their dayes, as Distaffes have their Gall,
So all men living ought to dwell at Hull,
For Hallifax cannot containe them all.
A statesman once corrupted is a Gun,
That ferrets Screachowls from Bellona's Beard,
To make a handsome Codpiece for the Sun
To were upon the pommell of his Sword.
Man unto Man, is Man; but Man to Man,
Is Herrings flesh, made of a yard of Ale,
With the ingredients of a Dripping pan,
Whiles Pancradge Church begets an Issue Male.
An Oxe was lately in a Mouse-trap taken;
Read but the booke of Weekly Newes, and note
How many stock-fishes were made fat Bacon,
Broyl'd on the Top-mast of a Mussell Boat,
New Hieroglyphick three-fold twisted Lines
Of things that were, and were not, how Augustus
With Ovids Metamorphoses combines,
To try us oftentimes, but never trust us.
The faculties of every humane soule
Are made of Turpentine and Venson bones:
Ingendred in the night-cap of an Owle

humane] human   pindust] glittering residue of filings, etc., resulting from
manufacture of pins   Bellona's] goddess of war   were] wear
Pancradge Church] St Pancras Church, in Needlers Lane in the City of
London   Issue Male] genealogist's term for a son   stock-fishes] dried
fish (usually cod)   Augustus] Roman emperor (ruled 31 BC – AD 14)

That gives a Glister to the Torrid-Zones:
For as a Pistoll lisps when he doth court
Three paire of guts, bound up in true loves knots,
So Easter Terme is curtold but in sport,
While Hobby-horses cur'd are of the Bots.
Then smoth thy brow with milk-white discontent,
And raise thy spirits up beneath thy feet:
For Shrovetide now hath swallow'd Jack-a-lent
Because few Marriners are in the Fleet.
I know I am a man abhorr'd of Bells
That ring in Conclave of an Heteroclite;
I know the Cuckolds thoughts of Bath and Wels,
Do fizzle like a Mil-stone in a Net.
I saw, but what I view'd, I never saw
A row of Teeth penfeatherd in a Trowt,
Whilst Perkins Horse orethrew a Case in Law,
And he himselfe got fee farme of the Gowt.
How can a Mayor Rule, but with a Lask,
That may squirt Steeples in the teeth of Fame?
For if they do, their touch-stone and their Flask
Will fill the Winde with Polecats of the name.
The clock doth strike when time bewrayes his hose,
And Oysters catch the cough with being kinde:
As Puttocks weare their Buttocks in their nose,
So Fables weare their Bables in their minde.

Glister] clyster, suppository or enema   Torrid-Zones] region of the earth
between the tropics   curtold] curtailed (literally, has its tail docked)   Bots]
a parasite-borne disease of horses   smoth] smooth   Jack-a-lent]
originally, a doll-like figure pelted with stones during Lent; more generally, a comic
personification of Lent, figuring in Carnival pageants   *Conclave*] Concave
Essence of Nonsense   Heteroclite] eccentric, person who diverges from
common standards   Bathe and Wels] Bath and Wells, diocese in West of
England   fizzle] make the sound of a quiet fart   penfeatherd] term used
for the half-developed quills of a young bird   Perkins Horse]
unidentified   fee farme] type of land-tenure involving fixed rent   Lask]
diarrhoea   of the name] famous   bewrayes] bewrays, exposes, reveals the
true character of   Puttocks] type of bird of prey; hence, rapacious people
Bables] baubles

I grant indeed, that whoso may and can,
Can never may, sith may doth can obey;
But he that can and will, may will as man,
But man can will, yet his will cannot may.
Call True the Taylor hither presently,
For he must make a mantle for the Moone:
Bid Atlas from his shoulders shake the sky,
And lend and send me his left handed spoone.
For Pride's a Pitchfork that the waine doth fill
Of Ursa Mayor (God of Apple-Cakes,)
Sloath is the Cucking stoole of Holborne hill,
Much like a Sope-boyler upon a Jakes.
Oh that I were in love with Bobbin-lace
Or great with child of Tullies purple Gowne;
Then to mine Ankles I would skrew my face,
To make a Paire of Boots for black Renowne.
Faine would I leave, but leave at me doth grin,
As doth a Custard when his nails doth ake;
Or like a blew Bore in a Pudding skin,
So I must manners leave for manners sake.
Then rest my Rimes, before my reason's done,
For women are all Wag tayles when they run:
   Who sets his wits my Sence to undermine, is
   A cunning man at Nonsence, farewell, Finis.

I grant . . . cannot may] these four lines carry a marginal annotation: 'Deep
Philosophy'   *obey*] abey *Essence of Nonsence*   True the Taylor] tailors
were proverbially dishonest: 'Whip, says the Tailor, whir, says the shears, /
Take a true Taylor and cut off his ears'; 'When Tailors are true there is little
good to sew' (Tilley, *Dictionary of Proverbs*, T19, T25)   Atlas] titan who
carried the heavens on his shoulders   *waine*] waile *Essence of Nonsence*;
waine *Nonsence upon Sence*   Ursa Mayor] Ursa Major, the Great Bear,
constellation also known as Charles's Wain   Cucking stoole] (not a misprint
for ducking-stool, but the original term): a chair to which miscreants were
tied, in which they were then either exposed to public ridicule, or ducked under
water. There was a well-known one at Holborn Ditch in London   Jakes]
lavatory   Bobbin-lace] lace made on a pillow with bobbins   Tullies]
Marcus Tullius Cicero, Roman orator and philosopher   Wag tayles]
wag-tails, a type of bird   Finis] 'the end'

*The third part of the fourth Edition to the five Senses,
or Sence aforesaid.*

Ile say no more, but what I mean to speak,
And speaking what I say shall silence break.
Mumbudget, let no words be utter'd neither,
Let's seperate our speeches close together.
Reach my fierce flye-flap, *Van Trump*, stand aloofe,
My Arms and Armour's close Committee Proofe;
Give me a Butterbox with not a rag on,
I'le pickle him like to a Dutch flap Draggon:
An Ordinance of Parliament shall scatter ye,
Our Ordinance is Ordnance, that can batter ye.
Me vat a whee, is Cambria Brittish French,
Dick shifts a Trencher, but Tom keeps the Trench.
An Annagram is John King, and King John,
Five quarters of one year is four to one:
May not a Miser wale a poor mans want,
And give him lodging, cloathing, and provant,
And hang himselfe, and give the Devill his due,
Perhaps the Newes is too good to be true.
I care not where mine Hostess, and mine Host lie,
T'have meat and drink for nothing, is not costly.
I could have written mad verse, sad verse, glad verse,
But you shall be contented now with bad verse;
I neither weep or sing of sweet Rebellion,
Or story old I list not now to tell ye on:
The Royall mad Lancastrians, and Yorkists

Mumbudget] phrase meaning 'keep mum', 'stay silent'; originally, a game
Van Trump] Maarten Tromp, admiral who led Dutch fleet against the British
in 1653   close Committee] from 'in close committee', phrase for committee
meetings held *in camera*   Butterbox] popular term of abuse for
Dutchmen   *not a rag*] not on rag *Essence of Nonsense*   flap Draggon]
flap-dragon, a flambéd raisin, quenched when eaten; also a contemptuous
term for a German or Dutchman (*OED* cites Taylor, elsewhere, in this
sense)   Me vat a whee] see Longer Notes, p. 291   Cambria] Wales
wale] choose   provant] provender, food

Scarce harm'd so much as some cornuted Forkists,
The most uncivill civill Goths and Vandals
Did not on their owne Countrey bring such scandals.
The Turks, the Jews, the Canibals and Tartars
Ne're kept such wicked, rude, unruly quarters.
Jerusalem's, Eleazer, John, and Simon
Did ne're yield Poet baser stuff to rime on.
Like bloudy Sylla, and consuming Marius,
One mischiefe did into another carry us.
Amongst all Trades (some thousands zealous Widgeons)
Were hardly more in number than Religions.
In Preachers Roomes were Preach'd, for which I woe am,
The basest people Priests like Jeroboam.
That one may say of London, what a Town is't?
It harbours in it many a Corbraind Brownist:
Tis scatter'd full of Sects, alas how apt is't
To be a Familist, or Anabaptist!
Whilst Knaves (of both sides) with Religions Mantle,
Have rifled England by patch, piece, and Cantle;
That I may say of thee O London, London,
What hath thy Wealth, Wit, Sword, & furious Gun
        done?
And what hath many a mothers wicked son done?
Whereby (against their wills) there's many undone.
Thrice happy had it been for our tranquility,

Scarce] Scare *Essence of Nonsence*   cornuted] cuckolded   Forkists]
apparently an invented term for those whose heads are 'forked', i.e. bearing
cuckold's horns   Goths and Vandals] barbarian tribes which attacked the
late Roman Empire   *Jerusalem's Eleazer*] Jerusalems, Eleazer *Essence of
Nonsence*: Eliezer was a priest in Jerusalem (1 Chron. 15: 24)   John, and
Simon] probably the Apostles John the Evangelist and Simon (Peter); or possibly
Simon (Peter) and his father, whose name was Jonas   Sylla . . . Marius]
Sulla and Marius, Roman generals, fought a bitter civil war until the latter's
death in 86 BC   Jeroboam] leader of revolt against Rehoboam, successor to
Solomon (see 1 Kings 11–15)   Corbraind] presumably a word coined from
'cor' or 'cor-fish', a small cod   Brownist] follower of Robert Browne
(1550?–1633?), radical Puritan and leader of 'separatist' movement   Familist]
member of 'Family of Love', radical Anabaptist movement founded in Holland
in 1566   Cantle] a portion cut out from a piece of cloth

If th'Authours of this incivility
Had been a little check'd by *Gregory Brandon*,
With each of them a hempen twisted band on.

Finis

Source: *The Essence of Nonsence upon Sence* (London, 1653) (collated with *Nonsence upon Sence* (London, 1651)). Both texts contain a poem of 101 lines on 'the sad death of a Scottish Nag', preceding the section entitled 'The Second Part to the same Sence'; this is not a nonsense poem, and is excluded here.

Gregory Brandon] famous hangman of London   Finis] 'the end'

18

JOHN TAYLOR AND ANON.

Non-sense

Oh that my Lungs could bleat like butter'd pease;
But bleating of my lungs hath caught the itch,
And are as mangy as the Irish Seas,
That doth ingender windmills on a Bitch.

I grant that Rainbowes being lull'd asleep,
Snort like a woodknife in a Ladies eyes;
Which maks her grieve to see a pudding creep
For creeping puddings onely please the wise.

Not that a hard-row'd Herring should presum
To swing a tyth pig in a Cateskin purse;
For fear the hailstons which did fall at Rome
By lesning of the fault should make it worse.

The first eight lines are from Taylor, *The Essence of Nonsence upon Sence* (poem
17, p. 204). Bodl. MS Ashmole 38 attributes the poem to 'Sir Jeffery
Nonsence', an adaptation of Taylor's 'Sir Gregory Nonsence', possibly
intending a reminiscence of Jeffery Hudson, the dwarf who entertained Queen
Henrietta Maria.   butter'd pease] apart from its literal meaning, this may
possibly refer to 'Buttered Peas', a popular English country dance (see
Walpole, *Letters*, i, p. 32)   ingender] engender   Snort] snore
woodknife] dagger, used by huntsmen for cutting up game   to see a pudding
creep] see Longer Notes, p. 293   hard-row'd] hard roed, with a hard roe
tyth pig] pig given in payment as tythe   Cateskin] cat-skin   lesning]
lessening

For 'tis most certain Winter wool-sacks grow
From geese to swans, if men could keep them so,
Till that the sheep shorn Planets gave the hint
To pickle pancakes in Geneva print.

Some men there were that did supose the skie
Was made of Carbonado'd Antidotes;
But my opinion is a Whales left eye,
Need not be coyned all in King *Harry* groates

The reason's plain for *Charons* westerne barge
Running a tilt at the subjunctive mood,
Beckned to Bednal Green, & gave him charge
To fatten padlockes with Antartick food:

The end will be the Millponds must be laded,
To fish for whitepots in a Country dance;
So they that suffered wrong & were upbraded
Shal be made friends in a left-handed trance.

Source: *Wit and Drollery, Jovial Poems*, ed. Sir John Mennes and James
Smith (London, 1656), pp. 153–4. Also in Bodl. MS Ashmole 38, fo.
140ʳ, with minor variants. Later copies (in an early 18th-century hand)
are in BL MS Add. 4457, fos. 106ʳ, 107ʳ.

Geneva print] see Longer Notes, pp. 290–91   Carbonado'd] scored with a
knife and broiled over a fire   all in King] all King *Wit and Drollery*; and in
King *MS Ashmole 38*   King Harry groates] groats (coins worth four pence)
from reign of Henry VIII   Charon] boatman of the underworld
westerne barge] type of barge used on Thames upstream from London
Beckned] beckoned   Bednal Green] Bethnal Green, district north-east of
City of London   fatten] fasten *Wit and Drollery*; fatten *MS Ashmole 38*
Antartick] antarctic   laded] emptied with a ladle   whitepots] type of
custard, made with cream

19

ANON.

Nonsense fragment

Which rangeth Heteroclites in the Irish-pale,
To keepe off Ulster-men from takeing Hull.
The times are strang, & strang times catch the pipp,
By eating Alpes by spoonfulls through a Quill,
O then bee wise, heare, see, & hang the lipp,
And answer if need be like a forrest Bill.
For what heart can but melt away to flint,
To see a pitchforke court the wild of Kent,
That gathers all the garbage of the Print,
To give a Glister to an Argument.
O would a verbe Deponent would untruss,
And in times face sluce eighteen parts of speech
Sith in her Codpiece fame keeps Brittaines burse
Whilst all the Shopps breeds vermine in her breech.
No more my Muse no more, now thrust thy nose

This fragment contains words and phrases from John Taylor's *The Essence of Nonsence upon Sence* (poem 17); a long extract from that text (with some minor alterations) is in the same MS, fos. 140–41.
Heteroclites] eccentrics, people who diverge from common standards
Irish-pale] area of early English dominion in Ireland   strang] strange
pipp] pip, disease of poultry or hawks   forrest Bill] cutting instrument used
by foresters   wild of Kent] Weald of Kent, area between North and South
Downs   Glister] clyster, suppository or enema   verbe Deponent] in
Latin grammar, a verb with passive form but active meaning   sluce]
sluice   Sith] since   burse] purse, or bourse (financial exchange)

Into that taile-peece of a Seet at Maw,
And there efsoones grow fat on butter'd prose,
Leaving thy rimes to Lads that live by law.
Sith well they wote that a lean Barrons roote
Eates like a Stockfish that hath lost his foote.

Source: Bodl. MS Ashmole 36, fo. 144ʳ.

Seet] set (of cards)   Maw] popular card-game   efsoones] eftsoons, again,
soon afterwards   Sith] since   wote] wot, knew   Stockfish] dried
fish

ANON.

A sonnett to cover my Epistles taile peece

Lo I the man whom Fates have serv'd on Sopps
With two splay foote couples in the edge of night,
Am made a spectacle of Mowes and Mopps,
While reason butters all my ribs with fright.
Yet lo my Genius, crown'd with frigid Zones,
Doth grinn like lodgicke when shee hath the squirt,
Soe all my reasons ranckle in my bones,
While for the pox, I sweat witt through my shirt.
The time hath bin when my fur'd numbers rann
Like Hauks that sing the sack of Troy, in June;
But now my Scull is made a dripping pann,
Where grimm Minerva scummers out of tune:
The sweetnes of my lines then, I suppose
Will draw your ears to vomitt in your Nose.

Dear friend, and there's an End.

Source: Bodl. MS Ashmole 36, fo. 140ʳ.

Mowes and Mopps] grimaces   frigid Zones] arctic and antarctic   the
squirt] diarrhoea   Minerva] goddess Athene   scummers] scumbers,
defecates

T. W.

'I am asham'd of Thee, ô Paracelsie'

I am asham'd of Thee, ô Paracelsie,
I understand thou dwell'st not beyond Chelsie;
But th'Alpes is my Country, and I come
Where the Equinoctiall is Solstitium:
Where Aetna's fiery furnace still disgorges,
More furious flames than any in my forge is.
The great Etruscan Emperour of Greece,
Or Ptolomy that wonne the golden fleece;
Or great Don Quixott, that swomme o're to Spaine,
Or else St George the Dragon that hath slaine,
Are nought to the Planets erraticall,
Wch are plaine netts to catch poore men with all.

Source: Nottingham University Library, Portland MS Pw v 37, p. 179:
it follows a version of 'Great Jack-a-Lent', and is entitled: 'T. W.
Another'. This 'T. W.' is perhaps intended as the initials of the author
(it cannot mean 'Taylor's *Workes*', since this poem is not contained
in that volume); but no suitable 'T. W.' has been identified.

Paracelsie] Paracelsus (1493–1541), chemical and medical writer   Solstitium]
the solstice   Ptolomy] there were 13 kings of Egypt called Ptolemy, but
this reference is probably to the 2nd-century geographer and astronomer

22

ANON.

Pure Nonsence

When *Neptune's* blasts, and *Boreas* blazing storms,
When *Tritons* pitchfork cut off *Vulcans* horns,
When *Eolus* boyst'rous Sun-beams grew so dark,
That *Mars* in Moon-shine could not hit the mark:
Then did I see the gloomy day of *Troy*,
When poor *Aeneas* legless ran away,
Who took the torrid Ocean in his hand,
And sailed to them all the way by land:
An horrid sight to see *Achilles* fall,
He brake his neck, yet had no hurt at all.
But being dead, and almost in a trance,
He threatned forty thousand with his lance.
Indeed 'twas like such strange sights then were seen:
An ugly, rough, black Monster all in green.
That all about the white, blew, round, square, sky
The fixed Stars hung by Geometry.
Juno amazed, and *Jove* surpris'd with wonder,
Caus'd Heaven to shake, and made the mountains
     thunder:
Which caus'd *Aeneas* once again retire,
Drown'd *Aetna's* hill, and burnt the Sea with fire.

Boreas] north wind   Tritons] sea-god, son of Neptune   Eolus] Aeolus,
god of winds   Aeneas] Trojan hero who fled from Troy   Achilles]
Greek hero who died at Troy

Nilus for fear to see the Ocean burn,
Went still on forward in a quick return.
Then was that broyle of *Agamemnon's* done,
When trembling *Ajax* to the battell come.
He struck stark dead (they now are living still)
Five hundred mushrooms with his martiall bill.
Nor had himselfe escap'd, as some men say,
If he being dead, he had not run away.
O monstrous, hideous Troops of Dromidaries,
How Bears and Bulls from Monks and Goblins varies;
Nay would not *Charon* yield to *Cerberus*,
But catch'd the Dog, and cut his head off thus:
Pluto rag'd, and *Juno* pleas'd with ire,
Sought all about, but could not find the fire:
But being found, well pleas'd, and in a spight
They slept at *Acharon*, and wak't all night:
Where I let pass to tell their mad bravadoes,
Their meat was toasted cheese and carobonadoes.
Thousands of Monsters more besides there be
Which I fast hoodwink'd, at that time did see;
And in a word to shut up this discourse,
A Rudg-gowns ribs are good to spur a horse.

Source: *Witt's Recreations Augments* (London, 1641), sigs. Y3^r–4^v.

Nilus] river Nile   broyle of Agamemnon's] the broil (quarrel) of
Agamemnon, commander of Greek forces at Troy, with Achilles, whose mistress
he stole   Ajax] Greek hero of Trojan War   Charon] boatman of the
underworld   Cerberus] dog guarding the underworld   Acharon]
Acheron, river of the underworld   carbonadoes] meat or fish scored with
a knife and broiled over a fire   Rudg-gown] slang term for constables (who
wore gowns made of rug, a coarse woollen cloth)

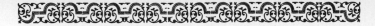

23

ANON.

Nonsense

Upon a dark, light, gloomy, sunshine day,
As I in *August* walkt to gather May,
It was at noon neer ten a clock at night,
The Sun being set, did shine exceeding bright,
I with mine eyes began to hear a noise,
And turn'd my ears about to see the voice,
When from a cellar seven stories high,
With loud low voice *Melpomene* did crie,
What sober madness hath possest your brains,
And men of no place, shall your easie pains
Be thus rewarded? passing *Smithfield* bars,
Cast up the blear-ey'd eyes down to the stars,
And see the Dragons head in Quartile move,
Now *Venus* is with *Mercury* in love,
Mars patient rages in a fustian fume,
And *Jove* will be reveng'd, or quit the room,
Mild *Juno*, beauteous *Saturn*, *Martia* free
At ten leagues distance now assembled be;

gather May] gather May-blossoms   Melpomene] muse of tragedy   *no*
place] no place? *Wits Interpreter*   Smithfield bars] barrier on the northern
edge of Smithfield (London cattle market), marking the boundaries between
the City Liberties and the county of Middlesex   Quartile] astrological term
for the aspect of two stars or planets when 90 degrees apart from each other
fustian fume] rage giving rise to invective (see Introduction, pp. 40–41)
Martia] a vestal virgin, executed for sexual transgression

Then shut your eyes and see bright *Iris* mount,
Five hundred fathoms deep by just account,
And with a noble ignominious train
Passes flying to the place were *Mars* was slain,
Thus silently she spake, whilst I mine eyes
First on the ground advanced to the skies,
And then not speaking any word reply'd
Our noble family is neer ally'd
To that renowned peasant *George a Green*,
Stout *Wakefield* Pinner, he that stood between
Achilles and the fierce *Eacides*,
And then withstood with most laborious ease,
Yet whilst that *Boreas* and kinde *Auster* lie
Together, and at once the same way flie,
And that unmoved wandring fixed star,
That bloody peace fortells, and patient war,
And scares the earth with fiery apparition,
And plants in men both good and bad conditions:
    I ever will with my weak able pen
    Subscribe myself your servant
                    French Ben:

Source: *Wits Interpreter: The English Parnassus*, ed. J. C[otgrave]
(London, 1655), p. 271.

George a Green, Stout Wakefield Pinner] Pinder (i.e. impounder of stray
animals) of Wakefield, character in Robin Hood ballads   Eacides]
Aeacides, descendants of Aeacus (such as Achilles, Peleus, Pyrrhus)
Boreas] north wind   Auster] south wind   French Ben] unidentified

24

T. C.

Thou that dwarft'st mountains into molehill sense

Upon the Gurmundizing Quagmires, and most Adiaphanous Bogs, of the Author's obnubilated Roundelayes.

Thou that *dwarft'st mountains* into *molehill* sense
With *Ell-broad* Marrow-bones of Eloquence;
Causing *thy* Eel-skin'd Glasses seem to be
But North-wind Blasts of *Mahomet's Nunnery.*
Break forth great *Argos* mast into my hand,
That I may *bob* for *Whales* upon *dry land?*
Send down the Mesenterick Huckle-bone
Of Crest-faln *Pancakes* which do cry and grone,
That ovall millstones are like tarbax't Stars
Spher'd so on purpose by *Saturn,* and eke *Mars.*
'Tis true indeed *Saturn* did leave his *Miter,*
To be Sow-gelded by's God-son Jupiter.
What then? should *Dunsmore's* Bulls fall from the sky?

Gurmundizing Quagmires] for the origin of this phrase, see poem 8, stanza 5 ('gurmundizing' means 'gourmandizing', eating gluttonously)
Adiaphanous] opaque   obnubilated] obscured by cloud   Roundelayes] type of short song with refrain   Argos mast] Argo was the name of the ship in which Jason and the Argonauts sailed   bob] to fish for eels, using a bunch of worms   Mesenterick] mesenteric, adjective from mesentery, part of the intestines   Huckle-bone] hip-bone   tarbax't] tar-boxed, treated with a tar-box (containing tar used as ointment for sheep)
Dunsmore's Bulls] the dun cow of Dunsmore was a mythical beast slain by Sir Guy of Warwick

And *Cart-ropes* into *Princes* secrets pry?
No sure: we mortals then may fall asleep
On feather'd *Dripping-pans*, playing Bo-peep.
But that's a work onely befits the Gods,
To *Weather-cock* their Eyes with fishing-rods.
Sail then (great Poet!) thither, where the mode is
To wear Black-pudding-*Points*, at th'*Antipodes*:
Rush forth into that Stage; and then it may be
Thou'lt *Crakanthorp* thy *Muse* with dull *Farnaby*.
Open our eyes with marble pick-tooths, then,
To see *thy* bed-rid Beetles turn to Men.
Grinde out *thy* Verses into meal-mouth'd Rhimes,
With *Camomil'd Horse-plum-trees* of the times.
Break out *thy* Muse's teeth; but be no caitiff,
To nickname *Lobsters* with the *case Ablative*:
Then, we shall see great Whiting mops in shrouds,
And *Planets* bounce *Conundrums* in the Clouds:
Then shall we see *thee* pass the Gallow *Tyburn*,
Creeping on Carret-tops, and bawl out, I burn,
I burn (great *Jove*) – with that, he staid his pace,

Black-pudding-Points] points were pieces of needlepoint lace
Crakanthorp] Richard Crakanthorpe (1567–1624), Oxford don, author of
standard textbooks on metaphysics (1619) and logic (1622)   Farnaby]
Thomas Farnaby (d. 1647), famous schoolmaster, author of standard textbooks
on rhetoric and grammar in 1630s and 1640s   Horse-plum-trees] in names
of fruits and plants, 'horse-' is used as a prefix denoting largeness and
coarseness (horse-bean, horse-chestnut, etc.); but 'horse-plum' does not
exist   Whiting mops] young whiting (fish)   Tyburn] place of execution
in London   Carret-tops] green tops of carrots

And heard a Lady call out thus, with grace;
  Dame *Gargamel* bids hye you home to supper,
  For great **Grangowsier's* Mule has broke his crupper.

* *In English, a Grandvisier, a grand Statesman in Turky.*

T.C. of Q.K.C.

Source: [Samuel Austin (ed.),] *Naps upon Parnassus. A sleepy Muse
nipt and pincht, though not awakened. Such Voluntary and Jovial Copies
of Verses, as were lately receiv'd from some of the Wits of the Universities,
in a Frolick, dedicated to* Gondibert's *Mistress by Captain* Jones *and others*
(London, 1658), sigs. B3ᵛ–B4ʳ.

Gargamel] Gargamelle, wife of Grangousier and mother of Gargantua (in
Rabelais)   Grangowsier's] Grangousier's

25

JAMES SMITH

Ad Johannuelem Leporem, Lepidissimum, Carmen Heroicum

I Sing the furious battails of the Sphaeres
Acted in eight and twenty fathom deep,
And from that (*a*) time, reckon so many yeares
You'l find (*b*) *Endymion* fell fast asleep.

And now assist me O ye (*c*) Musiques nine
That tell the Orbs in order as they fight,
And thou dread (*d*) *Atlas* with thine eyes so fine,
Smile on me now that first begin to write.

(A detailed discussion of this poem, interpreting it as an allegorical account
of the Battle of Naseby in the English Civil War, is in T. Raylor, *Cavaliers,
Clubs, and Literary Culture*, pp. 181–5. His suggestions are incorporated in
these notes, marked '(Raylor)'.)

Ad Johannuelem . . . heroicum] 'To the most charming Johnny Mennes, a
heroic song': 'leporem' is the accusative of 'lepos', the abstract noun from which
'lepidus' ('charming') is derived. Since 'lepos' could be translated as 'good
manners', this may be a word-play on 'Mennes', i.e. Sir John Mennes, Smith's
closest friend   Endymion] famously beautiful shepherd, visited by the
moon-goddess while he slept   Atlas] titan who carried heavens on his
shoulders

(*e*) *Pompey* that once was Tapster of *New-Inne*,
And fought with (*f*) *Caesar* on th' (*g*) *Aemathian* plaines,
First with his dreadfull (*g*) *Myrmidons* came in
And let them blood in the Hepatick veines.

But then an *Antelope* in Sable blew,
Clad like the (*h*) Prince of *Aurange* in his Cloke,
Studded with Satyres, on his Army drew,
And presently (*i*) *Pheanders* Army broke.

(*k*) *Philip*, for hardiness sirnamed *Chub*,
In Beauty equall to fork-bearing (*l*) *Bacchus*,
Made such a thrust at (*m*) *Phoebe*, with his Club,
That made the (*n*) *Parthians* cry, she will becack us.

Which heard, the *Delphick* Oracle drew nigh,
To wipe faire *Phoebe*, if ought were amiss,
But (*o*) *Heliotrope*, a little crafty spye,
Cry'd clouts were needless, for she did but piss.

Pompey] Roman general, defeated by Caesar in Civil War   Tapster] person
who draws beer in a tavern. 'Pompey' is the name of the tapster in *Measure
for Measure*. A reference to Cromwell, who was often accused by royalists of
having been a brewer (Raylor)   New-Inne] New Inn, in Farringdon,
London, one of the Inns of Chancery (societies for legal training, subsidiary
to the Inns of Court)   Aemathian plaines] Emathia was a general term for
Macedonia and Thessaly; Caesar's defeat of Pompey took place on the plains
of Thessaly   Myrmidons] industrious people from southern borders of
Thessaly   Hepatick] hepatic, pertaining to the liver   Prince of Aurange]
the Dutch princely family of Orange drew its name originally from the town of
Orange or Aurange, near Avignon. A reference to Prince Rupert of the Rhine;
his arms included quarters of sable and azure (Raylor)   Pheanders] the origin
of this name is unidentified; characters with similar names appear in d'Urfé's
L'Astrée (Silvander, Melander, Periander), but Pheander does not. Taylor used
the name as a comic title for Thomas Parsons (*Workes*, sig. Ff3'; on Parsons
see above, p. 156). A reference to Lord Fairfax (Raylor)   Philip] a reference
to Philip Skippon, parliamentary general at Naseby (Raylor)   Chub] dolt,
rustic simpleton   Phoebe] Diana, the moon-goddess   becack] smear
with excrement   Heliotrope] general name of flowers which turn to follow
the sun   clouts] pieces of cloth

A subtle Gloworme lying in a hedge
And heard the story of sweet cheek't (*p*) *Appollo*,
Snatch'd from bright (*q*) *Styropes* his Antick sledge
And to the butter'd Flownders cry'd out, (*r*) *Holla*.

Holla you pamper'd Jades, quoth he, look here,
And mounting straight upon a Lobsters thigh
An *English* man inflam'd with (*s*) double Beere,
Swore nev'r to (*t*) drink to Man, a Woman by.

By this time grew the conflict to be (*u*) hot,
Boots against boots 'gainst (*x*) Sandals, Sandals fly.
Many poor thirsty men went to the pot,
Feathers lopt off, spurrs every where did lie.

                               Caetera desiderantur.

(*a*) There began the *Utopian* accompt of years, *Mor: Lib.*
1 *circa finem.*

(*b*) *Endimion* was a handsome young Welshman, whom
one *Luce Moone* lov'd for his sweet breath; and would never
hang off his lips: but he not caring for her, eat abundance
of toasted cheese, purposely to make his breath unsavory;
upon which, she left him presently, and ever since 'tis
proverbially spoken 'as inconstant as *Luce Moone*'. The
Vatican coppy of Hesiod, reades her name, *Mohun*, but
contractedly it is *Moone. Hesiod. lib.* 4. *tom* 3.

Styropes] Steropes, 'lightning-maker', a Cyclops (one-eyed giant)   Antick]
antic, grotesque   double Beere] beer of twice normal strength   a Woman
by] in the presence of a woman   Caetera desiderantur] 'the rest is
missing'   Mor . . . finem] 'More, book 1, near the end'   Luce Moone]
probably referring to Luce Morgan, a notorious prostitute of Pickt-Hatch,
Clerkenwell (see 'On Luce Morgan a Common Whore', in *Wit and Drollery*,
sig. C2)   Mohun] a reference to Lord Mohun, who shifted allegiance from
King to Parliament in 1643 (Raylor)   Hesiod] early Greek poet

(c) For all the Orbes made Musick in their motion, *Berosus de sphaera. lib. 3.*

(d) *Atlas* was a Porter in *Mauretania*, and because by reason of his strength, he bore burthens of stupendious weight, the Poets fain'd, that he carried the heavens on his shoulders. Cicero *de nat. deorum. lib. 7.*

(e) There were two others of these names, Aldermen of *Rome. Tit. Liv. hist. lib. 28.*

(f) *Aemathia,* is a very faire Common in *Northamptonshire. Strabo. lib. 321.*

(g) These *Myrmidons* were *Cornish-men,* and sent by *Bladud,* sometimes King of this Realme, to ayd *Pompey. Caesar de bello civili lib. 14.*

(h) It seems not to be meant by *Count Henry,* but his brother *Maurice,* by comparing his picture to the thing here spoken of. *Jansen de praed. lib. 22.*

(i) *Pheander* was so modest, that he was called the Maiden

Berosus de sphaera lib. 3] Berosus was a Babylonian astronomer of the 3rd century BC; no work by him on 'the sphere' has survived   Mauretania] Roman province of north-western Africa, including Atlas mountains   de nat. Deorum] genuine work by Cicero, *On the Nature of the Gods*   Tit. Liv. hist.] history of Rome, *Ab urbe condita,* by Titus Livius (Livy)   Aemathia] Emathia, a general term for Macedonia and Thessaly (site of battle between Caesar and Pompey)   Northamptonshire] Naseby is in Northamptonshire (Raylor)   Strabo] Greek geographer (*c.*63 BC–AD 24)   Myrmidons] industrious people from southern borders of Thessaly   Bladud] mythical king of England, father of King Lear   Pompey] Roman general, defeated by Caesar in Civil War   Caesar de bello civili] Caesar, *The Civil Wars*   Count Henry . . . Maurice] Maurice of Nassau, prince of Orange, was stadholder of Holland and Zeeland 1585–1625; his half-brother and successor, Frederick-Henry, died in 1647. Both Prince Rupert of the Rhine and his brother Maurice were present at Naseby (Raylor)   Jansen de praed.] Cornelius Jansen (1585–1638), Flemish Catholic theologian; his only published work, *Augustinus* (1640), was partly on the theory of predestination ('de praed.')   Pheander] unidentified; characters with similar names appear in d'Urfé's *L'Astrée* (Silvander, Melander, Periander), but Pheander does not. Taylor used the name as a comic title for Thomas Parsons (*Workes,* sig. Ff3ʳ; on Parsons see above, p. 156). A reference to Lord Fairfax (Raylor)

Knight; and yet so valiant, that a French Cavaleer wrote his life, and called his Book, *Pheander* the *Maiden Knight*. *Hon. d'Urfee tom.* 45.

(*k*) This seemes not to be that King, that was Son of *Amintas*, and King of *Macedon*; but one who it seems was very lascivious: for I suspect there is some obscaene conceit in that word *Club* in the third verse following; besides, marke his violence.

(*l*) *Bacchus*, was a drunken yeoman of the Guard to Queen *Elizabeth*, and a great Archer; so that it seemes the Authour mistooke his halbert, for a forke.

(*m*) This was *Long-Megg* of *Westminster*, who after this conflict with *Phillip*, followed him in all his warres. *Justinian. lib.* 35.

(*n*) These were *Lancashire-men*, and sent by King *Gorbadug* (for this war seemes to have been in the time of the *Heptarchy* in *England*) to the side of *Caesar*. *Caesar lib. citat. prope finem.*

(*o*) And therefore, the herb into which he was turned, was called *Turnsole*. *Ovid Metam. lib.* 25.

(*p*) *Appollo*, was *Caesars* page, and a *Monomatapan* by

Hon. d'Urfee] Honoré d'Urfé (1567–1625), author of highly popular sentimental romance, *L'Astrée*   Son of Amintas] Philip of Macedon, father of Alexander the Great, was the son of Amyntas   Long-Megg of Westminster] famous virago of Elizabethan London (see *The Life and Pranks of Long Meg of Westminster* (London, 1582))   Justinian] Byzantine Emperor (483–565), responsible for codification of Roman law   Gorbadug] Gorboduc, mythical early King of Britain, tragic hero of a political morality play by Thomas Sackville and Thomas Norton (1561)   Heptarchy] the seven Angle and Saxon kingdoms of 5th- and 6th-century England   Caesar lib. citat. prope finem] 'Caesar, the book cited above, near the end'   Turnsole] name for flowers which turn to follow the sun; particularly, one such plant which yielded a purple dye   Metam.] *Metamorphoses*   Monomatapan] from Monomotapa, area of south-east Africa ('the kingdome of Monomotapa, wherein are manie golde mines': van Linschoten, *Discours of Voyages*, p. 212)

birth, whose name by inversion was *Ollopa*: which in the old language of that country, signifies as much as faire youth: but, *Euphoniae Gratia*, called *Apollo, Gor. Bec. lib. 46.*

(*q*) *Styropes*, was a lame Smiths-man dwelling in S. *Johns-street*; but how he was called *Bright*, I know not, except it were by reason of the Luster of his eyes.

(*r*) *Holla*, mistaken for *Apollo*.

(*s*) *Cervisia (apud Medicos vinum hordeaceum) potus est Anglis longè charissimus; Inventum Ferrarij Londinensis, Cui nomen Smuggo. Polydor. Virgil, de Invent. rerum. lib. 2.*

(*t*) *Impp. Germaniae, antiquitus solebant, statis temporibus, adire Basingstochium; ubi, de more, Jusjurandum solenne prae-stabant, de non viro propinando, praesente muliere; Hic Mos, jamdudum apud Anglos, pene vim legis obtinuit; quippe gens illa, longe humanissima morem istum, in hodiernum usque diem, magna Curiositate, pari Comitate conjunct, usurpant. Pancirol. utriusque imperij. lib. 6, cap. 5.*

(*u*) It seemes this was a great battail, both by the furie of

---

Euphoniae Gratia] 'for the sake of euphony'   Gor. Bec.] Goropius Becanus, Jan van Gorp (1518–72), Flemish writer of influential works on the origins of language   Styropes] Steropes, 'lightning-maker', a Cyclops (one-eyed giant)   S. Johns-street] street running north out of City of London   Cervisia . . . Smuggo] 'Beer (which medical writers call barley-wine) is by far the most preferred drink of the English. It was invented by a London blacksmith, whose name was Smugg'   Polydor . . . rerum] Polydore Vergil (*c.*1470–1555), Italian-born writer who settled in England; his *De inventoribus rerum* ('On the Inventors of Things') was published in 1499   Impp . . . usurpant] 'Anciently, the Emperors of Germany used to go at fixed times to Basingstoke, where, by custom, they solemnly gave their oath that they would not drink to a man's health, if a woman were present. This custom, for a long time now, has had almost the force of law among the English; indeed this people, being by far the most well-mannered of all, observe that custom up to this day with great punctiliousness, combined with equal courteousness.'   Pancirol. utriusque imperij.] Guido Panciroli (1523–99), Italian legal writer; his *Notitia utraque dignitatum, cum orientis, tum occidentis* (Venice, 1593), was later published under the title *Notitia dignitatum utriusque Imperii*

it, & the aydes of each side; but hereof read more, in
Cornel. Tacit. libe. de moribus German.

(*x*) This is in imitation of Lucan –
– *Signis Signa, & pila* – &c.
Pharsalia. lib. 1. *in principio.*

Source: *Wit Restor'd* (London, 1658), p. 35.

Cornel. . . German.] Cornelius Tacitus, book on the customs of the Germans
(i.e. his *Germania*)   Lucan . . . principio] 'battle-standards against
battle-standards, and javelins etc.', from Lucan's *Pharsalia* (epic poem about
Civil War between Caesar and Pompey), 'book 1, at the beginning' (the quotation
is genuine, from bk. 1, lines 6–7)

26

ANON.

A Fancy

When Py-crust first began to reign,
 Cheese-parings went to warre,
Red Herrings lookt both blew and wan,
 Green Leeks and Puddings jarre.
Blind *Hugh* went out to see
 Two Cripples run a race,
The Ox fought with the Humble Bee,
 And claw'd him by the face.

Source: *Sportive Wit: The Muses Merriment* (London, 1656), p. 48.

jarre] jar, come into conflict   Humble Bee] bumble-bee

27

ANON.

Interrogativa Cantilena

If all the world were paper,
And all the Sea were Inke;
If all the Trees were bread and cheese,
How should we do for drink?

If all the World were sand'o,
Oh then what should we lack'o;
If as they say there were no clay,
How should we take Tobacco?

If all our vessels ran'a,
If none but had a crack'a;
If Spanish Apes eat all the Grapes,
How should we do for Sack'a?

If Fryers had no bald pates,
Nor Nuns had no Dark Cloysters,
If all the Seas were Beans and Pease,
How should we do for Oysters?

Sack] sweet white wine from Spain or the Canaries

If there had been no projects,
Nor none that did great wrongs;
If Fidlers shall turn Players all,
How should we do for songs?

If all things were eternal,
And nothing their end bringing;
If this should be, then how should we,
Here make an end of singing?

Source: *Witt's Recreations Augmented*, sigs. X6ᵛ–7ʳ.

projects] schemes for making money, especially unpopular in early 17th-century
England because they often involved persuading the King to grant monopoly
powers; see the character of 'A Projector' in Butler, *Characters*, pp. 115–16
for songs?] for songs *Witt's Recreations Augmented*

ANON.

Prophecies

When the Fisherman drownes the Eele,
And the Hare bites the Huntsman by the heel:
When the Geese do drive the Foxe into his hole,
And the Thistle overtops the May-pole.
The Hering is at warre with the Whale,
And the Drunkard forsweares a pot of Ale:
And conscience is the Ruler of a Citty;
When the parson will his Tithes forgoe,
And the Parish will pay him, will, or no.
When the Usurer is weary of his gaine,
And the Farmer feedes the poor with his graine . . .

. . . When Charing-Crosse and Pauls Church meet,
And break their fast in Friday street:
When Ware and Waltham goe to Kent
Togither, there to purchase Rent.
When Islington and Lambeth joyne,
To make a voyage to the Groine:
And Southwarke with St. Katherines gree,

Friday street] street running from West Cheap to Old Fish street in City of
London   Ware] town in Hertfordshire   Waltham] village in
Essex   Groine] groyne, breakwater; a term for Corunna (La Coruña, port
in north-western Spain)   Southwarke with St. Katherines] Southwark
(district adjoining southern end of London Bridge) and St Katherine's by the
Tower (hospital near northern end of London Bridge)

To ride in post to Coventry:
When Turmele-street and Clarken-well,
Have sent all Bawdes and Whores to Hell:
And Long-ditch, and Long-lane do try,
Antiquities for honesty;
And Newgate weepes, and Bridewell greeves,
For want of Beggars, Whores, and Theeves.
And Tyburne doth to Wapping sweare,
Shall never more come Hang-man there:
When blinde men see, and dumbe men read,
Which seemes impossible indeed.
And by all rules that I can see,
I thinke in truth will never be.
Then, then, ye may say then,
Knaves now will be honest men.

Source: *Cobbes Prophecies* (London, 1614), sigs. B2ᵛ, D3ᵛ–4ʳ.

gree] agree   Turmele-street and Clarken-well] Turnmill street, in
Clerkenwell, district of London famous for brothels   Long-ditch] ditch
near Whitehall, Westminster   Long-lane] street in City of London
Newgate] prison in London   Bridewell] prison in London   Tyburne]
place of execution in London   Wapping] place of execution for pirates in
London

ANON.

Newes

Now Gentlemen if you will hear
Strange news as I will tell to you,
Where ere you go both far and near,
You may boldly say that this is true.

When *Charing-cross* was a pretty little boy,
He was sent to *Romford* to sell swine;
His mother made a Cheese, and he drank up the whey,
For he never lov'd strong beer, ale, nor wine.

When all the thieves in *England* died,
That very year fell such a chance,
That *Salisbury* plain would on horseback ride,
And *Parish-garden* carry the news to *France*.

When all the Lawyers they did plead
All for love, and not for gain,
Then 'twas a jovial world indeed,
The Blew Bore of *Dover* fetcht apples out of *Spain*.

Romford] Essex town famous for hog-market   Parish-garden] Paris
Garden, area on south bank of Thames famous for bear-baiting and
brothels   Blew Bore of Dover] unidentified; perhaps a tavern in Dover,
Kent

When Landlords they did let their Farms
Cheap, because his Tenants paid dear,
The weather-cock of *Pauls* turn his tail to the wind,
And Tinkers they left strong ale and beer.

When Misers all were griev'd in mind
Because that Corn was grown so dear,
The man in the moon made *Christmas pyes*,
And bid the seven stars to eat good chear.

But without a Broker or Cunny-catcher
Pauls church-yard was never free,
Then was my Lord Mayor become a house-thatcher,
Which was a wondrous sight to see.

When *Basingstoke* did swim upon Thames,
And swore all thieves to be just and true,
The Sumnors and Bailiffs were honest men,
And Pease and Bacon that year it snew.

When every man had a quiet wife
That never would once scold and chide,
Tom Tinker of *Turvey* to end all strife
Roasted a Pig in a blew Cowes hide.

Source: *Prince d'Amour*, pp. 178–9. (Also printed, under the title
'Nonsence', in *Merry Drollery, The First Part* (London, 1661)
pp. 18–19: that version has some minor variants, and also omits the
second half of stanza 5 and the first half of stanza 6, amalgamating the
two remaining halves into one stanza.)

Pauls] St Paul's Cathedral, London   Broker] retailer, second-hand dealer
or pawnbroker; also, a pimp   Cunny-catcher] coney-catcher, swindler or
sharper   Sumnors] sumners, summoning officers of a court   snew]
snowed   Tom Tinker] stock name for a blacksmith   Turvey] village
in Bedfordshire; 'The Tinker of Turvey' was a popular song (see *Merry Drollery,
The First Part*, pp. 17–18)

29

ANON.

A Bull Droll

Ile tell you a jest I never did know in my life
Of a man that was marry'd before he met with his wife.
He kist her and culd her, and led her hither and thither,
And marry'd they were before they came together,
Her belly was up before she was got with childe
Which made him with madness grow frantick, tame and
    wilde.
And she to excuse it told him then in scorne
T'was gotten some threescore years before it was borne.
My troth, quoth he, I never saw such another,
That the child should be gotten, before the father and
    mother.
Then upstart *Dick* that was both tame and wilde,
And furiously he began to excuse this child.
Quoth he about some fifty yeares agoe,
I met this child a walking to and fro,
With a basket of butter-milk hanging on his arme
And a Cloak of Snow to keep his body warme.
My little Boy quoth he, now we are met,
Wee'l walk a mile together, so down we set,
And as we sate me thought he walkt too fast,

Bull] comic illogicality   culd] culled, hugged, cuddled   *thither,*] thither.
Oxford Drollery   warme.] warme *Oxford Drollery*   *fast,*] fast. *Oxford
Drollery*

And by sitting still, did make the greater haste.
Then I in silence askt him whe'r he was able,
To let me know his life and's death from's cradle.
He sat him down and pausd a little while,
And with a sad and mournful look did smile.
Quoth he Ile tell you more then I do know,
And when you find it truth you'l swear 'tis so.
My father was single before he marryed a wife,
And Weaving of Oaken Planks was his trade of life.
My mother was a Justice of peace's Clarke,
And Joyning of bodies was her trade in the dark.
And I in that same manner was got I know,
Cause before I was born my mother did tell me so.

Source: *The Oxford Drollery* (Oxford, 1671), pp. 1–2. This is the first half of the poem only; the rest is based on scatological humour rather than nonsense.

cradle.] cradle *Oxford Drollery*

30

ANON.

Witley's Lies

From Barwick to Dover, ten thousand tymes over
I trewlye have travelled ten tymes on a daye.
From the top of pooles steeple in the sight of all people
To throwe my self headlong, I thought it a playe
I jumpe from Westminster, to the midste of all cheape
Ore the tops of the houses at one standing leape:
From thence downe to Greenwich in the sight of the
     manye
I bounde ore the barges, & never toucht anye.

From off Richmond castle 9 tymes into Scotland
Ile run in a morning at one breathing course
Ile march in a minuet twixt Norway & Goateland
And neere be beholden to the helpe of a horse
Ile dine with Duke Humphrey, this day at hye noone

Capital letters have been added to the beginnings of some lines, and full stops
to the ends of stanzas 1, 2, 4 and 5. Contractions have been expanded.
From Barwick . . . tymes over] Ray's *Collection of English Proverbs* (1678)
includes 'From *Barwick* to *Dover*, three hundred miles over', meaning 'from
one end of the land to the other' (p. 329)   Barwick] Berwick-upon-Tweed,
Northumberland   pooles] St Paul's Cathedral   cheape] Cheap, street in
City of London   Richmond castle] Norman castle at Richmond,
Yorkshire   minuet] minute   Goateland] Gothland, Sweden   dine with
Duke Humphrey] Humphrey, Duke of Gloucester (son of Henry IV), whose
tomb was popularly believed to be in St Paul's Cathedral; to dine with Duke
Humphrey was to go without dinner – originally, it seems, to linger at St Paul's
(a popular meeting-place) hoping to meet someone who could pay for a meal

The next night at supper I will meete you in Rome
Ile ride through the whole world to what place you can
    name
& Ile neer crosse river till I come at the same.

Ile walke upon Thames as well as drye land
And neere be beholden to the helpe of a boate
Ile goe at hye tyde from London to Gravesend
As light as a sculler I finelye shall floate
& soe on the river Ile goe with such skill
As slightlye uprightlye, as I were on the sand hill
From thence without danger Ile passe yarmouth sande
& briefelye I safely at Tinmouth will lande:

I likewise have studyed that learned vocation
To know how the planets & starres doe remove
Ile tell at a word what they doe in each nation
& for 7 yeares after what events there shall prove
& if French, Turke, or Spaniard, against us conspire
Ile beat their whole armyes with balles of hot fyre.
The shot of a Cannon I holde it a toy
For I slew 30,000 when I was but a boy.

In travell I likewise have beene most laborious
& traveld far further, than any I knowe
I used my practyse & wits soe industrious
Until Plutoes pallace moste plainelye I sawe
Whereas I grieved the tyme I did staye
A man with much terrour was taken away
When I came backe to England to the best of my thinking
I found the same fellow in an alehouse still drinking.

Gravesend] port on Thames estuary in Kent   yarmouth] port in
Norfolk   Tinmouth] Teignmouth, port in Devon; or Tynemouth, port in
Northumberland   Plutoe] Pluto, god of underworld

The victuals that would have Garganta sustained
Even for a whole 12 month I helde it a bit
For bring me a 1000 of waines strong by loading
& I at one mouth full will devour everye whitte
The hogsheades the greatest that are in the house
I drink of theise 40 at a mornings carouse
Ile blow from my nostrills such a boystrous gaile
As shall make 3 score thousand great ships for to saile.

I likewise have traveld through sword & through fyre
And paste such adventures as never were knowne
Of all sortes of people I hate a base lyar
That talkes of adventures, & never saw none
If you meete with such fellowes that will bragge, prate,
    & lye
Tell them but of my travels & thele cease presentlye
Thus wishing true souldiers all spur & increase
And a whippe for base lyars, & thus I doe cease.

Source: BL MS Sloane 1489, fo. 26. This MS contains a group of
poems from the late 1620s, some of them with Cambridge
connections.

Garganta] Gargantua   bit] bite, mouthful   paste] passed

31

ANON.

From the top of high Caucasus

From the top of high *Caucasus*,
To *Pauls wharf* near the Tower,
In no great haste I easily past
In less than half an hour.
The Gates of old *Bizantium*
I took upon my shoulders,
And them I bore twelve Leagues and more
In spight of *Turks* and Soldiers.
   Sigh, sing, and sob, sing, sigh, and be merry,
   Sighing, singing, and sobbing,
   Thus naked *Tom* away doth run,
   And fears no cold nor robbing.

From *Monsieur Tillies* Army,
I took two hundred Bannors,
And brought them all to *London* Hall
In sight of all the Tannors;
I past *Parnassus* Ferry
By the hill call'd *Aganip*,
From thence on foot without shooe or boot

Pauls wharf] wharf on the Thames, west of Tower of London   naked Tom]
stock name for an indigent madman   Tillies] Jean t'Serclaes, comte de Tilly
(1559–1632), general commanding the army of the Catholic League in the Thirty
Years' War: this reference suggests that the poem dates from *c*.1630   Aganip]
Aganippe, fountain sacred to the Muses, at foot of Mount Helicon

I past to the Isle of Ship,
    Sigh, sing, *&c.*

O're the *Piranean* Valley
'Twixt *Europe* and *St. Giles*,
I walk't one night by Sun-shine light
Which fifteen thousand miles is.
I Landed at *White Chapel*
Next to Saint *Edmonds Berry*
From thence I stept while *Charon* slept,
And stole away his Ferry.
    Sigh, sing, *&c.*

One Summers day at *Shrovetide*
I met old *January*,
Being male content, with him I went
To weep o're the old Canary.
The Man ith' Moon at *Pancrass*,
Doth yield us excellent Claret,
Having steel'd my nose, I sung old Rose,
Tush, greatness cannot carry it,
    Sigh, sing, *&c.*

I met the Turkish Sulton
At *Dover* near St. *Georges*
His train and him did to *Callis* swim
Without ships, Boats, or Barges.
I taught the King of *Egypt*
A trick to save his Cattle,

Isle of Ship] Sheppey, island off north coast of Kent   Piranean]
Pyrenean   St. Giles] St Giles, Cripplegate, in the City of London   White
Chapel] Whitechapel, district east of City of London   Saint Edmonds
Berry] Bury St Edmunds, town in Suffolk   Charon] boatman of the
underworld   Pancrass] St Pancras, in Needlers' Lane in the City of
London   old Rose] perhaps 'The Rose of England', a popular ballad (see
Chappell, *Popular Music*, i, p. 117)   St. Georges] parish in Southwark,
London   Callis] Calais

I'le Plough with dogs, and Harrow with Hogs,
You'd think it I do prattle,
   Sigh, sing, *&c.*

In a Boat I went on dry Land
From *Carthage* to St. *Albons*,
I saild to *Spain*, and back again
In a vessel made of Whalebones.
I met *Diana* hunting
With all her Nymphs attending,
In *Turnball* street with voices sweet
That honest place commending,
   Sigh, sing, *&c.*

Diogenes the Belman
Walkt with his Lanthorn duely,
Ith' term among the Lawyers throng
To find one that speaks truly,
The Sun and Moon eclipsed,
I very friendly parted,
And made the Sun away to run
For fear he should be Carted,
   Sigh, sing, *&c.*

Long time have I been studying,
My brains with fancies tearing,
How I might get old *Pauls* a hat,
And a Cross-cloth for old *Charing*.
Thus to give men and women
In cloaths full satisfaction,
These fruitless toyes robb'd me of joyes,

Thurball Street] alternative name of Turnmill Street in Clerkenwell, London,
famous for brothels   Diogenes] Cynic philosopher   Carted] carried in a
cart through the streets, for exposure to public ridicule: a form of punishment,
especially for prostitutes   old Pauls] St Paul's Cathedral   old Charing]
Charing Cross, the memorial cross at the western end of the Strand, London

And keeps my brains in action,
   Sing, sing, *&c.*

Source: *Prince d'Amour*, pp. 164–7.

32

ANON.

Cure for the Quartain Ague

The Aphorismes of Galen I esteeme them as strawes
Profound pispot peepers all be ye mute:
The old quartane ague breakes all physick lawes
The Emperick scarse will purchase a cute.
Perusing of late a worme eaten booke
Brought hither from Cynthia downe in Charles waine;
A soveraigne medicine thence I have tooke
To cure the Quartane feaver againe.

First take a Physitian, that will not exceed
Probatum est, speaking more than he knowes;
Nor hath more skill in his tongue than his head:
His passion on patient the greatest bestowes

MS Tanner (which dates from the early 1640s) gives a fuller version of the
poem; MS Egerton omits stanzas 2, 4 and 5, and combines a selection of lines
from stanzas 7 and 8 into a single stanza. MS Tanner is used as the copy-text
here; however, a few evidently superior readings are taken from MS Egerton,
as are the first four lines of the poem, which are absent from MS Tanner.
The version in *The Second Part of Merry Drollery* is simplified and corrupted in
several places; it omits the seventh stanza, but includes a new stanza between
the second and third stanzas here.
Quartain Ague] intermittent fever with paroxysm every three days   Galen]
Greek medical writer (AD 130–200)   pispot peepers] practitioners of
uroscopy, medical diagnosis by examination of urine   Emperick] Empiric,
physician who relies on observation and experience; also, a quack   cute]
cur   Cynthia] Diana, the moon-goddess   Charles waine] constellation,
also called Ursa Major, the Great Bear   Probatum est] 'it is proved'

Three Midsomer mornes in one lett him pray,
To Apollo, the moone being full in the wane,
And Schola Salerna twice back lett him say,
It hath power to cure the fever againe.

Then lett him take from him a drop, & a halfe
Of putrifi'd blood, & peirce not the skin;
Only open a vaine in the heele of the calfe
Some half a yeare 'fore the fitt doth beginne
To sweat eleven minutes in an Oven lett him lie
Heat with a Northwind, & a shower of raine,
And sleepe every night with the half of an eye;
It will cure the Quartane fever againe.

To keepe his body alway soluble, & loose,
That he never be subject in's body to be bound,
Lett him drinke woodcocks water in the quill of a
       goose,
And always untrusse, when he goes to the ground.
Thus being prepar'd, lett the Doctor proceed
With other ingredients to cure his paine,
And professe noe more art, than ere he did read:
To cure the Quartane fever againe.

Then lett him take the wind from a crowes wing,
As shee flies over Caucasus hill:
With the precious stone in Gyges his ring.
Mixe all these together in an honest windmill.
Then boile them all well from a pint to a quart
In a travellers mouth, that cannot faine:

Schola Salerna] famous medieval medical text giving prescriptions for common
ailments in Latin verse, produced by the medical school at Salerno (Italy) and
translated by Sir John Harington as 'The School of Salernum'   untrusse]
untruss, undo fastenings of garments   Gyges his ring] Gyges found a magic
ring which rendered him invisible; he used it to murder the king of Lydia and
marry the queen

And having thus done, give them him next his heart,
It will cure the Quartane fever againe.

Then take three handfulls of a Popes holy shaddow,
When Sol is new entred into the dogs taile,
Three shreekes of an Owle, three kawes of a Caddow,
With the braines, & the heads of three penny nailes
Fry these altogether in a meale sive,
With the sweat of the outside of a french-beane:
And this to the patient morne, & even lett him give,
It will cure the Quartane fever againe.

Take twice two opinions of our latest divines,
That in points of religion doe all well agree:
A pint of plaine dealing of Lawyers lines:
Three leapes of a Lawyer, that never took fee;
A blast of a Bishop, that gold doth refuse;
Foure wise words from an Aldermans braine:
Mixe them with the puritie found in the stewes;
It will praesently cure the fever againe.

Take three merry thoughts of a bride the first night,
When she lies with her groome to purge Melancholy;
Three gingles of the silver spurres of a knight,
Three Puritans faces not counterfett holy,
Take three youthfull capers of a good old oxe;
And through a joyn'd stoole all these lett him straine;
And then drink the juice through the taile of a foxe;
It will cure the Quartane fever againe.

Sol] astrological term for the Sun   *dogs taile*] dogdaies *MS Tanner*; dogs
taile *MS Egerton*   Caddow] jackdaw   *french-beane*] French braine *MS
Tanner*; french-beane *MS Egerton*   *silver spurres of a knight*] spure of a pauls
spright *MS Egerton*; silver spurres of a knight *MS Tanner*   *not counterfett
holy*] that counterfeit holy *MS Egerton*; not counterfett holy *MS Tanner*
joyn'd stoole] joint-stool, stool made of parts joined or fitted together

Moreover, for I should strive to be briefe,
Take three honest thrummes from a weaver's shuttle,
Three snipps of a tailors sheeres, that is not a theefe,
A cut-purses thumbe, his hone, & his whittle.
The mind of a miller, that never took tole
Burne them altogether, in Barnewelle poole,
It will cure the Quartane fever againe.

And lastly, this counsell an old author gives;
Take the bloud of a beetle, in the aire as she flies;
Who, like a Physitian, on excrement lives,
And therewith lett th'Empirick anoint his quick eyes.
And this being practised, he shall see soone
All naturall mysteries, both perfect and plaine,
And know as much Physick, as the man in the Moone,
To cure the Quartane fever againe.

Source: Bodl. MS Tanner 465, fos. 85ᵛ–86, collated with BL MS
Egerton 2421, fos. 21ᵛ–22ʳ. (Another version is in *The Second Part of
Merry Drollery, or A Collection of Jovial Poems, Merry Songs, Witty
Drolleries. Intermix'd with Pleasant Catches* (London, n.d. [1661]),
pp. 94–6.)

thrummes] thrums, ends of the warp-threads on a weaver's loom   hone]
whetstone   whittle] sharp knife   Barnewelle poole] bathing pool in
Cambridge   *bloud of a beetle*] wind of a beetle *MS Tanner*; bloud of a beetle
MS Egerton   *th'Emperick*] quacksilver *MS Egerton*; th'Empirick *MS
Tanner*: an Empiric was a physician who relied on observation and experience;
also, a quack.

33

ANON.

How to get a Child without help of a Man

A Maiden of late, whose name was sweet *Kate*,
Was dwelling in *London*, near to *Aldersgate*:
Now list to my Ditty, declare it I can,
She would have a Child without help of a man.

To a Doctor she came, a man of great fame,
Whose deep skill in Physick report did proclaime,
I pray, Master Doctor, shew me, if you can,
How I may conceive without help of a man.

Then listen, quoth he, since so it must be,
This wondrous strong medicine I'll shew presently,
Take nine pound of Thunder, six legs of a Swan,
And you shall conceive without help of a man.

The wooll of a Frog, the juyce of a Log,
Well parboyl'd together in the skin of a hog,
With the Egge of a Mooncalf, if get it you can,
And you shall conceive without help of a man.

Aldersgate] street on north-western side of City of London   *I pray*] Quoth
she *New Academy*   Mooncalf] congenital idiot

The love of false Harlots, the Faith of false Varlets,
With the Truth of decoys, that walk in their Scarlet,
And the Feathers of a Lobster well fry'd in a pan,
And you shall conceive without help of a man.

Nine Drops of rain, brought hither from *Spaine*,
With the blast of a Bellows quite over the Maine,
With eight quarts of brimstone, brew'd in a beer Can,
And you shall conceive without help of a man.

Six pottles of Lard squeez'd from a Rock hard,
With nine Turky Eggs, each as long as a Yard,
With a Pudding of hailstones bak'd well in a Pan,
And you shall conceive without help of a man.

These Medicines are good, and approved hath stood,
Well tempered together with a Pottle of blood,
Squeez'd from a Grasshopper, and the naile of a Swan,
To make Maids conceive without help of a man.

Source: *Merry Drollery, or A Collection of Jovial Poems, Merry Songs, Witty Drolleries. Intermix'd with Pleasant Catches. The First Part* (London, n.d. [1661]), pp. 160–61 (collated with *The New Academy of Complements. With an exact collection of the newest and choicest songs à la mode, both amorous and jovial* (London, 1671), pp. 226–7).

decoys] prostitutes, used to trap victims for swindling or extortion   pottles]
one pottle was half a gallon

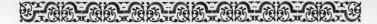

MARTIN PARKER

A Bill of Fare

*For, a Saturday nights Supper, A Sunday morning Breakfast,
and a Munday Dinner, Described in a pleasant new merry
Ditie. To the tune of* Cooke Laurell, *or,* Michaelmas Terme.

I'le tell you a Jest, which you'l hardly beleeve:
No matter for that, you shall hear't, right or wrong,
A hungry appetite may perhaps grieve
To heare such a Banquet set forth in a Song.
He rather would have it then heare on't, hee'l say,
But I cannot promise him such a faire sight;
All that I can doe, is with words to display,
What we had to Supper on Saturday night.

Inprimis, foure Fancies, two boyld, and two roast,
A large dish of Endimions (good for one's drinke)
Six Pelican Chickens as hote as a toast,

Cooke Laurell] Cock Lorrel was a popular song from Jonson's masque *The
Gypsies Metamorphosed*, giving a fanciful-satirical list of ingredients for a feast
(Jonson, *Works*, vii, pp. 601–3; Chappell, *Old English Popular Music*, ii, pp. 40–41).
Because of this association, the name was often given as 'Cook' instead of
'Cock'   Michaelmas Terme] tune unidentified   Inprimis] imprimis, in
the first place (word used at start of documents, e.g. inventories)   Endimions]
Endymion was a famously beautiful shepherd, visited by the moon-goddess
while he slept. The context here (following 'Fancies') suggests that 'Endimions'
might mean dreams or slumbers (*OED* records 'endymiony' in this sense)

And six Birds of Paradise, brave meate I thinke,
A couple of Phenix, a Cocke and a Hen,
That late from *Arabia* had tane their flight.
I think such a Banquet was ne're made for men,
As we had to Supper on Saturday night.

Two paire of Eliphants Pettitoes boyld
A greene Dragon Spitchcock (an excellent dish)
One messe by the Cooke was like to be spoil'd,
And yet, by good hap 'twas to every one's wish:
It was a Rhenoceros boyld in Alegant,
To all who did taste it, gave great delight:
Judge whether we have not occasion to vaunt
Of this our rare Supper on Saturday night.

A Calves head was roast with a pudding i'th belly
(Of which all the women did heartily feed)
A dish of Irish Harts hornes boyld to a Jelly,
(Which most men esteem'd as a good dish indeed)
I had almost forgotten to name sowc'd Owle,
Brought up to the Master o'th Feast as his right,
He lov'd it he said above all other Fowle,
And this was our Supper on Saturday night.

The next in due course was foure golden Horshooes,
Exactly dissolved through a Woodcocks bill,
Six Camelions in greene-sawce (Maids commonly chuse
This dish every day if they may have their will.)
The chine of a Lyon, the haunch of a Beare,
Well larded with Brimstone and Quicksilver bright:
Judge Gentlemen, was not this excellent cheere,
That wee had to Supper on Saturday night.

Pettitoes] a term normally used for pigs' trotters   Spitchcock] spatchcock,
a fowl split open and grilled   Alegant] Alicant, a variety of red wine, from
Alicante in Spain   greene-sawce] sauce made with green herbs and vinegar

A whole Horse sowst after the Russian manner,
Twelve Pigs of a strange Capadocian Bitch,
Six dozen of Estridges rost (which a Tanner
Did send out of *Asia* by an Old Witch).
The Leg of an Eagle carbonadoed (in Snow)
The Pluck of a Grampoise stew'd till it was white,
And thus in particular I let you know,
What we had to Supper on Saturday night.

Then came in an Ell of a Jackanapes taile,
Serv'd in upon Sippits as dainty as may be:
O that is a dainty, which rather then faile,
Might well serve to feast an Utopian Lady:
Twelve Maids were stew'd in the shell of a Shrimp,
And cause it was meat that was held very light,
They had for their Sawce a salt pickled Pimpe,
And this was our Supper on Saturday night.

The second part, To the same tune.

Two Beares sowst pig fashion, sent whole to the board,
And 4 black swans serv'd by 2 in a dish,
With a Lobster fried in steaks take my word,
I know not well whether it was Flesh or Fish,
Two Cockatrices, and three Baboones boyld,
Two dry Salamanders, a very strange sight,
A Joale of a Whale soundly butter'd and oyl'd,
And this was our Supper on Saturday night.

Capadocian] from Cappadocia, area of central Anatolia (modern Turkey)
Estridges] ostriches   carbonadoed] scored with a knife and broiled over a
fire   Pluck] heart, liver and lungs   Grampoise] grampus, name used for
several varieties of small whale   Sippets] small pieces of toasted or fried bread,
served in broth   Joale] jowl

A good dish of Modicums, I know not what,
In *Barbary* Vinegar boyld very soft,
I mus'd how my Hostis became so huge fat,
I find tis with eating these Modicums oft:
A Grosse of Canary birds roasted alive,
That out of the dishes (for sport) tooke their flight,
And every one present to catch them did strive:
This was our rare Supper on Saturday night.

A shoale of Red-herrings with bels 'bout their neckes,
Which made such rare sport that I never saw such,
They leaped and danced with other fine tricks,
A man may admire how they could doe so much.
Two Porposes parboild in May-dew and Roses,
That unto the smell yeelded so much delighte,
Some (fearing to lose them) laid hold on their noses:
All this was at Supper on Saturday night.

Three dozen of Welsh Embassadors bak't,
Which made such a nois it was heard through y.e town
Some hearing the eccho their foreheads so ak't,
That many a smile was orecome with a frowne:
A dish of Bonitoes, or Fish that can flie,
That out of the Indes came hither by flight,
To close up our stomacks, a Gridiron Pye
We had to our Supper on Saturday night.

But what commeth after must not be forgotten,
The Fruit and the Cheese as they follow by course,
A West-Indian Cheese (not a bit of it rotten,
Thats made of no worse than the milke of a Horse)
A dish of Pine-apples, two bushels at least,
An hundred of Cokernuts for our delight.

Modicums] moderate portions, or salted titbits eaten to whet the thirst
Hostis] hostess   Pine-apples] see Longer Notes, p. 292

The world may admire at this wonderfull Feast,
Which we had at Supper on Saturday night.

Six Pumpians codled with exquisite Art,
To pleasure the palate of every one there.
Then we at the last had a great Cabbage Tart;
Thus have I exactly described our Cheere:
What all this amounted to, I cannot tell,
It cost me just nothing, no faith not a mite,
The Master o'th Feast (whom I know very well)
Did pay for this Supper on Saturday night.

Wee rose from our mirth with the 12 a clock Chimes,
Went every one home as his way did direct;
And I for my part on the morning betimes,
Had a Breakfast prepar'd, which I did not expect:
My wife, because she was not bidden to Supper,
(It seemes by the story) she bare me a spight:
The Breakfast she gave me, to you I will utter,
It passed our Supper on Saturday night.

Sunday morning Breakfast.

First I had a dish of Maundering broath,
So scolding hote that I could not abide it,
But I like a patient man (though I was loath)
Must swallow all down, cause my wife did provide it,
A many small Reasons she put in the same,
Her Nose yeelded Pepper that keenly did bite:
Thought I here's a Breakfast, I thank my good dame
That passes our Supper on Saturday night.

Pumpians] pompions, pumpkins

A great Carpe Pye, and a dish of sad Pouts,
With Crocodile Vinegar, sawce very tart,
Quoth she, thou last night wast among thy sound trouts,
Now fall to thy Breakfast, and comfort thy heart:
Then had I a Cup full of stout Wormwood Beere,
It seemes that in Physicke she has good insight,
This shewd me the difference 'twixt the homely cheere
And our dainty Supper on Saturday night,

Munday Dinner.

On this sorry Fare all that day I did feed,
And on Munday morning, on purpose to win her,
I went and got money to furnish her need,
And now you shall heare what I had to my Dinner:
A Pye made of Conies, with Ducks and Pigs eyes,
With a deale of sweet Hony my taste to delight:
With sweet Lambe and Chicken my mind to suffice,
These passed my Supper on Saturday night.

Another Pye made with a many Sheepes eyes,
With sweet Sugar Candy that pleased my pallet,
These severall Banquets my Muse did advise,
And with her assistance I made this mad Ballett.
There's no man that's wise will my paines reprehend
For most married men will confesse I say right;
Yet on no occasion this Ditie was pen'd,
But to show our rare Supper on Saturday night.

Source: BL, Roxburghe Ballads, i, 18, 19 (printed in *The Roxburghe Ballads*, ed. C. Hindley, 2 vols. (London, 1873–4), i, pp. 93–9).

JOHN TAYLOR

A Bill of Fare

A Bill of Fare, invented by the choicest Pallats of our time, both for Worth and Wit, wherein are appointed such Rare and Admirable Dishes, as are not to bee had every where; and may be expected dayly at the Five pound Ordinary: as it came to my hands I give it to you freely (Gentlemen) with some Additions of Dishes of mine owne.

Four Phantasmes, two boil'd and two roasted.
One Dish of Cadalsets.
A stew'd Torpedo.
One Dish of Andovians.
One Phoenix in white Broath.
One fore-legge of a Green Dragon bak'd.
Four Pellican Chickens.
Two Dottrells broyl'd.
A Dish of Elephants Pettitoes.
A Rhinorceros boyld in Allecant.

Five pound Ordinary] an ordinary was a fixed-price meal at an
eating-house   Cadalsets] this word, not in *OED*, is presumably a coinage
from the Spanish 'cadalso', meaning scaffold or gibbet   Torpedo] electric
ray (a fish)   Andovians] unidentified; perhaps a printer's error for 'Anchovias',
anchovies: Taylor referred elsewhere to 'The Pickled *Herring*, and the *Anchovea*
rare' (*Taylor's Travels*, sig. D7')   Dottrells] dotterels, a type of plover
Pettitoes] a term normally used for pigs' trotters   Allecant] Alicant, a variety
of red wine, from Alicante in Spain

A Calves Head roast with a Pudding in the belly.

A sowst Owle.

A Dish of Irish Harts Horne boil'd into Jelly, with a
    golden Horse-shooe dissolv'd in it.

One Lobster fry'd in steaks.

Nine Soales of a Goose.

Three Ells of a Jackanapes taile.

Two Cockatrices.

Two dryed Sallamanders.

One boild Eele-pie.

A Dish of Quishquillions.

A Dish of *Modicums* boild with *Bonum*.

A Dish of Bounties with Sorrell-soppes.

A Gull pickled.

A Tantablin with an Onion.

A Sallet of Goose-grease and Chickweed-fruite.

A *West-India* Cheese.

One Hundred of Coaker-Nuts.

Fifty Pine-apples.

Twelve Palmitaes.

Source: *Taylor's Feast*, sigs. G6–7ʳ.

Quishquillions] *OED* records the adjectives 'quisquilious' and 'quisquilian',
meaning 'of the nature of rubbish or refuse', but does not give a substantival
form   Modicums boild with Bonum] 'modicum' means 'moderate', and
'bonum' 'good'. 'Modicum' also had a gastronomic meaning: a moderate
portion, or a salted titbit to whet the thirst   Sorrell-soppes] bread soaked
in sorrel-flavoured sauce (used as an accompaniment to chicken)
Tantablin] tantadlin or tantoblin, a fruit tart   Goose-grease] goose-grass,
a popular name for wild tansy and similar plants which were fed to geese
Pine-apples] see Longer Notes, p. 292   Palmitaes] palmettos, a name given
to various sorts of small fruit-bearing palm-trees, especially in America

35

MARTIN PARKER

An Excellent New Medley (i)

An Excellent New Medley,
Which you may admire at (without offence)
For every line speakes a contrary sence.
To the tune of Tarletons Medley.

In Summer time when folkes make Hay,
All is not true which people say,
The foole's the wisest in the play,
    tush take away your band:
The Fidlers boy hath broke his Bass,
Sirs is not this a pittious case,
Most gallants loath to smell the Mace
    of Woodstreet.

The Citty followes Courtly pride,
Jone sweares she cannot *John* abide,
Dicke weares a Dagger by his side.
    come tell us what's to pay.
The Lawyers thrive by others fall,

sence.] sences. *Roxburghe Ballads*   Tarletons] Richard Tarlton, famous actor
and jester to Queen Elizabeth (see Nungezer, *Dictionary of Actors*)   Mace of
Woodstreet] Wood Street Counter was a debtor's prison in the City of London;
'mace' here puns on the sweet-smelling spice and the staff or club carried by
the constables who arrested debtors

The weakest alwaies goes to'th wall,
The Shoomaker commandeth all
    at's pleasure.

The Weaver prayes for Huswives store,
A pretty woman was *Jane Shore.*
Kicke the base Rascalls out o'th doore:
    peace, peace, you bawling Curres.
A Cuckold's band weares out behinde,
Tis easie to beguile the blinde,
All people are not of one minde,
    hold Carmen.

Our women cut their haire like men,
The Cocke's ore-mastred by the Henne
There's hardly one good friend in ten,
    turne on your right hand:
But few regard the cryes o'th poore,
Will spendeth all upon a whore,
The Souldier longeth to goe ore,
    brave knocking.

When the fifth *Henry* sail'd to France,
Let me alone for a Countrey dance,
Nell doth bewaile her lucklesse chance,
    fie on false hearted men:
Dicke Tarleton was a merry wagge,
Harke how that prating asse doth bragge,
John Dory sold his ambling Nagge,
    for Kicke-shawes.

Jane Shore] Jane Shore (d. 1527), famous beauty and tragic figure, mistress of
Edward IV, persecuted after his death   Dicke Tarleton] Richard Tarlton,
famous actor and jester to Queen Elizabeth (see Nungezer, *Dictionary of
Actors*)   John Dory] fictional French pirate, hero of popular ballad
Kicke-shawes] quelquechoses, dainty dishes

The Saylor counts the Ship his house,
I'le say no more but dun's the Mouse,
He is no man that scornes a Louse,
   vaine pride undoes the Land:
Hard hearted men make Corne so deare,
Few Frenchmen love well English beere,
I hope ere long good newes to heare,
     hey Lusticke.

Now hides are cheape, the Tanner thrives,
Hang those base men that beate their wives.
He needs must that the Devill drives,
   God blesse us from a Gun:
The Beadles make the lame to runne,
Vaunt not before the battle's wonne,
A Cloud sometimes may hide the Sunne,
     chance medley:

The second part to the same tune.

The Surgeon thrives by fencing schooles,
Some for strong liquor pawne their tooles,
For one wise man ther's twenty fooles,
   oh when shall we be married?
In time of youth when I was wilde,
Who toucheth Pitch, must be defild,
Moll is afraid that shee's with childe,
     peace *Peter*.

The poore still hope for better daies,
I doe not love these long delayes,

Lusticke] merry, jolly

All love and charity decayes,
 in the daies of old:
I'me very loth to pawne my cloake.
Meere poverty doth me provoke,
They say a scald head is soone broke,
  poore trading.

The Dutchmen thrive by Sea and Land,
Women are ships and must be mand,
Lets bravely to our Colours stand,
 Courage, my hearts of gold:
I read in moderne Histories,
The King of Swedens Victories,
At Islington ther's Pudding pies,
  hot Custards.

The Tapster is undone by chalke.
Tush tis in vaine to prate and talke,
The Parrat pratles, walke knaves, walke,
 Duke *Humfrey* lies in Pauls,
The Souldier hath but small regard,
Ther's weekely newes in *Pauls* Churchyard,
The poore man cries the world growes hard,
  cold Winter.

From Long-lane cloathe and Turnestile boots
O fie upon these scabbed cootes,
The cheapest meat is Reddish rootes,
 come, all these for a penny:
Light my Tobacco quickly heere,

mand] manned Duke Humfrey lies in Paul's] Humphrey, Duke of
Gloucester (son of Henry IV), whose tomb was popularly believed to be in
St Paul's Cathedral; to dine with Duke Humphrey was to go without dinner
– originally, it seems, to linger at St Paul's (a popular meeting-place) hoping
to meet someone who could pay for a meal Long-lane] street in the City
of London Reddish] radish

There lies a pretty woman neere,
This boy will come to naught I feare,
    proud Coxcombe.

The world is full of odious sinnes,
'Tis ten to one but this horse winnes,
Fooles set stooles to breake wise mens shinnes,
   this man's more knave than foole:
Jane ofte in private meets with *Tom*,
Husband ya're kindly welcome home,
Hast any money? lend me some,
    Ime broken.

In ancient times all things were cheape,
'Tis good to looke before thou leape,
When Corne is ripe, 'tis time to reape,
   once walking by the way.
A jealous man the Cuckoo loaths,
The gallant complements with oathes,
A wench will make you sell your cloaths.
    run Broker.

The Courtier and the country man,
Let's live as honest as we can.
When *Arthur* first in Court began,
   His men wore hanging sleeves.
In *May* when Grasse and Flowers be green
The strangest sight that ere was seene.

Broker] retailer, second-hand dealer or pawnbroker; also, a pimp

God blesse our gracious King and Queene,
    from danger.

                            Amen.

Finis.   M.P.

Source: BL, Roxburghe Ballads, i, 112, 13 (printed in *Roxburghe Ballads*, i, pp. 67–73).

Finis] 'the end'   M.P.] Martin Parker

36

MARTIN PARKER (?)

An Excellent New Medley (ii)

An excellent new Medley
To the tune of the Spanish Pavin.

When Philomel begins to sing,
The grasse growes green & flowres spring,
Me thinks it is a pleasant thing,
   to walk on Primrose hill.
Maides have you any Connie-skins
To sell for Laces or great Pinnes
The Pope will pardon veniall sinnes:
     Saint *Peter*.

Fresh fish and newes grew quickly stale:
Some say good wine can nere want sale,
But God send poore folkes Beere & Ale,
   enough untill they die
Most people now are full of pride.
The Boy said no but yet he lyde:

Pavin] pavane, stately dance   Philomel] Philomela, raped by her
brother-in-law Tereus and then silenced by having her tongue cut out, was
turned into a nightingale   Primrose hill] hill north of London
Connie-skins] coney-skins, rabbit-skins

His Aunt did to the Cuck-stoole ride
    for scolding.

Within oure Towne faire Susan dwells:
Sure Meg is poysond, for she swels,
My friend pull off your bozzards bells,
    and let the haggard fly.
Take heed you play not at Tray-trip.
Shorte heeles forsooth will quickly slip.
The beadle makes folke with his whip,
    dance naked.

Come tapster tell us whats to pay,
Jane frownd and cryde good Sir, away,
She tooke his kindenesse, yet said nay,
    as Maidens use to do,
The man shall have his Mare agen,
When all false knaves prove honest men.
Our *Sisly* shall be Sainted then,
    true *Roger.*

The Butcher with his masty Dog
At Rumford you may buy a Hog,
I faith *Raph Goose* hath got a clog,
    his wench is great with childe.
In Pillory put the Bakers head,
For making of such little bread,
Good conscience now a dayes is dead,
    Pierce plowman.

Cuck-stoole] cucking-stool, a chair to which miscreants were tied, and either
exposed to public ridicule, or ducked under water   bozzards]
buzzard's   haggard] hawk caught when adult   Tray-trip] trey-trip, a
game at dice   Sisly] Cicely (Cecilia)   masty] mastiff   Rumford]
Romford, Essex town famous for hog-market   Raph Goose hath got a
clog] meaning uncertain; possibly a reference to the proverbial saying about
shoeing geese (performing unnecessary labours)   Pierce plowman] *Piers
Plowman*, satirical-allegorical poem by Langland

The Cutpurse and his Companie
Theeves finde receivers presently:
Shun Brokers, Bawdes and Usury,
    for feare of after-claps.
Lord, what a wicked world is this
The stone lets Kate she cannot pisse:
Come hither sweet and take a kisse
        in kindnesse.

In *Bath* a wanton wife did dwell,
She had two buckets to a well,
Would not a dog for anger swell,
    to see a pudding creepe:
The Horse-leach is become a Smith,
When halters faile, then take a With:
They say an old man hath no pith,
        Round *Robin*.

Simon doth suck up all the Egges,
Franke never drinks without Nutmegs,
And pretty *Parnell* shewes her legs,
    as slender as my waste.
When faire *Jerusalem* did stand,
The match is made give me thy hand,
Maulkin must have a cambrick band
        blew starched.

The cuckow sung hard by the doore,
Gyll brawled like a butter-whore

Brokers] retailers, second-hand dealers or pawnbrokers; also, pimps
after-claps] unexpected blows, after the recipient has ceased to be on his
guard   lets] impedes   Would . . . a pudding creepe] see Longer Notes,
p. 293   Horse-leach] horse-doctor   With] withe, withy, tough and
flexible twig (e.g. of willow), used for making bands or halters   Maulkin]
Malkin, Mawkin, diminutive of Maud, used as name of sluttish or lower-class
women in proverbial expressions   cambrick] cambric, type of fine white
linen   butter-whore] scolding butter-woman

Cause her buckeheaded Husband swore
   the Miller was a knave.
Good Poets leave of making playes
Let players seek for Souldiers payes
I doe not like the drunken fraies,
     in Smithfield.

Now Roysters spurs do gingle brave,
John Sexton playd the arrand knave.
To digge a Coarse out of the Grave,
   and steal the sheet away.
The wandring Prince of stately *Troy*,
Greene sleeeves were wont to be my joy,
He is a blinde and paultry boy
     god *Cupid*.

Come hither friend and give good eare,
A leg of mutton stuft is rare,
Take heed you do not steal my Mare,
   it is so hot it burns.
Behold the tryall of your love,
He took a scrich-Owle for a Dove,
This man is like ere long to prove
     A Monster.

Tis merry when kinde Maltmen meet:
No Cowards fight but in the street,
Mee thinkes this wench smels very sweet,
   of Muske, or somewhat else.
There was a man did play at Maw,
The whilest his wife made him a daw,

---

buckeheaded] horned like a young stag, i.e. cuckolded   Smithfield] district
of City of London containing a cattle market, close to the brothels of
Clerkenwell   Roysters] roisters, roisterers, swaggering or riotous men
Coarse] corpse   Maw] card game   daw] jackdaw; here in its metaphorical
meaning, simpleton

Your case is altered in the law
    quoth *ployden*.

The Weaver will no shuttle shoote,
Goe bid the Cobler mend my boot
He is a foole will go afoot
    and let his Horse stand still.
Old *John a Nokes* and *John a Stiles*,
Many an honest man beguiles.
But all the world is full of wiles
    and knavery.

Of treason and of Traytors spight
The house is haunted with a sprit,
Now *Nan* will rise about midnight,
    and walke for *Richards* house.
You Courtly states and gallants all,
Climbe not too hie for feare you fall:
If one please not another shall,
    King *pipping*.

Diana and her darlings deere,
The Dutchmen ply the double Beere:
Boyes ring the bels & make good cheere
    When *Kempe* returnes from *Rome*,
O man what meanes thy heavie looke
Is *Will* not in his Mistris booke
Sir *Rouland* for a refuge took
    Horne-Castle

Your case is altered . . . quoth ployden] see Longer Notes, p. 294   John a
Nokes and John a Stiles] proverbial names for simple country folk, also used in
fictitious examples of legal cases   King pipping] Pepin, early King of
France   double Beere] beer of double strength   *Boyes ring*] Boyes rings
Roxburghe Ballads   Kempe] Will Kemp, famous Elizabethan actor and
clown; having danced from London to Norwich in 1599, he possibly undertook
a similar stunt-journey to Italy   Horne-Castle] Horncastle, town in Lincs;
used here probably with bawdy overtones

Rich people have the world at will
Trades fade, but Lawiers flourish still,
Jacke would be married until *Gyll*:
    but care will kill a Cat.
Are you there Sirrah with your Beares
A Barbers shop with nittie haires.
Doll, *Phyllis* hath lost both her eares
    for coozning.

Who list to lead a souldier's life?
Tom would eat meat but wants a knife,
The Tinker swore that *Tib* his wife,
    would playe at uptailes all
Beleeve my word without an Oath
The Tailor stole some of her cloath:
When *George* lay sick & *Joane* made him broath
    with Hemlocke.

The Patron gelt the parsonage,
And *Esau* sold his heritage,
Now *Leonard* lack-wit is foole age,
    to be his Fathers heire.
Ther's many scratch before it itch,
Saul did ask counsel of a Witch.
Friend, ye may have a Bacon flitch
    at *Dunmow*.

King *David* plaid on a Welch Harpe,
This threed will never make a good warpe

---

coozning] cozening, fraud   Tib] shortened form of 'Isabel', used as generic
name for lower-class woman   uptailes all] 'Up-tails all', name of a popular
song, used as a proverbial phrase for jovial and good spirits, but here probably
with bawdy meaning   gelt] gelded, cut down the income of   Leonard
lack-wit] character invented by Martin Parker, as son-in-law to Taylor's Sir
Gregory Nonsence (see poem 12)   Saul did ask counsel of a Witch] see
1 Samuel 28   flitch at Dunmow] flitch of bacon traditionally awarded as a prize
for outstanding marital harmony and fidelity at Dunmow, Essex   threed] thread

At wise mens word's each foole will carpe
  and shoote their witlesse bolts.
Jone like a Ram, wore hornes and wooll.
Knew you my Hostis of the Bull,
Squire Curio once was made a gull
    in *Shoreditch*.

The blackamores are blabber lipt,
At *yarmouth* are the Herrings shipt,
And at Bride-well the beggers whipt,
   a man may live and learne,
Grief in my hearte doth stop my tongue,
The poore man still must put up wrong,
Your way lies there then walk along,
    to *Witham*.

There lies a Lasse that I love well,
The Broker hath gay clothes to sell,
Which from the Hangmans budget fell,
   are you no further yet?
In Summer times when Peares be ripe,
Who would give sixpence for a Tripe,
Play Lad or else lend me thy Pipe
    and Taber.

Saint *Nicholas* Clarkes wil take a purse,
Young children now can sweare and curse
I hope yee like me nere the worse,
   for finding fault therewith.
The servant is the Masters mate.
When gossips meet, ther's too much prate

Hostis] hostess   Squire Curio] perhaps a reference to Curio, an attendant on the Duke of Illyria in Shakespeare's *Twelfth Night*   Shoreditch] eastern district of City of London   Bride-well] London prison   Witham] small town near Chelmsford, Essex   Broker] second-hand dealer   budget] bag, purse   Saint Nicholas Clarkes] highwaymen

Poor *Lazarus* lies at *Dives* gate
    halfe starved,

Make haste to Sea, and hoyst up sailes
The hogs were servd with milking pales
From filthy sluts, and from all Jayles,
    good Lord deliver us all.
I scorne to ride a raw-boned Jade,
Fetch me a Mattock and a Spade,
A *Gravesend* Toste will soone be made,
    Saint *Dennis*.

But for to finish up my Song,
The Ale-wife did the brewer wrong,
One day of sorrow seems as long
    as ten daies do of mirth,
My Medly now is at an end,
Have you no Bowles or Trayes to mend
Tis hard to finde so true a friend
    as *Damon*.

Source: BL, Roxburghe Ballads, i, 14 (printed in *Roxburghe Ballads*, i, pp. 74–81)

Lazarus ... Dives gate] see Luke 16: 19–31   *Jayles*] Joayles *Roxburghe Ballads*   Gravesend Toste] Gravesend is a port in Kent, on the Thames estuary; this possibly refers to a farewell drink (or binge) by sailors putting to sea

37

ANON.

A New Merry Medley

A New Merry Medley Containing a fit of Innocent Mirth in Melancholy Times, together with a Health to the Man *in the Moon.*

Here is a New Medley of Pastime enough,
My Grand mother was an Old wife in a Ruff,
I will go to the Captain and fall on my Knees,
Shon ap Morgan loves Leeks and hur good tosted sheese,
And *Jockey* to *Genny* he prov'd a saw Loon,
Here's a health in full Bowls to the Man in the Moon.

There was a Young Damsel both Bonny and Brown,
If I live to grow Old for I find I grown down,
Fourpence half-penny Farthing. A Taylors no man,
Now there was an Old Prince and his name was K. *John*
I would have a Figgary but where is my Wife,
A dish of good meat is the stay of mans life.

Shon ap Morgan] John ap Morgan, stock name for Welshman (this line imitates Welsh pronunciation)   a saw Loon] perhaps a mock-Scottish version of 'a sorry lown' (term used for inferior or stupid people)   Figgary] vagary, frolic

There was a Blind Beggar that long Lost his sight,
Fairest *Cynthia* the Beauty was *Strephon*'s delight,
Now a Coach cannot pass in the street for a Carr,
For *Pegy*'s gone over the Sea with a Soldier;
Let us go from the Temple away to the Bed,
I will tell you I have a Colts Tooth in my Head.

I am a stout Pavior and Stones I can lay,
Now arise my dear *Cloris* 'tis all abroad day,
Now I am a Maid and a very good Maid,
Pray remember last Winter I learn'd you our Trade:
And how vain are the sordid Intreagues of the Town,
Pritty *Nancy* will never take less than a Crown.

The Merry-Gold opens and spreads with the Sun,
I am Marry'd good People and yet I'm undone;
True Blew will ne'r stain, let the Bottles go round,
Oh the Arrows of *Cupid* fair *Phillis* did wound;
Young Gallants will Tipple, nay, Hector and Swear,
Pritty *Sue* was catcht Napping, as *Moss* catch'd his Mare.

There was a Bold Keeper that Chased the Deer,
The Person he Kisses Young *Nancy* we hear:
Sweet *Katy* of *Windsor* she Rid to the Mill,
My thing is mine own and I'll keep it so still;
This is my dearest Love how do ye like of her hoe,
Wipping Tom is a coming fair *Sillo* my Foe.

The Pudding and Dumpling is burnt to the Pot,
Pretty *Nancey* I'll treat thee and pay the whole shot,

Cynthia] Diana, the moon-goddess   Strephon] shepherd in Sidney's
Arcadia, in love with Urania   Colts Tooth] desire to commit youthful
indiscretion   Pavior] paviour, pavement-layer   Merry-Gold]
marigold   as Moss catch'd his Mare] the proverbial saying, 'To take one
napping, as Mosse took his mare' came from a popular ballad, first printed in
1570 (Tilley, *Dictionary of Proverbs*, M1185)   Person] parson   Sillo]
unidentified

Here is Silver and Gold and tother thing too,
Precious Bells I and Curril sweet Ladys for you;
Therefore buy my fine Fancies, oh buy them up soon,
That I may sell all my New Songs a ver boon.

Source: *The Pepys Ballads*, ed. W. G. Day, 5 vols. (Cambridge, 1987),
v, p. 403. Another version of this medley, with minor variants, is in
ibid., v, p. 401.

I and Curril] aye, and coral   a ver boon] meaning uncertain

38

ANON.

A New made Medly

A New made Medly Compos'd out of sundry songs, For Sport and Pastime for the most ingenious Lovers of Wit and Mirth. To the tune of State and Ambition

State and Ambition, all Joy to great *Caesar*,
   Sawney shall ne'er be my *Colly* my Cow;
All hail to the shades, all joy to the Bridegroom,
   and call upon *Dobin* with Hi, je, ho.
Remember ye Whigs what was formerly done,
   and *Jenny* come tye my bonny Cravat;
If I live to grow old, for I find I go down,
   for I cannot come every day to Wooe.

Jove in his Throne was a Fumbler, *Tom Farthing*,
   and *Jockey* and *Jenny* together did lye;
Oh Mother *Roger*, Boys, fill us a Bumper,
   for why will you dye, my poor *Caelia*, ah! why?

tune of State and Ambition] popular song, of which the first line begins this
poem   Sawney] name commonly used for comic Scottish characters in
popular songs   Tom Farthing] term for a congenital idiot   Jockey] name
commonly used for comic Scottish characters in popular songs

Hark! how the thundring Cannons do roar,
   Ladies of *London*, both wealthy and fair,
Charon make hast, and Ferry me over,
   Lilli burlero, bullen a lah.

Cloris awake, Four-pence-half-penny-farthing,
   give me the Lass that is true Country bred,
Like *John* of *Gaunt*, I walk in *Covent'garden*,
   I am a Maid, and a very good Maid.
Twa bonny Lads was *Sawney* and *Jockey*,
   the Delights of the Bottle, and Charms of good Wine
Wading the Water so deep, my sweet *Moggy*,
   cold and raw, let it run in the right Line.

Old *Obadiah* sings *Ave Maria*,
   sing lulla-by-Baby, with a Dildo;
The Old Woman and her Cat sate by the Fire,
   now this is my Love, d' y' like her ho?
Old *Charon* thus preach'd to his Pupil *Achilles*,
   and under this Stone here lies *Gabriel John*:
Happy was I at the sight of fair *Phillis*,
   what should a young Woman do with an old Man.

There's old Father *Petres* with his Romish Creatures.
   there was an old Woman sold Puddings & Pies
Cannons with Thunder shall fill them with wonder
   I once lov'd a Lass that had bright rowling eyes.
There's my Maid *Mary* she do's mind her Dairy,
   I took to my heels, and away I did run,

Charon] boatman of the underworld   Lilli burlero, bullen a lah] refrain of
a popular song, said to be based on words used by Irish rebels in massacres of
Protestants in 1641 but first printed in 1686 (see Chappell, *Old English Popular
Music*, ii, pp. 58–60)   John of Gaunt] third son of Edward III   Old
Obadiah . . . Maria] see Longer Notes, p. 292   Father Petres] Edward Petre
(1631–99), Catholic priest and confessor to James II

And bids him prepare to be happy to morrow,
 alas! I don't know the right end of a Gun.

My Life and Death do's lye both in your Power,
 and every Man to his Mind, *Shrowsbury* for me;
On a Bank of a Brook as I sate fishing,
 shall I dye a Maid now, and ne'er Married be.
Uds bobs, let *Oliver* now be forgotten,
 Jone is as good as my Lady in the dark:
Cuckold's are Christians, Boys, all the World over,
 and here's a full Bumper to *Robin John Clark*.

Source: *Pepys Ballads*, v, p. 411.

Uds bobs] jocular oath, from 'Ods bodikins', 'God's little body'   Oliver]
Oliver Cromwell

39

JOSEPH BROOKESBANK

Monosyllables

I

An ew *all* in *ale*, oh it is an od age!
All are in aw; or in ire at it
An ell of ice in the sky is at an ace of py
I ake in one eye, you two (so sly) *use us* so ill.
Wo is me! I see an ax in an eg, and am in aw.
Ly by an ew, or an ax; in eye of a fo.
Fy go up, he is to dy; or ly in a py.

II

If the wind blow, then the blew *lamb* will blay
That wilde asse doth blay without blee
Shee with the bitl brow, did brew rich good ale.
It will cloy that mad crew to chew all clay.
That crow in the drag net, did claw his cray
Draw you the line as you drew it to winde it on a clew
He flew to flay the *calfs*, but his knife had a flaw
You are free to flee from a fray, tho the glew flow ore

ew] ewe   blay] blea, bleat   blee] colour   bitl] beetle   glew] glue

The Gray will gnaw the Glow-worm with-out glee
You know this knee doth grow as that grew
I *pray* let your plow stray, if you pray for a *prey*
She will shew me, as I did shew you, how to stay an ox
Stay not, they had need to come on slow that slew the
    man
They bear sway at the stew, and spew at the spaw
Tho he is in hast, he I trow see's the ice thaw
Make you a tray of that tree, to keep whey in Troy
She ayds mee, there-fore give her one *gold* ouch
What ayld thee, to see it oyl'd with these oyls?
I see the *old* man loves salt, and sels it well.
He own'd those *awls*, that he may prick *all* these owls.
His *Aunt* aims to give him an ounce of Pearl.
It was aird with more aires then one at that time.
He puts an owsl, in those that are ours.
For all his outs, he owns more than he oweth.

Source: Brookesbank, *An English Monosyllabary* (London, 1651), sigs.
A6ᵛ, B5.

Gray] grey (horse)   spaw] spa   ouch] clasp, brooch   owsl] ouzel,
blackbird

40

GEORGE DALGARNO

Mnemonic verses

I

When I *sit down* upon a *hie place*, I'm *sick* with *light* and
    heat
For the many thick moistures, doe *open wide* my *Emptie*
    pores
But when I *sit* upon a *strong borrowed* Horse, I *ride* and
    run most *swiftly*
Therefore if I can *purchase* this *courtesie* with *civilitie*, I
    care not the *hirers barbaritie*
Becauce I'm *perswaded* they are *wild villains, scornfully
    deceiving modest* men
Neverthelesse I *allowe* their *frequent wrongs*, and will
    encourage them with *obliging exhortations*
Moreover I'l *assist* them to *fight* against *robbers*, when I
    have my *long crooked* sword.

II

We'l *call* this *old mad* man, and *tickle* him till he *fart* for
    laughter
The pleasant mirth of *itching*, will make him *scratch* his
    white snowie beard
Sharp byting wounds, will *bury* his *lustfull desires*
We'll *feed* his *lean barren* corps, with *fresh savoury dinners*
Filthie stinking roasts, *move* him *fall* a *vomiting*
We'l *penetrate* him with *fearfull thunder*, and *kindle*
    unhappy flames in him
We'l *prove* he *divorced* his wife for *dancing*, and *inchanted*
    her to *refuse* his *kindnes*.

III

Another *error* of *proud fingers*, is to *defloure* maids with
    wrestling temptations
They *forbid* them to *spin* and *twist*, but *trie touching* and
    smelling
Another *hindrance is put*, which *drives* them to *forsake*
    this *advantage*
Another *disputation* is *diligentlie brought*, how a *drop*
    stickes in a *steep* place
The *hollownes* being *washed perishes*, and *sends* out
    environing sinkings
A *bald* man may *dip* a *bleired*, and *cast* him *revengefully*
    among the *planting*
Another *carrier* may stretch him out and *plucke* him, and
    separate his *sound* from his *colour*.

bleired] bleared, with eyes dimmed or inflamed   *plucke him*] plucke, him
Ars signorum

IV

I saw the *sun* rising in the *south east*, and a *hairie cat*
 barking at her

Shee made the *sea* and the *hils* like *blood*, and the *hornes*
 of the *sheep* like *trees*

The wings of the best *kind* of *foules*, covered the *fountaines*
 with the *feathers* of their *taile*

I put the *wheat barley* and *pease*, through my *kinsmans*
 cheeks to his *stomack*

The *bridegroome* my *schismaticall master*, stood in the *door*
 & threw *stones* over the *wall* at me.

I *needled* a hole in his *paps*, and *fingered* his *bastard beard*

I *sworded* his *arme* from the *elbowe* downe, and *faded* the
 kings goose for him.

Source: *Ars signorum* (London, 1661), 'Tables of the Universal
Character'.

NOTES,
BIBLIOGRAPHY,
INDICES

LONGER NOTES

Bell-Swagger . . . at Mims]
Mimms (now South Mimms) is a small town (in Taylor's time, a village), in Hertfordshire, near St Albans, on the main road from London. In Fletcher's *Wit without Money* (*c*.1614), the reluctant servant prays that the innkeepers of St Albans will be too drunk to entertain his mistress, and adds: 'Let Mims be angry at their St. bel-swagger, / And we pass in the heat on't, and be beaten, / Beaten abominably, beaten horse and man, / And all my lady's linen sprinkled / With suds and dish-water!' (Beaumont and Fletcher, *Works*, ed. Dyce, iv, p. 139). Alexander Dyce was baffled by this, and merely cited a note on this passage in the 1778 edition: 'some local custom, tumultuously celebrated, is plainly alluded to in this speech . . . but we have in vain endeavoured to trace its memory'. Sugden interprets 'St. Bel' as the sanctus or saunce bell, rung in Catholic churches during the celebration of Mass, which is 'used for anything trifling . . . Hence St. Bel swagger means the silly, trifling roystering of the drunken inn-keepers of St Albans' (*Topographical Dictionary*, s.v. 'Mims'); but this explanation seems very forced. John Taylor refers to some sort of chaotic practice at Mimms in his *Part of This Summer's Travels* (1639): 'Onely at *Mims*, a Cockney boasting bragger / In mirth, did aske the women for *Bel-swagger*, / But strait the females, like the *Furies fell*, / Did curse, scold, raile, cast dirt, and stones pell mell' (p. 1). Taylor's own explanation for this, given at some length in this work, is that a local squire called Belswagger had got all the women in the village with child. It is possible, however, that this story was nothing more than a popular rationalization of an earlier folk-practice, on which the comment of the 18th-century editors of Beaumont and Fletcher may be the wisest one available.

Dick Swash]
'Swash', an onomatopoeic word referring to a heavy blow, gives rise to the word 'swashbuckling', implying ostentatiously heavy blows on

bucklers. Nashe refers in his dedicatory epistle to *Have with you to Saffron Walden* (1596) to 'Dick Swash, or Desperate Dick, that's such a terrible Cutter at a chyne of beefe, and devoures more meate at Ordinaries in discoursing of his fraies and deep acting of his slashing and hewing, than would serve half a dozen Brewers Dray-men' (*Works*, iii, p. 5). Henry Parrot paints a similar picture of urban braggadoccio in his *The Mous-Trap* (1606): '*Dick Swash* (or *Swaggering Dick*) through Fleetstreet reeles / With *Sis* & *Bettrice* waiting at his heeles: / To one that would have tane the wall, he swore, / Doost thou not see my punck and Paramore?' / (sig. E4ᵛ) From this it would appear that 'Dick Swash' was a generic term for a swaggering, boastful swordsman. Philip Gosson had complained in his *School of Abuse* (1579; ed. Arber, p. 46): 'the skil of Logicians, is exercysed in caveling, the cunning of Fencers applied to quarrelling: . . . Every Duns will be a Carper, every Dick Swash a common Cutter'; and a mid 16th century ballad had included the line 'Dick Swashe keepes Salisbury plane, syr', which seems to refer to the activities of a highwayman (Wright (ed.), *Songs and Ballads*, p. 209).

elbow itches]
Scratching one's elbow was a gesture of annoyance, defiance or swagger: see Nashe, *Works*, iv, p. 261, where McKerrow notes a passage by Deloney: 'O how that word makes me scratch my elbo! . . . See how it makes my blood rise'. Tilley also notes the saying, 'My elbow itches, I must change my bedfellow': *Dictionary of Proverbs*, E98; and a mock-love poem attributed to John Hoskyns includes the lines, 'I know that I shall dye love so my harte bewitches, / it makes mee howle and crye oh how my elbow itches' (Osborn, *Life of Hoskyns*, p. 301).

Geneva print]
Originally this referred to the distinctive typeface (roman, and rather small) of the Geneva Bible. In the early 17th century, the term began to be used as a figurative (and derogatory) way of referring to Puritan behaviour or appearance. In particular, it was used for the small and precisely folded ruffs favoured by Puritans, which were called 'in print' because of the exactness of their folds. Thus John Earle, in his 'character' of 'A She Precise Hypocrite' (1628), observed: 'She is a Non-conformist in a close stomacher and ruffle of Geneva print' (*Microcosmography*, pp. 72–3). At some later stage, in the 18th century, 'Geneva print' became a jocular term for gin (a drink originally known

as 'geneva', from Dutch 'jenever', juniper). Partridge (*Dictionary of Historical Slang*) dates this development to the early 17th century, referring to Massinger. His reference is presumably to a passage in *The Duke of Millaine* (1623), I. i. 9–12: 'And if you meet / An officer preaching of sobriety, / Unlesse he read it in *Geneva* print, / Lay him by the heeles' (Massinger, *Plays and Poems*, i, p. 219). That certainly sounds like an allusion to gin. However, the term for the drink, 'Geneva', did not become current in England until the early 18th century: the first citations for 'Geneva', 'Hollands Geneva' and 'gin' in the *OED* are dated 1706, 1714 and 1714 respectively. Obviously the jocular use of 'Geneva print' to mean gin cannot pre-date the use of 'Geneva' itself. So although the phrase 'To pickle pancakes in Geneva print' (poem 18) would make more sense as a reference to gin, we should probably interpret it as making nonsense (by referring either to typography, or to puritanism) instead.

Jacke Drum]
'Jack Drum's entertainment' was a proverbial phrase for ejecting a guest (Tilley, *Dictionary of Proverbs*, J12). Taylor used it elsewhere: 'Not like the entertainment of *Jacke Drum*, / Who was best welcome when he went his way' (Taylor, *Workes*, sig. Gg4ᵛ). In Marston's play *Jack Drum's Entertainment* (1601), the phrase is used by the character Jack Drum, steward to Sir Edward Fortune, implying that this was his own way of treating unwelcome visitors: 'I beseech you give him *Jacke Drums* entertainment: Let the Jebusite depart in peace' (I, i). In proverbial usage, however, Jack Drum was the person so treated. The character in Marston's play took his name from the proverb, and not vice-versa.

me vat a whee]
The Welsh for 'God preserve you', 'Duw cadw chwi', underwent a process of Chinese whispers in the English literature of this period. Nashe wrote in his dedicatory epistle to *Have with you to Saffron Walden* (1596): 'Dick, no more at this time, but *Nos-da diu catawhy*' (*Works*, iii, p. 17; 'Nos-da' is 'goodnight'.) Fletcher and Massinger gave it as 'Du cat a whee' in *The Custom of the Country* (c.1620), I. ii. 21, and Beaumont and Fletcher used it in other plays of the same period (see Dyce's note in Beaumont and Fletcher, *Works*, ed. Dyce, iv, p. 411). Taylor's 'me vat a whee' seems to be a further distortion of Fletcher's version.

Monday hang himselfe]
These lines borrow from a famous comic epitaph on a Mr Munday,
who hanged himself: 'Hallowed be the Sabbaoth, / And farewell all
worldly pelf, / The weeke begins on Tuesday, / For Munday hath
hang'd himselfe' (*Witts Recreation*, sig. Bb7ʳ). An earlier version of
these lines is contained in a group of poems of the 1620s: BL MS
Stowe 962, fo. 166ᵛ.

mulsacke pies]
This is probably an error for 'Woolsack': Jonson refers to 'Woolsack
pies' (*Alchemist*, V. iv. 41), meaning pies from the Woolsack tavern,
probably the one outside Aldgate. Otherwise 'mulsacke' might possibly
mean 'mulled sack' (sack was a type of sweet wine); alternatively, the
editors of Corbet, *Poems*, note that Mulsacke was the name of a famous
chimney-sweep of the early 17th century (p. 164).

Old Obadiah sings Ave Maria]
Obadiah Walker (1616–99) became Master of University College,
Oxford, in 1676. Suspected for some time of 'popery', he made public
his conversion to Roman Catholicism in 1686, and became a key
supporter of James II's unpopular pro-Catholic policy in the university.
The young wits of Christ Church composed a lampooning verse,
taught it to a simpleton and persuaded him to sing it at Walker's
door:

> Oh, old Obadiah
> Sing Ave Maria
> But so will not I-a
> For why-a
> I had rather be a fool than a knave-a

Pine-apples]
Until the 17th century this term referred only to the common pine-cone
(or to pine-nuts); then it was applied to the tropical fruit because of
its similar shape. The contexts suggest that Parker and Taylor are
referring to the fruit (a great rarity – like the coconuts which they also
mention – unobtainable in large quantities); if so, these references
pre-date the earliest citation in the *OED* by nearly 30 years.

to see a pudding creep]
Tilley records the proverbial saying 'It would vex a dog to see a pudding creep' (*Dictionary of Proverbs*, D491); the earliest source noted by him is the 'Excellent New Medley' (poem 36), which he dates to *c.*1629. Two lines from one of the comic poems prefixed to *Coryats Crudities* suggest a possible origin for this puzzling image: 'Tom Thumbe is dumbe, untill the pudding creepe, / In which he was intomb'd then out doth peepe' (sig. lr; the poem is by James Field). One popular episode in the story of Tom Thumb involves the hero falling into a mixing-bowl and being made part of a pudding. In the earliest printed versions of this story which have survived (R. Johnson, *History of Tom Thumbe* (1621); *Tom Thumbe, his Life and Death* (1630)), the strange movements of the pudding startle Tom Thumb's mother, who, fearing that it is bewitched, gives it to a passing tinker. It would appear that in some earlier version of the story, the movement of the pudding had caused surprise or alarm to a watching dog. We know that other versions of the story were circulating: Nashe referred in *Pierce Penilesse* to 'a Treatise of *Tom Thumme*' (*Works*, i, p. 159). But none of these earlier versions has come down to us in print.

Trundle's Sussex Dragon]
John Trundle (d. 1626) was a London publisher specializing in ballads, news-pamphlets and other such popular materials (see G. D. Johnson, 'John Trundle and the Book-Trade'). Taylor, a personal friend of Trundle (Capp, *World of John Taylor*, p. 45), played on his name in *Taylors Motto* (1621), where he said that he gained material for his own poetry when reading all kinds of publications, even when 'monstrous newes came Trundling in my way' (*Workes*, sig. Ee6r). This was probably a reference to Trundle's most notorious production, a pamphlet by 'A. R.' entitled *True and wonderfull. A Discourse relating a strange and monstrous Serpent (or Dragon) lately discovered, and yet living, to the great annoyance and divers slaughter, both of Men and Cattell, by his strong and violent poyson, In Sussex two miles from Horsam, in a woode called S. Leonards Forrest, and thirtie miles from London, this present month of August 1614* (London, 1614). After a solemn discussion of the accounts of dragons given by classical authors, the pamphlet briefly described the terror wrought by the creature near Horsham, and observed: 'This Serpent (or Dragon as some call it) is reputed to be nine foote or rather more in length' (sig. B3v). The 'Sussex Dragon' was quickly 'laughed out of existence' (Shaaber, *Forerunners of the*

Newspaper, p. 154); it became a proverbial example of sensationalist news-mongering, and was ridiculed by Jonson in his *Newes from the New World* in 1620 (*Works*, vii, p. 515: 'your printed Conundrums of the serpent in *Sussex*'). As late as 1652 a ballad could announce: 'Heer's no Sussex Serpent to fright you here in my Bundle, nor was it ever Printed for the Widdow *Trundle*' (Johnson, 'John Trundle and the Book-Trade', p. 193).

Your case is altered . . . quoth ployden]
This proverbial saying (Tilley, *Dictionary of Proverbs*, C111) arises from an anecdote, probably apocryphal, about the great jurist Edmund Plowden or Ployden (1518–85), whose *Commentaries* (legal reports from the 1550s to the 1570s, with comments and analysis) were a standard authority. According to James Howell (*Paroimiographia*, p. 17), a client asked Plowden if he could bring an action for trespass after someone's hogs had entered his land; Plowden agreed that he would have a strong case. The client then explained that the hogs were Plowden's own: hence his famous remark. (A more elaborate explanation, involving an attempt to trap Plowden into attending an illegal Roman Catholic Mass, is given by Ray, *Collection of English Proverbs*, pp. 225–6.)

MANUSCRIPT SOURCES

This list is confined to recording those MSS cited in the editorial materials of this book.

Bodleian Library, Oxford

Ashmole 36: poems 14, 17, 19, 20
Ashmole 37: poem 14
Ashmole 38: poem 18
CCC 328: poem 14
Eng. poet. e. 97: poem 14
Rawl. poet. 117: poem 14
Rawl. poet. 160: poem 14
Tanner 465: poems 14, 32

British Library, London

Add. 4457: poem 18
Add. 25303: Hoskyns speech
Egerton 2421: poems 14, 32
Sloane 1489: poem 30
Stowe 962: epitaph on Munday

Nottingham University Library, Nottingham

Portland Pw v 37: poems 10, 21

BIBLIOGRAPHY

This bibliography is confined to listing those works which have been referred to in the Introduction, notes and other editorial material of this book. Anonymous works are listed by title. The seventeenth-century 'drolleries' are also listed by title; where the names of editors or principal authors are known, cross-references to the relevant titles are supplied in entries under their names.

The Academy of Complements (London, 1650).

Allen, D. C., *The Star-Crossed Renaissance: The Quarrel about Astrology and Its Influence in England* (Durham, NC, 1941).

Amades, J., 'El habla sin significado y la poesía popular disparatada', *Revista de dialectologia y tradiciones populares*, xv (1959), pp. 274–91.

Andriotes, N. P., *Glossike laographia* (Athens, 1940).

Angeli, G., *Il mondo rovesciato* (Rome, 1977).

Apuleius, *Metamorphoses*, ed. and trans. J. A. Hanson, 2 vols. (Cambridge, Mass., 1989).

Arber, E. (ed.), *A Transcript of the Registers of the Company of Stationers of London, 1554–1640 A.D.*, 5 vols. (London, Birmingham, 1875–94).

Artus, T., *Relation de l'isle des hermaphrodites* (Paris, 1605).

Ashton, J. (ed.), *Humour, Wit, and Satire of the Seventeenth Century* (London, 1883).

Atkinson, G., *The Extraordinary Voyage in French Literature before 1700* (New York, 1920).

Aubrey, J., *'Brief Lives', chiefly of Contemporaries, set down by John Aubrey, between the Years 1669 and 1696*, ed. A. Clark, 2 vols. (Oxford, 1898).

Ault, N. (ed.), *Elizabethan Lyrics*, 3rd edn. (London, 1949).

—*Seventeenth Century Lyrics*, 2nd edn. (London, 1950).

[Austin, S. (ed.),] *Naps upon Parnassus. A sleepy Muse nipt and pincht, though not awakened. Such Voluntary and Jovial Copies of Verses, as were lately receiv'd from some of the Wits of the Universities, in a Frolick, dedicated to* Gondibert's *Mistress by Captain* Jones *and others* (London, 1658).

Babcock, B. A. (ed.), *The Reversible World: Symbolic Inversion in Art and Society* (Ithaca, NY, 1978).

Bakhtin ['Bakhtine'], M., *L'Oeuvre de François Rabelais et la culture populaire au moyen âge et sous la renaissance,* trans. A. Robel (Paris, 1970).

Baroja, J. C., *El carnaval (analisis historico-cultural)* (Madrid, 1965).

du Bartas, G., *Divine Weekes and Workes,* trans. J. Sylvester (London, 1611).

Baskervill, C. R., *The Elizabethan Jig and Related Song Drama* (Chicago, 1929).

Beaumont, F., and J. Fletcher, *Works,* ed. A. Dyce, 11 vols. (London, 1843–6).

—*The Dramatic Works in the Beaumont and Fletcher Canon,* ed. F. Bowers, 9 vols. (Cambridge, 1966–94).

Bell, R. (ed.), *Poems of Robert Greene and Christopher Marlowe* (London, 1856).

Benayoun, R. (ed.), *Le Nonsense* (Paris, 1977).

Bercé, Y.-M., *Fête et révolte: des mentalités populaires du XVI⁰ au XVIII⁰ siècle* (Paris, 1976).

Billington, S., *A Social History of the Fool* (Brighton, 1984).

—*Mock Kings in Medieval Society and Renaissance Drama* (Oxford, 1991).

Birlinger, A., 'Ein scherzhaftes Rezept', *Zeitschrift für deutsches Althertum,* xv (1872), pp. 510–12.

Blau, J. L., *The Christian Interpretation of the Cabala in the Renaissance* (New York, 1944).

Boccaccio, G., *Il Decamerone,* ed. A. Rossi (Bologna, 1977).

Böhme, F. M., *Altdeutsches Liederbuch: Volkslieder der Deutschen nach Wort und Weise aus dem 12. bis zum 17. Jahrhundert* (Leipzig, 1877).

Böhmer, G. (ed.), *Die verkehrte Welt: Le Monde renversé: The Topsy-Turvy World,* catalogue of an exhibition held by the Goethe-Institut, Amsterdam, Paris, London and New York (1985).

Bolte, J., and P. Polívka, *Anmerkungen zu den Kinder- und Hausmärchen der Brüder Grimm*, 5 vols. (Leipzig, 1913–32).

Bond, R. P., *English Burlesque Poetry, 1700–1750* (Cambridge, Mass., 1932).

Boorde, A., *Merie Tales of the Mad Men of Gotam*, ed. S. J. Kahrl, with R. Johnson, *The History of Tom Thumbe*, ed. C. F. Bühler, Renaissance English Text Society (Evanston, Illinois, 1965).

Brewer, E. C., *Dictionary of Phrase and Fable*, 2nd edn. (London, 1894).

—*The Reader's Handbook of Famous Names in Fiction, Allusions, References, Proverbs, Plots, Stories, and Poems*, rev. edn. (London, 1923).

Bristol, M. D., *Carnival and Theater: Plebeian Culture and the Structure of Authority in Renaissance England* (New York, 1985).

Broadbent, J. (ed.), *Signet Classic Poets of the Seventeenth Century*, 2 vols. (New York, 1974).

Broich, U., *The Eighteenth-Century Mock-Heroic Poem* (Cambridge, 1990).

Brookesbank, J., *An English Monosyllabary* (London, 1651).

Brown, H., *Rabelais in English Literature* (Cambridge, Mass., 1933).

Browne, Sir Thomas, *Works*, ed. S. Wilkin, 3 vols. (London, 1910).

Bruni, R., Campioni, R., and D. Zancani, *Giulio Cesare Croce dall' Emilia all' Inghilterra: cataloghi, biblioteche e testi* (Florence, 1991).

Bullokar, J., *An English Expositor: Teaching the Interpretation of the Hardest Words in our Language* (London, 1616).

Il Burchiello, *Le rime*, ed. A. Doni (Venice, 1566).

Burton, R., *The Anatomy of Melancholy* (London, 1883).

Butler, S., *Characters and Passages from Note-Books*, ed. A. R. Waller (Cambridge, 1908).

Le Cabinet satyrique, ou recueil parfaict des vers picquans & gaillards de ce temps (Paris, 1633).

Caesar, *The Civil Wars*, ed. and trans. A. G. Peskett (Cambridge, Mass., 1966).

Cammaerts, É., *The Poetry of Nonsense* (New York, 1925).

Camporesi, P., *La maschera di Bertoldo: G. C. Croce e la letteratura carnevalesca* (Turin, 1976).

—*Bread of Dreams: Food and Fantasy in Early Modern Europe*, trans. D. Gentilcore (Cambridge, 1989).

Canter, H. V., 'The Figure of Adynaton in Greek and Latin Poetry', *American Journal of Philology*, li (1930), pp. 32–41.

Capp, B., *The World of John Taylor the Water-Poet, 1578–1653* (Oxford, 1994).

Carkesse, J., *Lucida intervalla* (London, 1679).

Case, A. E., *A Bibliography of English Poetical Miscellanies, 1521–1750* (Oxford, 1935).

Cavendish, M., *Poems and Fancies* (London, 1653).

Chambers, E. K., and F. Sidgwick (eds.), *Early English Lyrics, Amorous, Divine, Moral and Trivial* (London, 1907).

Chappell, W., *Popular Music of the Olden Time: A Collection of Ancient Songs, Ballads, and Dance Tunes, illustrative of the National Music of England*, 2 vols. (London, 1853–9).

—*Old English Popular Music*, ed. H. Ellis Wooldridge, 2 vols. (London, 1893).

Chesterton, G. K., 'A Defence of Nonsense', in E. Rhys (ed.), *A Century of English Essays* (London, n.d.).

Chevaldin, L. E., *Les Jargons de la farce de Pathelin* (Paris, 1903).

Cicero, *De natura deorum*, ed. and trans. H. Rackham (Cambridge, Mass., 1967).

Clark, A. (ed.), *The Shirburn Ballads 1585–1616* (Oxford, 1907).

Cleveland, J., *Poems*, ed. B. Morris and E. Withington (Oxford, 1967).

Cobbes Prophecies, his Signes and Tokens, his Madrigalls, Questions, and Answeres, with his spirituall Lesson, in Verse, Rime, and Prose (London, 1614).

Cocchiara, G., *Il paese di Cuccagna e altri studi di folklore* (Turin, 1956).

—*Il mondo alla rovescia* (Turin, 1963).

Colie, R., *Paradoxa epidemica: The Renaissance Tradition of Paradox* (Princeton, NJ, 1966).

Corbet ['Corbett'], R., *Poems*, ed. J. A. W. Bennett and H. R. Trevor-Roper (Oxford, 1955).

Cornwallis, Sir William, *Essayes of Certaine Paradoxes* (London, 1616).

Coryate, T., *Coryats Crudities Hastily gobled up in five Moneths of travell*... *Newly digested in the hungry aire of Odcombe in the County of Somerset, & now dispersed to the nourishment of the travelling Members of this Kingdome* (London, 1611).

—*Coryats Crambe* (London, 1611).

C[otgrave], J. (ed.), *Wits Interpreter* (London, 1655).

Cotton, C., *Scarronides: Or, Virgile Travestie* (London, 1664).

Croce, G. C., *Dono, over presente, di varii, e diversi capricci bizzari* (Bologna, n.d. [164?]).

—*Nel tempo che la luna buratava, operetta bellissima, dove s'intendano alcune stantie ridicolose* (Bologna, n.d. [164?]).

—*La scatola* (Bologna, n.d. [164?]).

—*Spalliera in grottesco alla burchiellesca* (Bologna, n.d. [164?]).

Crocioni, G., 'Il "Menzionero" di Baldassare da Fossombrone', *Il rinascita*, vi, no. 31 (1943), pp. 224–57.

Curtius, E. R., *European Literature and the Latin Middle Ages*, trans. W. Trask (London, 1953).

Dalgarno, G., *Ars signorum* (London, 1661).

Dane, J. A., *Parody: Critical Concepts versus Literary Practices, Aristophanes to Sterne* (Norman, Oklahoma, 1988).

Davis, N. Z., 'The Reasons of Misrule: Youth Groups and Charivaris in Sixteenth-Century France', *Past and Present*, no. 50 (1971), pp. 41–75.

Dekker, T., *The Raven's Almanacke* (London, 1609).

—*The Non-Dramatic Works*, ed. A. B. Grosart, 5 vols. (London, 1884–6).

—*The Dramatic Works*, ed. F. Bowers, 4 vols. (Cambridge, 1953–61).

Delepierre, O., *Macaronéana, ou mélanges de littérature macaronique* (Paris, 1852).

—*De la Littérature macaronique, et de quelques raretés bibliographiques de ce genre*, Miscellanies of the Philobiblion Society, ii, no. 14 (London, 1854).

—*Tableau de la littérature du centon chez les anciens et chez les modernes*, 2 vols. (London, 1875).

Dickson, A., *Valentine and Orson: A Study in Late Medieval Romance* (New York, 1929).

Dictionary of National Biography, 63 vols. (London, 1885–1900).

DNB: see *Dictionary of National Biography.*

Dobson, W. T., *Poetical Ingenuities and Eccentricities* (London, 1882).

Dornavius, C. (ed.), *Amphitheatrum sapientiae socraticae joco-seriae* (Hanover, 1619).

Dugdale, Sir William, *Origines juridiciales, or Historical Memorials of the English Laws* (London, 1666).

Dutoit, E., *Le Thème de l'adynaton dans la poésie antique* (Paris, 1936).

Earle, J., *Microcosmography: Or, A Piece of the World Discovered in Essays and Characters*, ed. H. Osborne (London, n.d.).

Elam, K., *Shakespeare's Universe of Discourse* (Cambridge, 1984).

del Encina, J., *Obras completas*, ed. A. M. Rambaldo, 4 vols. (Madrid, 1978–83).

Erasmus, D., *The Praise of Folie*, trans. Sir Thomas Chaloner, ed. C. H. Miller, Early English Texts Society, cclvii (London, 1965).

Euling, K., 'Ein Quodlibet', *Zeitschrift für deutsche Philologie*, xxii (1890), pp. 312–17.

—'Eine Lügendichtung', *Zeitschrift für deutsche Philologie*, xxii (1890), pp. 317–20.

'Evesdropper, Adam', *Platoes Cap* (London, 1604).

An Excellent Recipe to make a Compleat Parliament or (if you please) a New Senate fitted to the English-Man's Palate (London, 1659).

Facetiae facetiarum, hoc est joco-seriorum fasciculus, 2 vols. (Frankfurt, 1615).

Faral, E., *Les Jongleurs en France au moyen âge* (Paris, 1910).

Farley-Hills, D., *The Benevolence of Laughter: Comic Poetry of the Commonwealth and Restoration* (London, 1974).

Farmer, J. S. (ed.), *Musa pedestris: Three Centuries of Canting Songs and Slang Rhymes (1536–1896)* (New York, 1964).

Finkelpearl, P. J., *John Marston of the Middle Temple* (Cambridge, Mass., 1969).

'Finkenritter', *Das Volksbuch vom Finkenritter*, ed. J. Bolte (Zwickau, 1913).

Fischer, H., *Studien zur deutschen Märendichtung*, 2nd edn., ed. J. Janota (Tübingen, 1983).

Flögel, K. F., *Geschichte der Groteskekomischen* (Leipzig, 1788).

— *Geschichte der Hofnarren* (Leipzig, 1789).

— *Geschichte der Burlesken* (Leipzig, 1794).

Forster, L., *The Icy Fire: Five Studies in European Petrarchism* (Cambridge, 1969).

'Fouleweather, Adam', *A Wonderfull strange and miraculous Astrologicall Prognostication* (London, 1591).

Fowler, A. (ed.), *The New Oxford Book of Seventeenth Century Verse* (Oxford, 1992).

France, A, *The Arcadian Rhetorike* (London, 1588).

Fucilla, J. G., 'Petrarchism and the Modern Vogue of the figure Adynaton', *Zeitschrift für romanische Philologie*, lvi (1936), pp. 671–81.

Fulwell, U., *Dramatic Writings*, ed. J. S. Farmer (London, 1906).

Gaignebet, C., *Le Carnaval: essais de mythologie populaire* (Paris, 1974).

Garapon, R., *La Fantasie verbale et le comique dans le théâtre français du moyen âge à la fin du XVIIᵉ siècle* (Paris, 1957).

Garzoni, T., *The Hospitall of Incurable Fooles*, trans. anon. (London, 1600).

Gesta Grayorum, ed. W. W. Greg, Malone Society Reprints (Oxford, '1914' [1915]).

Gildon, C. (ed.), *The Post-boy rob'd of all his Mail: or, the Pacquet broke open* (London, 1692).

Gilman, S. L., *The Parodic Sermon in European Perspective: Aspects of Liturgical Parody from the Middle Ages to the Twentieth Century*, Beiträge zur Literatur des XV. bis XVIII. Jahrhunderts, vi (Wiesbaden, 1974).

Giovanelli, E. (ed.), *Antologia burchiellesca* (Rome, 1949).

Glapthorne, H., *Plays and Poems*, ed. R. H. Shepherd, 2 vols. (London, 1874).

Gosson, S., *The Schoole of Abuse; and A Short Apologie of the Schoole of Abuse*, ed. E. Arber (London, 1868).

Grammatical Drollery, consisting of Poems and Songs, ed. W. Hicks (London, 1682).

The Great Eater of Graye's-Inn (London, 1652).

Greene, R., *Life and Complete Works*, ed. A. B. Grosart, 15 vols. (London, 1881–6).

Grigson, G. (ed.), *The Faber Book of Nonsense Verse, with a Sprinkling of Nonsense Prose* (London, 1979).

Guerrini, O., *La vita e le opere di Giulio Cesare Croce* (Bologna, 1879).

Guiraud, P., *Le Jargon de Villon ou le gai savoir de la Coquille* (Paris, 1968).

von der Hagen, F., *Minnesänger: deutsche Liederdichter des zwölften, dreizehnten und vierzehnten Jahrhunderts*, 4 vols. (Leipzig, 1838).

Hall, J., *Another World and Yet the Same*, trans. J. M. Wands (New Haven, Conn., 1981).

Hammerstein, R., *Diabolus in musica* (Munich, 1974).

Harington, Sir John, *A New Discourse of a Stale Subject, Called the Metamorphosis of Ajax*, ed. E. S. Donno (London, 1962).

—see also *School of Salernum.*

Hauffen, A., 'Zur Litteratur der ironischen Enkomien', *Vierteljahrschrift für Litteraturgeschichte*, vi (1893), pp. 161–85.

Haughton, H. (ed.), *The Chatto Book of Nonsense Poetry* (London, 1988).

Hensley, C. S., *The Later Career of George Wither* (The Hague, 1969).

Herodotus, *Histories*, trans. H. Carter (London, 1962).

Hicks: see *Grammatical Drollery.*

Hildebrandt, R., *Nonsense-Aspekte der englischen Kinderliteratur* (Hamburg, 1962).

'Homer', *Batrachomyomachia Homero vulgo attributa*, ed. A. Baumeister (Göttingen, 1852).

Hoskyns ['Hoskins'], Sir John, *Directions for Speech and Style*, ed. H. H. Hudson (Princeton, NJ, 1935).

Howard, H., Earl of Northampton, *A Defensative against the Poyson of Supposed Prophecies* (London, 1583).

Howell, J., *Paroimiographia: Proverbs, or, Old Sayed Sawes and Adages* (London, 1659), printed with his *Lexicon Tetraglotton, an English-French-Italian-Spanish Dictionary* (London, 1660).

Hutchinson, P., *Games Authors Play* (London, 1983).

Hutton, R., *The Rise and Fall of Merry England: The Ritual Year, 1400–1700* (Oxford, 1994).

Ingram, A, *The Madhouse of Language: Writing and Reading Madness in the Eighteenth Century* (London, 1991).

Jansen, C., *Augustinus*, 3 vols. (Louvain, 1640).

Jauss, H. R., *Untersuchungen zur mittelalterliche Tierdichtung* (Tübingen, 1959).

Johnson, G. D., 'John Trundle and the Book-Trade, 1603–1626', *Studies in Bibliography*, xxxix (1986), pp. 177–99.

Johnson, R., *The History of Tom Thumbe*, ed. C. F. Bühler, with A. Boorde, *Merie Tales of the Mad Men of Gotam*, ed. S. J. Kahrl, Renaissance English Text Society (Evanston, Illinois, 1965).

Jonson, B., *Works*, ed. C. H. Herford and P. Simpson, 11 vols. (Oxford, 1925–52).

—*Complete Plays*, ed. G. A. Wilkes, 4 vols. (Oxford, 1981–2).

Jump, J., *Burlesque* (London, 1972).

Kalff, G., *Het Lied in de middeleuwen*, 2nd edn. (Leiden, 1884).

Kane, E. K., *Gongorism and the Golden Age: A Study of Exuberance and Unrestraint in the Arts* (Chapel Hill, NC, 1928).

Karrer, W., *Parodie, Travestie, Pastiche* (Munich, 1977).

Kellermann, W., 'Über die altfranzösichen Gedichte des uneingeschränkten Unsinns', *Archiv für das Studium der neueren Sprachen und Literaturen*, ccv (1968–9), pp. 1–22.

Kempe, A. J. (ed.), *The Loseley Manuscripts* (London, 1835).

Kenner, H., 'Seraphic Glitter: Stevens and Nonsense', *Parnassus: Poetry in Review* (1976), no. 2, pp. 153–9.

Kent, W. (ed.), *An Encyclopaedia of London*, rev. edn. (London, 1951).

Kernan, A., 'The Plays and the Playwrights', in J. L. Barroll, A. Leggatt, R. Hosley and A. Kernan, *The Revels History of Drama in English*, iii (London, 1975), pp. 237–474.

Kinch, C. E., *La Poésie satirique de Clément Marot* (Paris, 1940).

Kitchin, G., *A Survey of Burlesque and Parody in English* (Edinburgh, 1931).

Knowlson, J., *Universal Language Schemes in England and France 1600–1800* (Toronto, 1975).

Kocher, P. H., 'Nashe's Authorship of the Prose Scenes in *Faustus*', *Modern Languages Quarterly*, iii (1942), pp. 17–40.

Köhler, R., *Kleinere Schriften zur neueren Litterateurgeschichte, Volkskunde und Wortforschung*, 3 vols. (Berlin, 1900).

Kruger, S. K., *Dreaming in the Middle Ages* (Cambridge, 1992).

Kunzle, D., 'World Upside Down: The Iconography of a European Broadsheet Type', in B. A. Babcock (ed.), *The Reversible World: Symbolic Inversion in Art and Society* (Ithaca, NY, 1978), pp. 39–94.

Lactantius, *Opera omnia*, ed. S. Brandt and G. Laubmann, 2 vols., Corpus scriptorum ecclesiasticorum latinorum, xix, xxvii (Vienna, 1890–95).

Lalanne, F., *Curiosités littéraires* (Paris, 1845).

Landi, O., *Paradossi, cioè, sententie fuori del comun parere* (n.p., 1543).

Långfors, A. (ed.), *Deux recueils de sottes chansons*, Annales academiae scientiarum fennicae, ser. B, liii, no. 4 (Helsinki, 1945).

Lanza, A., *Polemiche e berte letterarie nella Firenze del primo quattrocento: storia e testi* (Rome, 1971).

Laroque, F., *Shakespeare's Festive World: Elizabethan Seasonal Entertainment and the Festive Stage*, trans. J. Lloyd (Cambridge, 1991).

von Lassberg, J., *Lieder-Saal: Sammlung altdeutscher Gedichte*, 4 vols. (n.p., 1820; photo-reproduction, Hildesheim, 1968).

Lecercle, J.-J., *Philosophy of Nonsense: The Intuitions of Victorian Nonsense Literature* (London, 1994).

Lehmann, P., *Die Parodie im Mittelalter* (Munich, 1922).

Leishman, J. B. (ed.), *The Three Parnassus Plays* (London, 1949).

Lemprière, J., *Classical Dictionary of Proper Names mentioned in Ancient Authors Writ Large*, 3rd edn., ed. R. Willets (London, 1984).

Le Roy Ladurie, E., *Carnival in Romans: A People's Uprising at Romans, 1579–1580*, trans. M. Feeney (London, 1980).

Liede, A., *Dichtung als Spiel: Studien zur Unsinnspoesie an den Grenzen der Sprache*, 2 vols. (Berlin, 1963).

The Life and Pranks of Long Meg of Westminster (London, 1582).

Lindsay, J. (ed.), *Loving Mad Tom: Bedlamite verses of the XVI and XVII Centuries* (London, 1927).

van Linschoten, J. H., *Discours of the Voyages into the Easte and west Indies*, trans. anon. (London, 1598).

Linthicum, M. C., *Costume in the Drama of Shakespeare and His Contemporaries* (Oxford, 1936).

Livy, *[Ab urbe condita]*, ed. and trans. B. O. Foster, F. G. Moore, E. T. Sage and A. C. Schlesinger, 14 vols. (Cambridge, Mass., 1967).

Lucan, *Pharsalia*, ed. and trans. J. D. Duff (Cambridge, Mass., 1969).

Lucian, *Works*, ed. and trans. A. M. Harmon, 8 vols. (Cambridge, Mass., 1961).

MacDonald, M., *Mystical Bedlam: Madness, Anxiety, and Healing in Seventeenth-Century England* (Cambridge, 1981).

Marlowe, C., *Tamburlaine the Great, Parts 1 and 2*, ed. J. Jump (London, 1967).

Marot, C., *L'Enfer, les coq-à-l'ânes, les élégies*, ed. C. A. Mayer (Paris, 1977).

Marston, J., *Jack Drum's Entertainment*, The Tudor Facsimile Texts, ed. J. S. Farmer (London, 1912).

—*Plays*, ed. H. H. Wood, 3 vols. (Edinburgh, 1934–9).

—*Poems*, ed. A. Davenport (Liverpool, 1961).

Martín, A. L., *Cervantes and the Burlesque Sonnet* (Berkeley, Calif., 1991).

Massèra, F. (ed.), *Sonetti burleschi e realistici dei primi due secoli*, 2 vols. (Bari, 1920).

Massinger, P. *Plays and Poems*, ed. P. Edwards and C. Gibson, 5 vols. (Oxford, 1976).

Mätzner, E., *Altenglische Sprachproben*, 2 vols. (Berlin, 1867–1900).

Mazzeo, J. A., *Renaissance and Seventeenth-Century Studies* (New York, 1964).

Mazzi, C., *Il Burchiello, saggio* (Bologna, 1877).

Mennes, Sir John: see *Wit and Drollery*.

Merry Drollery, or A Collection of Jovial Poems, Merry Songs, Witty Drolleries. Intermix'd with Pleasant Catches. The First Part (London, n.d. [1661]).

—see also *The Second Part of Merry Drollery*.

Messina, M., 'Domenico di Giovanni detto il Burchiello: sonetti inediti', *Biblioteca dell' 'Archivum Romanicum'*, ser. 1, xxxiii (Florence, 1952).

Metge, B., *Obra completa*, ed. L. Badia and X. Lamuela, 2nd edn. (Barcelona, 1975).

Miller, H. K., 'The Paradoxical Encomium with Special Reference to its Vogue in England, 1600–1800', *Modern Philology*, liii (1956), pp. 145–78.

Il modo novo da intendere la lingua zerga cioè parlar furbesco (Venice, 1549).

Molière, J.-B., *Le Bourgeois gentilhomme*, ed. F. A. Wilson (Walton-on-Thames, 1984).

Montaiglon, A. (ed.), *Recueil de poésies françaises des XVᵉ et XVIᵉ siècles*, 16 vols. (Paris, 1865–78).

de Montluc, A., comte de Cramail, *Les Jeux de l'inconnu, augmenté de plusieurs pièces en ceste dernière edition* (Rouen, 1645).

More, Sir Thomas, *Utopia*, ed. E. Surtz and J. H. Hexter (New Haven, Conn., 1965).

Müller-Fraureuth, C., *Die deutschen Lügendichtungen bis auf Münchhausen* (Halle, 1881).

Nashe, T., *Works*, ed. R. B. McKerrow, rev. F. P. Wilson, 5 vols. (Oxford, 1966).

The New Academy of Complements. With an exact collection of the newest and choicest songs à la mode, both amorous and jovial (London, 1671).

The New Grove Dictionary of Music and Musicians, ed. S. Sadie, 20 vols. (London, 1980).

Nicholl, C., *A Cup of News: The Life of Thomas Nashe* (London, 1984).

Notestein, W., *Four Worthies: John Chamberlain, Anne Clifford, John Taylor, Oliver Heywood* (London, 1956).

Novati, F., *Studi critici e letterari* (Turin, 1889).

Nungezer, E., *A Dictionary of Actors and of Other Persons Associated with the Public Representation of Plays in England before 1642* (New Haven, Conn., 1929).

Odenius, O., 'Mundus inversus: några inledande bibliografiska anteckningar kring tre mellansvenska bildvarianter', *Arv: tidskrift för nordisk folkminneforskning*, x (1954), pp. 142–70.

OED: see *The Oxford English Dictionary*.

Oesterley, H. (ed.), *Shakespeare's Jest Book: A Hundred Mery Talys, from the Only Perfect Copy Known* (London, 1866).

Opie, I., and P. Opie (eds.), *The Oxford Dictionary of Nursery Rhymes*, rev. edn. (Oxford, 1980).

Orvieto, P., 'Sulle forme metriche della poesia del non-senso relativo e assoluto', *Metrica*, i (1978), pp. 203–18.

Osborn, L. B., *The Life, Letters, and Writings of John Hoskyns 1566–1638* (New Haven, Conn., 1937).

Overbury, Sir Thomas, *The Miscellaneous Works*, ed. E. F. Rimbault (London, 1856).

Ovid, *Tristia; Ex Ponto*, ed. and trans. A. L. Wheeler, 2nd edn., rev. G. P. Goold (Cambridge, Mass., 1988).

The Oxford Companion to Classical Literature, 2nd edn., ed. M. C. Howatson (Oxford, 1989).

The Oxford English Dictionary, 12 vols. (Oxford, 1933).

The Oxford Drollery (Oxford, 1671).

Panciroli, G., *Notitia utraque dignitatum, cum orientis, tum occidentis* (Venice, 1593).

Parker, M., *The Legend of Sir Leonard Lack-Wit, sonne in law to Sir Gregory Nonsence* (London, 1633).

Parrot, H., *The Mous-Trap* (London, 1601).

Partridge, E., *A Dictionary of Historical Slang*, ed. J. Simpson (Harmondsworth, 1972).

Peacham, H., *The Truth of our Times* (London, 1638).

Peers, E. A., *Elizabethan Drama and Its Mad Folks* (Cambridge, 1914).

The Pepys Ballads, ed. W. G. Day, 5 vols. (Cambridge, 1987).

Periñan, B., *Poeta ludens: disparate, perqué y chiste en los siglos XVI y XVII* (Pisa, 1979).

Petzold, D., *Formen und Funktionen der englische Nonsense-Dichtung im 19. Jahrhundert*, Erlanger Beiträge zur Sprach- und Kunstwissenschaft, xliv (Nuremberg, 1972).

Phillips, J. (ed.): see *Sportive Wit*.

Picot, E., 'La Sottie en France', *Romania*, vii (1878), pp. 236–326.

—(ed.), *Recueil général des sotties*, 3 vols. (Paris, 1902–12).

Plowden, E., *Les Commentaires, ou Reports* (London, 1588).

Poeschel, J., 'Das Märchen vom Schlaraffenlande', *Beiträge zur Geschichte der deutschen Sprache und Literatur*, v (1878), pp. 389–427.

Pons, É., 'Les Langues imaginaires dans le voyage utopique: un précurseur: Thomas Morus', *Revue de littérature comparée*, x (1930), pp. 589–607.

—'Les Langues imaginaires dans le voyage utopique: les "jargons" de Panurge dans Rabelais', *Revue de littérature comparée*, xi (1931), pp. 185–218.

Porter, L. C., *La Fatrasie et le fatras: essai sur la poésie irrationnelle en France au moyen âge* (Geneva, 1960).

Porter, R., 'Bedlam and Parnassus: Mad People's Writing in Georgian England', in G. Levine (ed.), *On Culture: Essays in Science and Literature* (Madison, Wisconsin, 1987), pp. 258–84.

Previtera, C., *La poesia giocosa e l'umorismo dalle origini al rinascimento* (Milan, 1939).

Le Prince d'Amour; or the Prince of Love. With a Collection of Several Ingenious Poems and Songs by the Wits of the Age (London, 1660).

The Princeton Encyclopaedia of Poetry and Poetics, rev. edn., ed. A. Preminger (Princeton, NJ, 1974).

A Prognostication for ever of Erra Pater, a Jewe . . . verie profitable to keepe the bodie in health (London, 1606).

Puttenham, G., *The Arte of English Poesie*, ed. G. D. Willcock and A. Walker (Cambridge, 1936).

R., A., *True and Wonderfull. A Discourse relating to a strange and monstrous Serpent (or Dragon) lately discovered, and yet living, to the great annoyance and divers slaughters both of Men and Cattell, by his strong and violent poyson, In Sussex two miles from Horsam, in a woode called S. Leonards Forrest, and thirtie miles from London, this present month of August 1614* (London, 1614).

Ravenscroft, T., *Pammelia: Musicks Miscellanie* (London, 1609).

Ray, J., *A Collection of English Proverbs Digested into a convenient Method for the speedy finding any one upon occasion*, 2nd edn. (Cambridge, 1678).

Raylor, T., *Cavaliers, Clubs, and Literary Culture: Sir John Mennes, James Smith, and the Order of the Fancy* (Newark, NJ, 1994).

Riehe, A., *The Senses of Nonsense* (Iowa City, 1992).

Robbins, R. H. (ed.), *Secular Lyrics of the XIVth and XVth Centuries* (Oxford, 1952).

Robinson, C., *Lucian and His Influence in Europe* (London, 1979).

Rohou, J., 'Le Burlesque et les avatars de l'écriture discordante (1635–1655)', in I. Landy-Houillon and M. Menard (eds.), *Burlesque et formes parodiques* (Seattle, 1987), pp. 349–65.

Le Roman de Renart, ed. M. Roques, 6 vols. (Paris, 1948–63).

Ross, A., *Virgilius evangelisans* (London, 1634).

Rouch, M., 'Bibliografia delle opere di Giulio Cesare Croce', *Strada maestra*, xvii (1984), pp. 229–72.

The Roxburghe Ballads, ed. C. Hindley, 2 vols. (London, 1873–4).

Russell, R., *Generi poetici medioevali*, Studi e testi di bibliologia e critica letteraria, viii (Naples, 1982).

Il Sacchetti, *Il libro delle rime*, ed. A. Chiari (Bari, 1936).

Sainéan, L., *L'Argot ancien (1455–1850)* (Paris, 1907).

—*La Langue de Rabelais*, 2 vols. (Paris, 1922–3).

—*L'Influence et la réputation de Rabelais: interprètes, lecteurs et imitateurs. Un rabelaisien (Marnix de Sainte-Aldegonde)* (Paris, 1930).

Salmon, V., *The Works of Francis Lodwick: A Study of his Writings in the Intellectual Context of the Seventeenth Century* (London, 1972).

Sanvisenti, B., *I primi influssi di Dante del Petrarca e del Boccaccio sulla letteratura spagnuola* (Milan, 1902).

Scarron, C., *Typhon* (Paris, 1644).

—*L'Énéide travestie* (Paris, 1648).

Schäfer, J., *Early Modern English Lexicography*, 2 vols. (Oxford, 1989).

Schama, S., *Landscape and Memory* (London, 1995).

The School of Salernum, trans. Sir John Harington (Salerno, 1953).

Schröder, E., 'Die "Lügenpredigt" und das "Quodlibet"', *Anzeiger für deutsches Altertum und deutsche Literatur*, i (1930), p. 214.

Schouwink, W., 'When Pigs Consecrate a Church: Parodies of Liturgical Music in the *Ysengrimus* and some Medieval Analogies', *Reinardus: Yearbook of the International Reynard Society*, v (1992), pp. 171–81.

Schultz-Gora, O., 'Das Adynaton in der altfranzösischen und provenzialischen Dichtung nebst Dazugehörigen', *Archiv für das*

Studium der neueren Sprachen, year 87, clxi (n.s., lxi) (1932), pp. 196–209.

The Second Part of Merry Drollery, or A Collection of Jovial Poems, Merry Songs, Witty Discourses. Intermix'd with Pleasant Catches (London, n.d. [1661]).

Secret, F., *Les Kabbalistes chrétiens de la renaissance* (Paris, 1964).

Sewell, E., *The Field of Nonsense* (London, 1952).

Shaaber, M. A, *Some Forerunners of the Newspaper in England 1476–1622* (Philadelphia, 1929).

Shakespeare, W., *Complete Works*, ed. W. J. Craig (London, 1930).

Sidney, Sir Philip, *The Countess of Pembroke's Arcadia*, ed. A. Feuillerat (Cambridge, 1926).

Silverstein, T. (ed.), *English Lyrics before 1500* (York, 1971).

Smith, C. C., 'The Seventeenth-Century Drolleries', *Harvard Library Bulletin*, vi (1952), pp. 40–51.

Smith, J.: see *Wit and Drollery*.

Southey, R., *The Lives and Works of the Uneducated Poets*, ed. J. S. Childers (London, 1925).

Sparke, M., *The Crums of Comfort* (London, 1628).

Sportive Wit: The Muses Merriment. A New Spring of Lusty Drollery, Joviall Fancies, and A la mode Lamponnes, on some Heroick persons of these late Times, Never before exposed to the publick view, [ed. J. Phillips,] (London, 1656).

Stammler, W., and K. Langrosch (eds.), *Die deutsche Literatur des Mittelalters: Verfasserlexicon*, 5 vols. (Berlin, Leipzig, 1933–55).

Stapleton, T., *Tres Thomae seu de S. Thomae apostoli rebus gestis, de S. Thoma archiepiscopo cantuarensi & martyre, D. Thomae Mori Angliae quondam cancellarii vita* (n.p., 1588).

Steiner, W., *The Colors of Rhetoric: Problems in the Relation between Modern Literature and Painting* (Chicago, 1982).

Stengel, E. (ed.), *Codicum manu scriptum Digby 86 in bibliotheca bodleiana asservatum* (Halle, 1871).

Stewart, S., *Nonsense: Aspects of Intertextuality in Folklore and Literature* (Baltimore, 1979).

Stow, J., *Survey of London*, ed. H. B. Wheatley (London, 1956).

Strachan, M., *The Life and Adventures of Thomas Coryate* (London, 1962).

Strecker, K. (ed.), *Die Cambridger Lieder*, Monumenta Germaniae historica (Berlin, 1926).

Sugden, E. H., *A Topographical Dictionary of the Works of Shakespeare and His Fellow Dramatists* (Manchester, 1925).

Swift, J., *Gulliver's Travels, 1726*, ed. H. Davis, rev. edn. (Oxford, 1959).

Tacitus, *Agricola; Germania; Dialogus*, ed. and trans. M. Hutton and W. Peterson (Cambridge, Mass., 1970).

Tartaro, A., *Il primo quattrocento toscano* (Bari, 1971).

Taylor, J., *The Sculler, rowing from Tiber to Thames* (London, 1612).

—*Laugh, and be Fat: or, a Commentary upon the Odcombyan Banket* (London, 1613).

—*Odcombs Complaint* (London, 1613).

—*The Nipping and Snipping of Abuses* (London, 1614).

—*Jack a Lent His Beginning and Entertainment: with the mad pranks of his Gentleman-Usher Shrove-Tuesday that goes before him, and his Foot-man Hunger attending* (London, 1620).

—*The Praise, Antiquity, and Commodity of Beggery* (London, 1621).

—*Taylors Goose* (London, 1621).

—*The Great O'Toole* (London, 1622).

—*Sir Gregory Nonsence his Newes from No Place* (London, 1622).

—*All the Workes* (London, 1630).

—*The Great Eater* (London, 1630).

—*The Honorable, and Memorable Foundations* (London, 1636).

—*Taylors Travels and Circular Perambulation* (London, 1636).

—*The Carriers Cosmographie* (London, 1637).

—*Taylors Feast: Contayning Twenty-seaven Dishes of meate* (London, 1638).

—*Part of This Summers Travels* (London, 1639).

—*Mad Fashions, Od Fashions* (London, 1642).

—*Aqua-Musae: or, Cacafogo, Cacadaemon, Captain George Wither Wrung in the Withers* (Oxford, 1644).

—*Crop-Eare Curried, or, Tom Nashe his Ghost* (n.p. [Oxford], n.d. [1644]).

—*Mercurius Infernalis: or Orderlesse Orders, Votes, Ordinances, and*

Commands from Hell, established by a Close Committee of the Divell and his Angels (Oxford, 1644).

—*Mercurius Nonsensicus* (n.p. [London], 1648).

—*Nonsence upon Sence* (n.p. [London], 1651).

—*Nonsence upon Sence, or, Sence upon Nonsense: Chuse you either, or neither* (London, 1652).

—*The Essence, Quintessence, Insence, Innocence, Lye-sence, & Magnificence of Nonsense upon Sence: or, Sence upon Nonsense* (London, '1653' [1654]).

—*Works*, ed. C. Hindley (London, 1872).

da Tempo, A., *Trattato delle rime volgari*, ed. G. Giron (Bologna, 1970).

Thomas, K., 'The Place of Laughter in Tudor and Stuart England', *The Times Literary Supplement*, no. 3906 (21 Jan. 1977), pp. 77–81.

Tigges, W. (ed.), *Explorations in the Field of Nonsense*, DQR Studies in Literature, iii (Amsterdam, 1987).

Tilley, M. P., *A Dictionary of the Proverbs of England in the Sixteenth and Seventeenth Centuries* (Ann Arbor, Michigan, 1950).

Tom Thumbe, his life and death, in W. C. Hazlitt (ed.), *Remains of Early Popular Poetry*, 4 vols. (London, 1864–6), ii, pp. 175–92.

Toscan, J., *Le Carnaval du langage: la lexique érotique des poètes de l'équivoque de Burchiello à Marino (XVᵉ–XVIIᵉ siècles)*, 4 vols. (Paris, 1981).

Ungureanu, M., *La Bourgeoisie naissante. Société et littérature bourgeoises d'Arras aux XIIᵉ et XIIIᵉ siècles*, Mémoires de la commission des monuments historiques du Pas-de-Calais, viii, no. 1 (Arras, 1955).

d'Urfé, H., *L'Astrée*, ed. H. Vaganay, 5 vols. (Lyon, 1925–8).

'de Vaux': see de Montluc.

Vavasseur, F., *De ludicra dictione liber in quo tota jocandi ratio ex veterum scriptis aestimatur* (Paris, 1658).

Vergil, P., *De inventoribus rerum* (n.p., 1499).

Verhulst, S., *La frottola (XIV–XV sec.): aspetti della codificazione e proposte esegetiche*, Rijksuniversiteit te Gent, Werken uitgegeven door de Faculteit van de Letteren en Wijsbegeerte, clxxvii (Ghent, 1990).

Vidaković-Petrov, K., *Kultura španskih jevreja na jugoslovenskom tlu: XVI–XX vek*, 2nd edn. (Sarajevo, 1990).

Virgil, *Works*, ed. and trans. H. R. Fairclough, 2 vols. (Cambridge, Mass., 1967).

Wackernagel, *Deutsches Lesebuch*, 5 vols. (Basel, 1872–8).

Waddell, H., *The Wandering Scholars*, 7th edn. (London, 1934).

Walpole, H., *Letters*, ed. J. Wright, 6 vols. (London, 1840).

Wardroper, J. (ed.), *Love and Drollery* (London, 1969).

Watkins, R., 'Il Burchiello (1404–1448) – Poverty, Politics, and Poetry', *Italian Quarterly*, xiv, no. 54 (1970), pp. 21–57.

Wells, C., 'The Sense of Nonsense', *Scribner's Magazine*, xxix (Jan.–June 1901), pp. 239–48.

—*A Nonsense Anthology* (New York, 1958).

Welsford, E., *The Fool: His Social and Literary History*, 2nd edn. (London, 1968).

Westphal-Wihl, S., 'Quodlibets: Introduction to a Middle High German Genre', in H. Heinen and I. Henderson (eds.), *Genres in Medieval German Literature*, Göppinger Arbeiten zur Germanistik, no. 439 (Göppingen, 1986), pp. 157–74.

Whitlock, B. W., *John Hoskyns, Serjeant-at-Law* (Washington, DC 1982).

Wigfall Green, A., *The Inns of Court and Early English Drama* (New Haven, Conn., 1931).

Wilson, F. P. (ed.), *Pantagruel's Prognostication*, Luttrell Reprints, no. 3 (Oxford, 1947).

Wilson, T., *The Arte of Rhetorique, 1560*, ed. G. H. Mair (Oxford, 1909).

Wither, G., *Campo-Musae* (London, 1643).

Wit and Drollery, [ed. Sir John Mennes and J. Smith] (London, 1656).

Wit Restor'd (London, 1658).

Wits Interpreter: The English Parnassus, ed. J. C[otgrave] (London, 1671).

Witts Recreations (London, 1667).

Witt's Recreations Augmented (London, 1641).

Wood, A., *The Life and Times of Anthony Wood, Antiquary, of Oxford*,

1632–1695, Described by Himself, ed. A. Clark, 5 vols., Oxford Historical Society, xix, xxi, xxvi, xxx, xl (Oxford, 1891–1900).

Wood, A. C., *A History of the Levant Company* (London, 1935).

Wright, L. B., 'Madmen as Vaudeville Performers on the Elizabethan Stage', *Journal of English and Germanic Philology*, xxx (1931), pp. 48–54.

Wright, T., *A History of Caricature and Grotesque in Literature and Art* (London, 1875).

—and J. O. Halliwell (eds.), *Reliquiae antiquae: Scraps from Ancient Manuscripts, Illustrating chiefly Early English Literature and the English Language*, 2 vols. (London, 1841–3).

Ysengrimus, ed. and trans. J. Mann, Mittellateinische Studien und Texte, xii (Leiden, 1987).

Ziolkowski, J., *Talking Animals: Medieval Latin Beast Poetry, 750–1150* (Philadelphia, 1993).

Zumthor, P., 'Fatrasie et coq-à-l'âne', in G. De Poerck, M. Piron, et al. (eds.), *Fin du moyen âge et renaissance: mélanges de philologie offerts à Robert Guiette* (Antwerp, 1961), pp. 5–18.

—*Essai de poétique médiévale* (Paris, 1972).

INDEX OF AUTHORS OF
THE NONSENSE POEMS

(by poem-number)

INDEX OF TITLES AND
FIRST LINES OF
THE NONSENSE POEMS

(by poem-number)

INDEX TO
THE INTRODUCTION